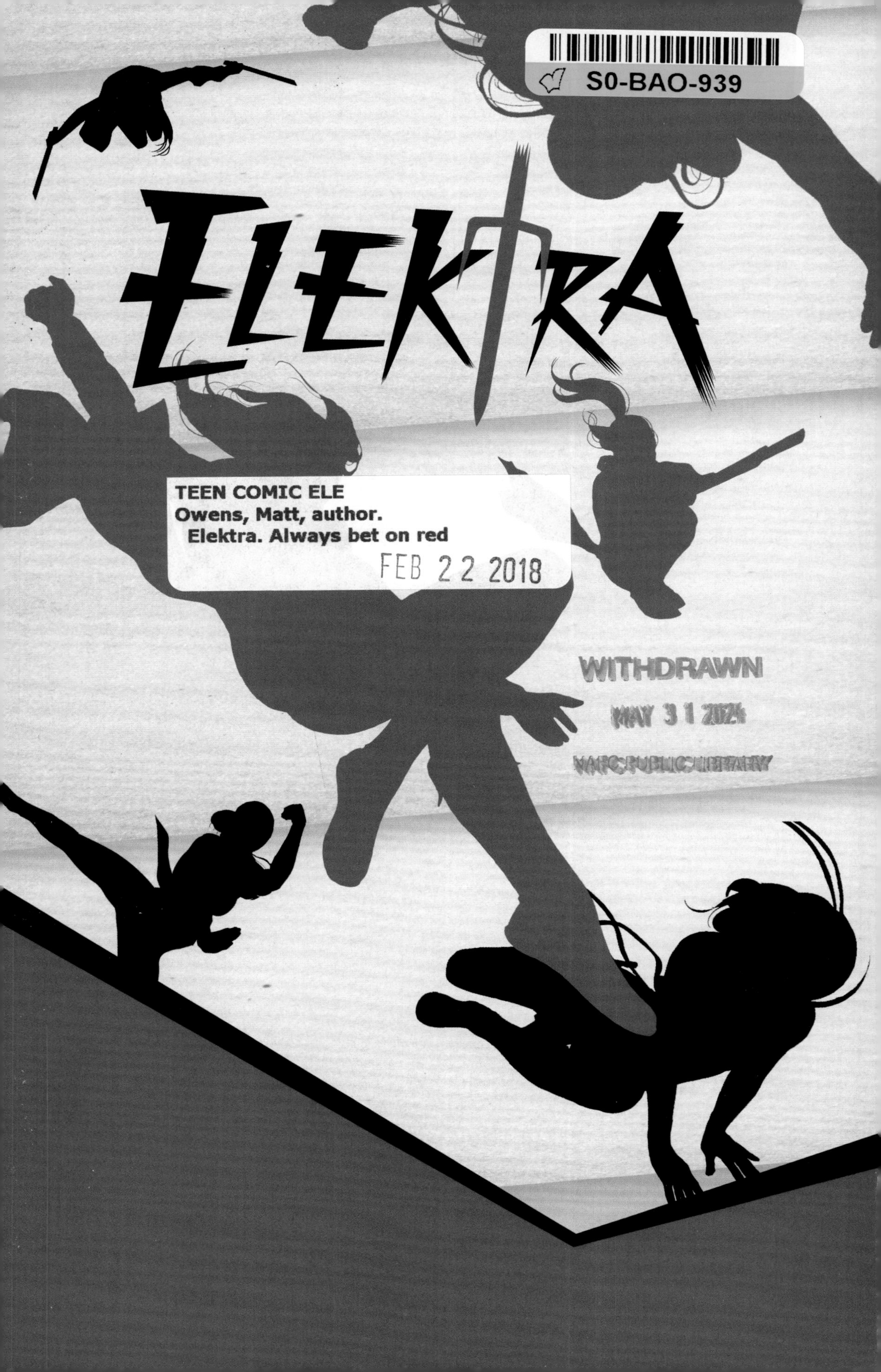
ELEKTRA

The costumed vigilante known as DAREDEVIL has been fighting crime in the dark streets and on the foggy, cold rooftops of New York City for years. In that time he's fought some deadly men and women: assassins, crime lords, killers and thieves. One of Daredevil's most complicated relationships is with the ninja-assassin known as...

# ELEKTRA

## *Always Bet on Red*

### *Matt Owens*
**WRITER**

### *Juann Cabal*
WITH *Martin Morazzo* (#4)
**ARTISTS**

### *Antonio Fabela*
WITH *Marcio Menyz* (#1)
& *Jordan Boyd* (#3)
**COLOR ARTISTS**

### *VC's Cory Petit*
**LETTERER**

### *Elizabeth Torque*
**COVER ART**

### *Christina Harrington*
**ASSISTANT EDITOR**

### *Mark Paniccia*
**EDITOR**

COLLECTION EDITOR **JENNIFER GRÜNWALD** | ASSISTANT EDITOR **CAITLIN O'CONNELL**
ASSOCIATE MANAGING EDITOR **KATERI WOODY** | EDITOR, SPECIAL PROJECTS **MARK D. BEAZLEY**
VP PRODUCTION & SPECIAL PROJECTS **JEFF YOUNGQUIST** | SVP PRINT, SALES & MARKETING **DAVID GABRIEL**
BOOK DESIGNER **JAY BOWEN**

EDITOR IN CHIEF **AXEL ALONSO** | CHIEF CREATIVE OFFICER **JOE QUESADA**
PRESIDENT **DAN BUCKLEY** | EXECUTIVE PRODUCER **ALAN FINE**

ELEKTRA: ALWAYS BET ON RED. Contains material originally published in magazine form as ELEKTRA #1-5. First printing 2017. ISBN# 978-1-302-90564-4. Published by MARVEL WORLDWIDE, INC., a subsidiary of MARVEL ENTERTAINMENT, LLC. OFFICE OF PUBLICATION: 135 West 50th Street, New York, NY 10020. Copyright © 2017 MARVEL No similarity between any of the names, characters, persons, and/or institutions in this magazine with those of any living or dead person or institution is intended, and any such similarity which may exist is purely coincidental. **Printed in Canada.** DAN BUCKLEY, President, Marvel Entertainment; JOE QUESADA, Chief Creative Officer; TOM BREVOORT, SVP of Publishing; DAVID BOGART, SVP of Business Affairs & Operations, Publishing & Partnership; C.B. CEBULSKI, VP of Brand Management & Development, Asia; DAVID GABRIEL, SVP of Sales & Marketing, Publishing; JEFF YOUNGQUIST, VP of Production & Special Projects; DAN CARR, Executive Director of Publishing Technology; ALEX MORALES, Director of Publishing Operations; SUSAN CRESPI, Production Manager; STAN LEE, Chairman Emeritus. For information regarding advertising in Marvel Comics or on Marvel.com, please contact Vit DeBellis, Integrated Sales Manager, at vdebellis@marvel.com. For Marvel subscription inquiries, please call 888-511-5480. **Manufactured between 7/21/2017 and 8/22/2017 by SOLISCO PRINTERS, SCOTT, QC, CANADA.**

10 9 8 7 6 5 4 3 2 1

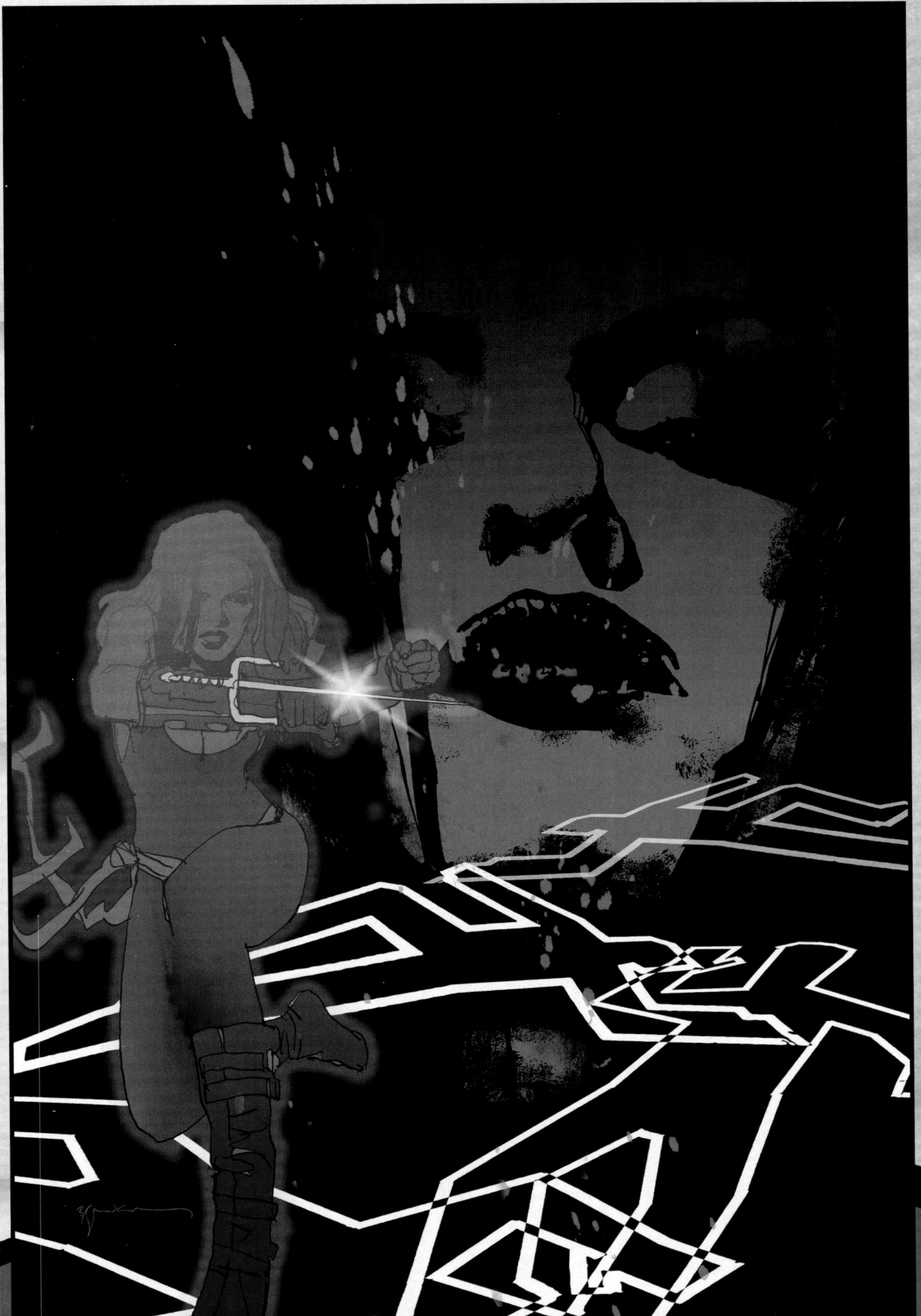

**#1 VARIANT BY** *Bill Sienkiewicz*

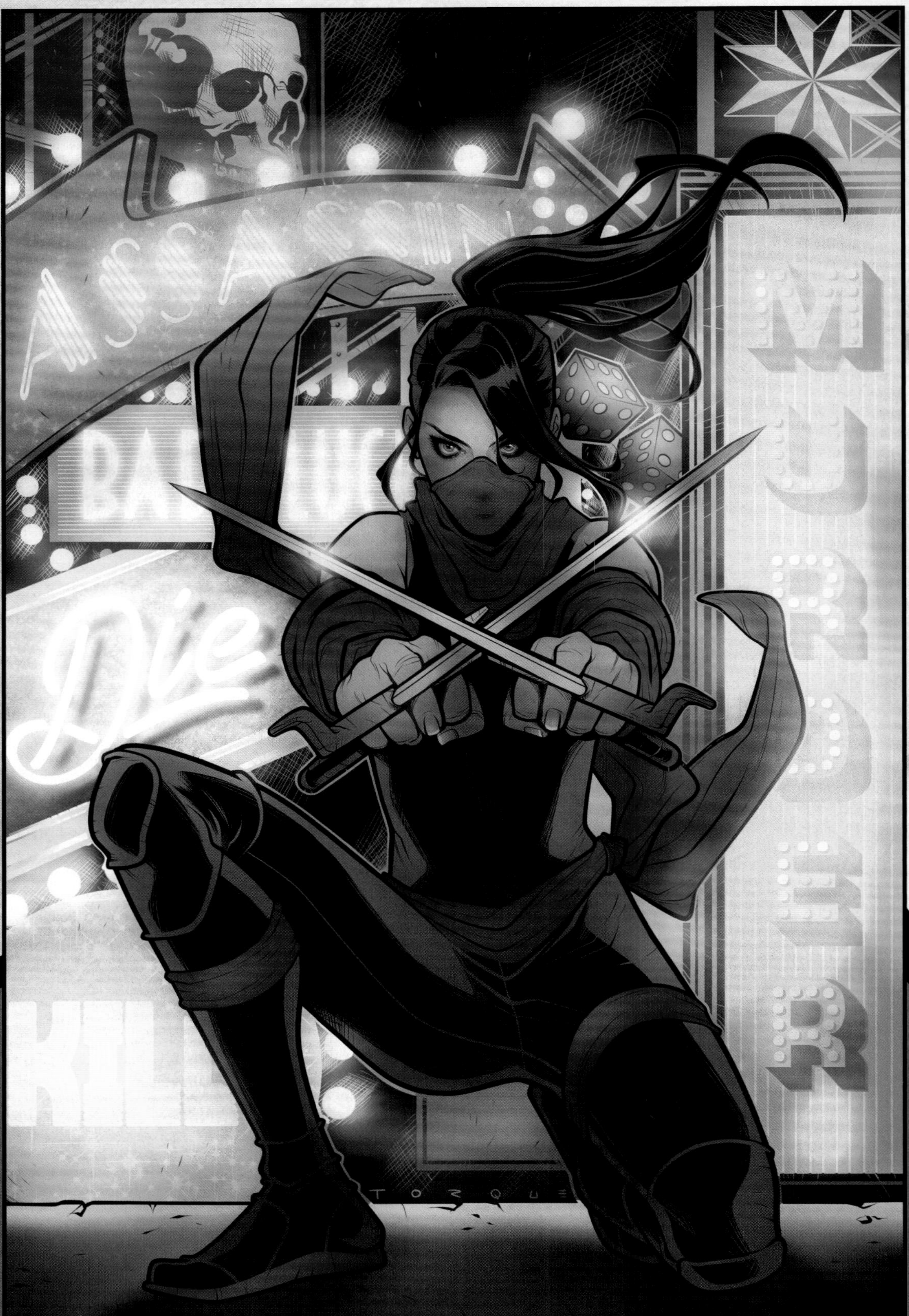
ASSASSIN
Die
MURDER
TORQUE

"WELCOME BACK TO THE *MIDWAY CASINO!*
M MIDWAY
"THE BRIGHTEST SHINING BEACON IN ALL OF LAS VEGAS!
Jackpot 7
"AND THOSE BRIGHT LIGHTS CAST SOME *DARK* SHADOWS."

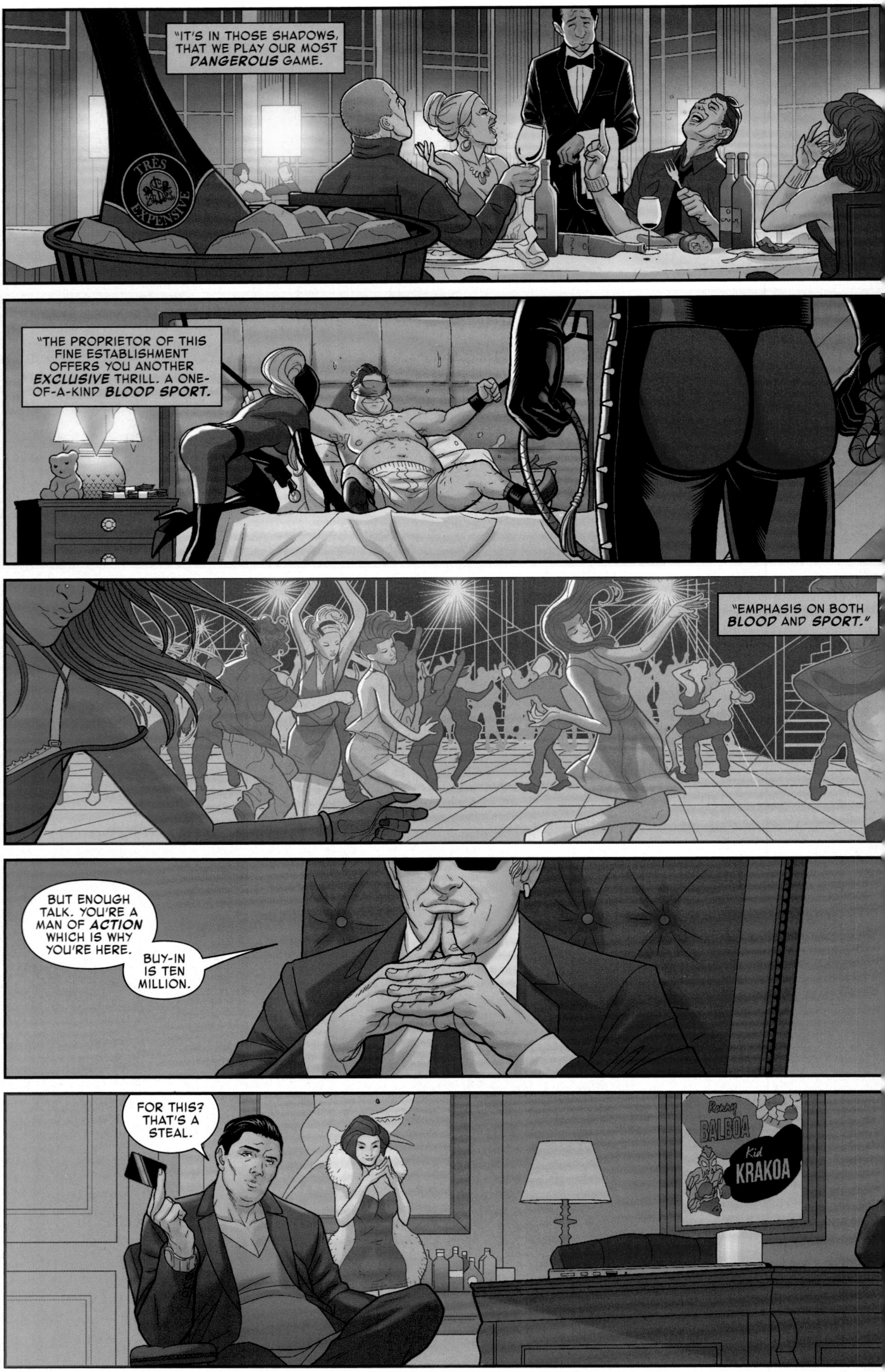
"IT'S IN THOSE SHADOWS, THAT WE PLAY OUR MOST DANGEROUS GAME.
TRÈS EXPENSIVE
"THE PROPRIETOR OF THIS FINE ESTABLISHMENT OFFERS YOU ANOTHER EXCLUSIVE THRILL. A ONE-OF-A-KIND BLOOD SPORT.
"EMPHASIS ON BOTH BLOOD AND SPORT."
BUT ENOUGH TALK. YOU'RE A MAN OF ACTION WHICH IS WHY YOU'RE HERE.
BUY-IN IS TEN MILLION.
FOR THIS? THAT'S A STEAL.
Ronny
BALBOA
Kid
KRAKOA

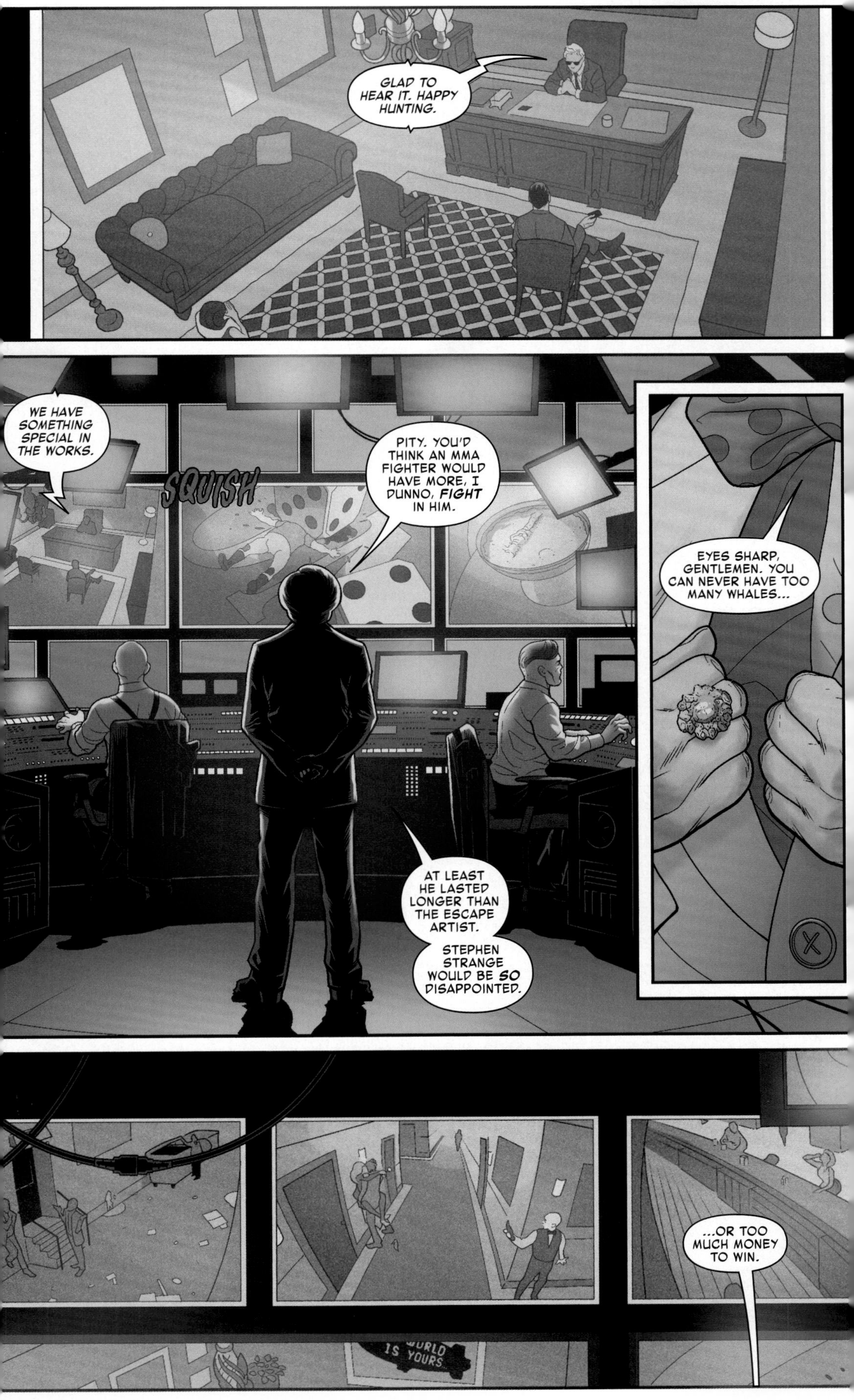
GLAD TO HEAR IT. HAPPY HUNTING.
WE HAVE SOMETHING SPECIAL IN THE WORKS.
SQUISH
PITY. YOU'D THINK AN MMA FIGHTER WOULD HAVE MORE, I DUNNO, FIGHT IN HIM.
AT LEAST HE LASTED LONGER THAN THE ESCAPE ARTIST.
STEPHEN STRANGE WOULD BE SO DISAPPOINTED.
EYES SHARP, GENTLEMEN. YOU CAN NEVER HAVE TOO MANY WHALES...
...OR TOO MUCH MONEY TO WIN.

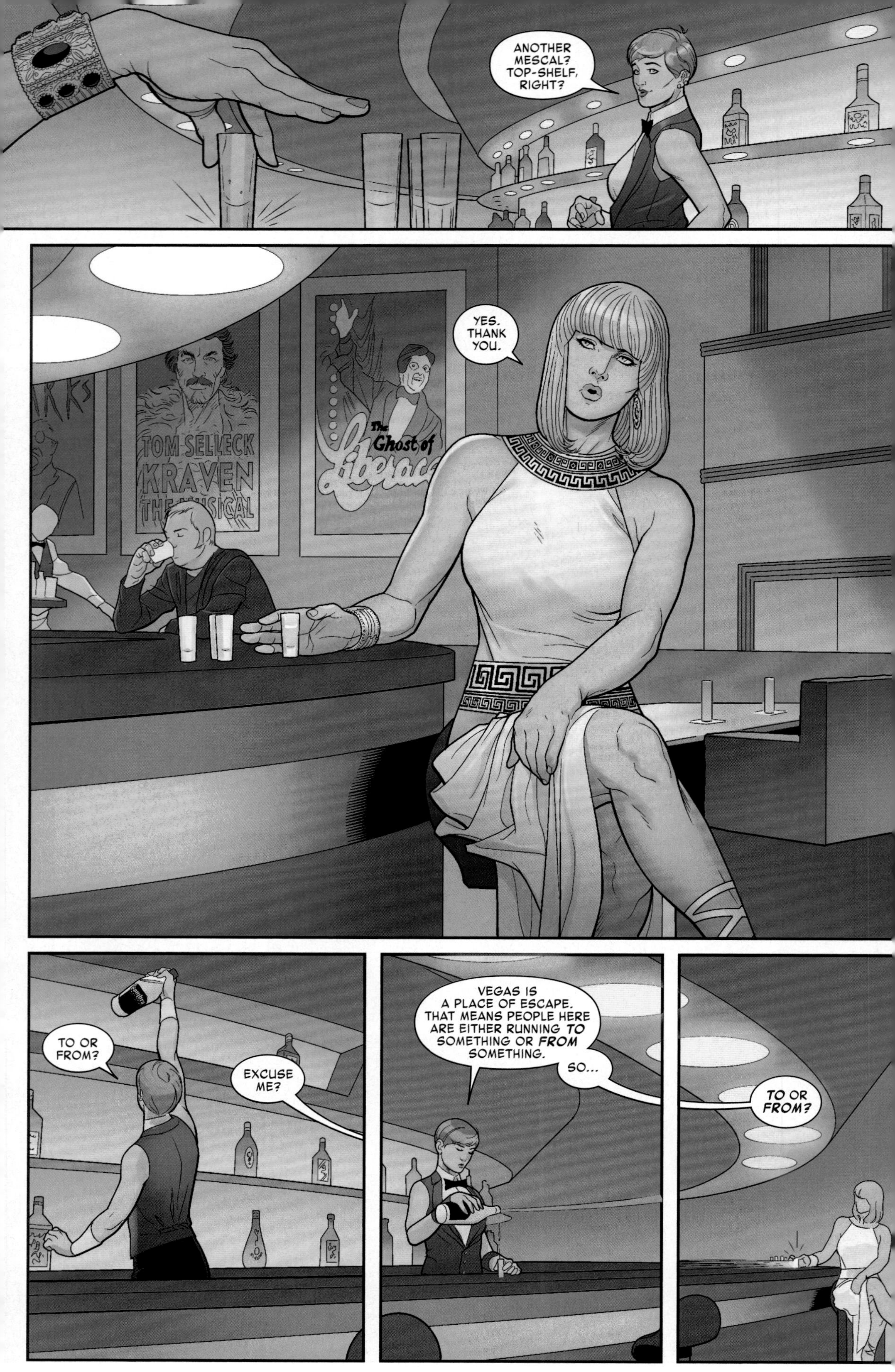
ANOTHER MESCAL? TOP-SHELF, RIGHT?
TOM SELLECK
KRAVEN
THE MUSICAL
The Ghost of Liberace
YES. THANK YOU.
TO OR FROM?
EXCUSE ME?
VEGAS IS A PLACE OF ESCAPE. THAT MEANS PEOPLE HERE ARE EITHER RUNNING TO SOMETHING OR FROM SOMETHING.
SO...
TO OR FROM?

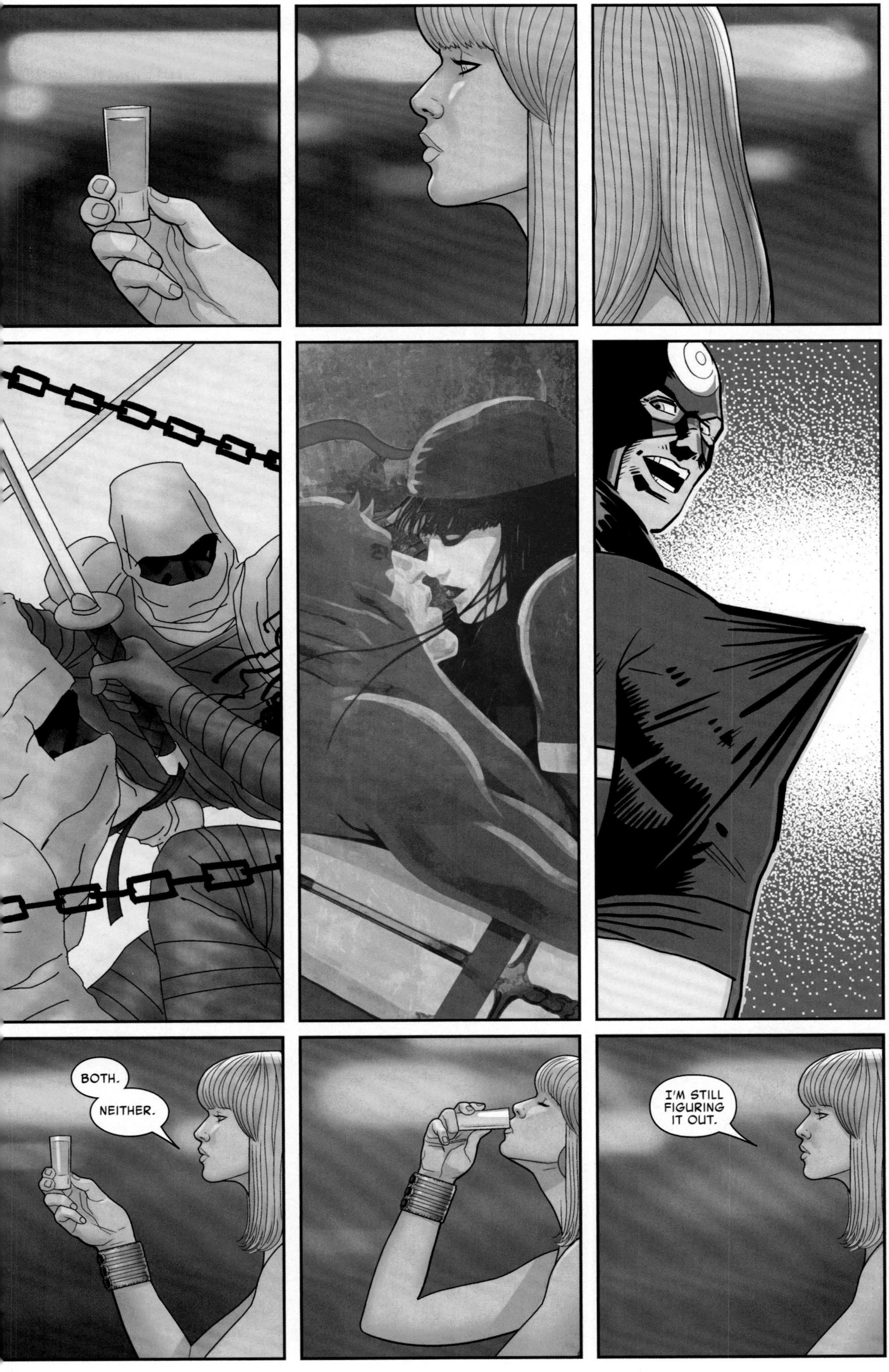
BOTH.
NEITHER.
I'M STILL FIGURING IT OUT.

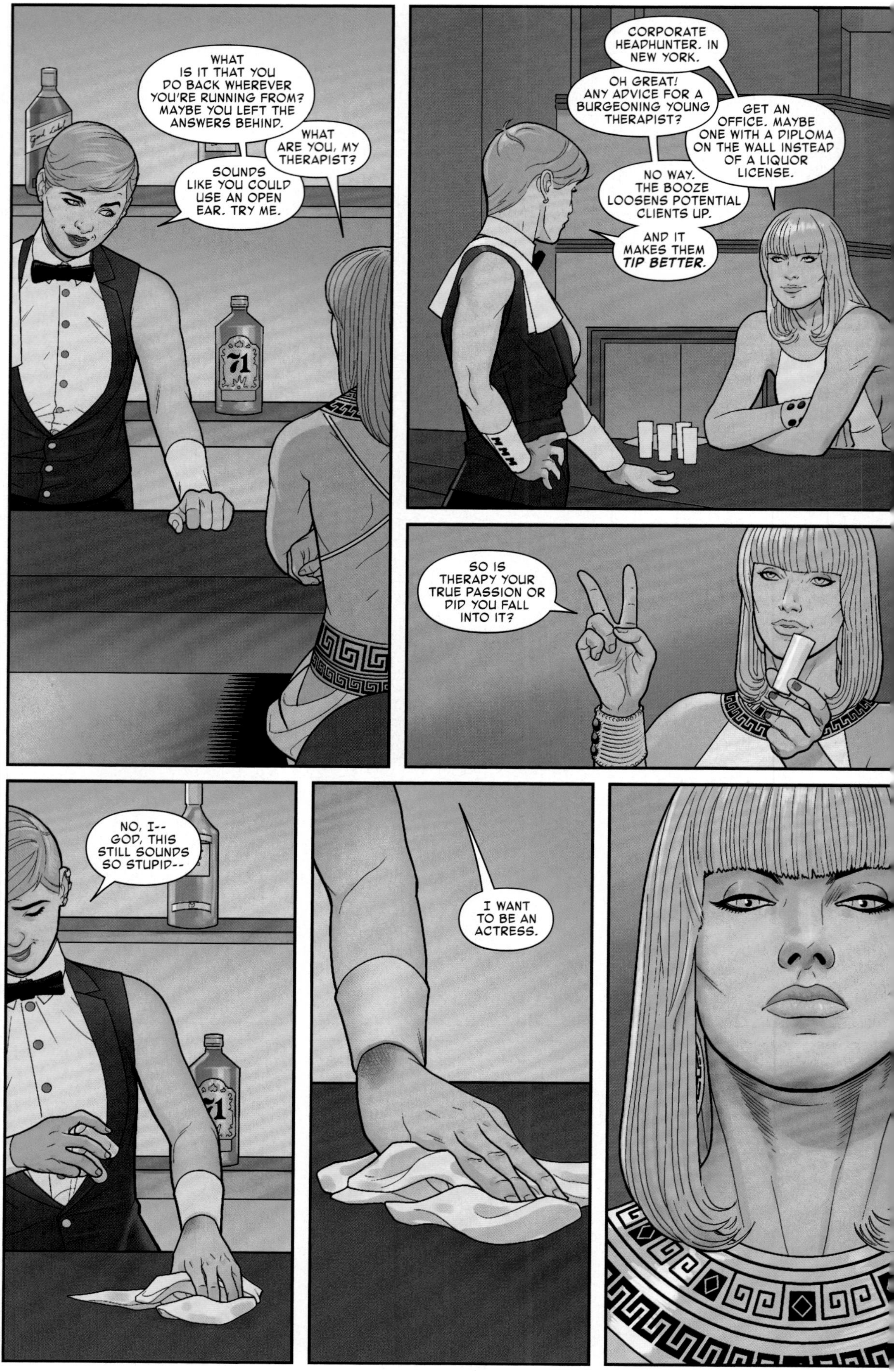
WHAT IS IT THAT YOU DO BACK WHEREVER YOU'RE RUNNING FROM? MAYBE YOU LEFT THE ANSWERS BEHIND.
WHAT ARE YOU, MY THERAPIST?
SOUNDS LIKE YOU COULD USE AN OPEN EAR. TRY ME.
CORPORATE HEADHUNTER. IN NEW YORK.
OH GREAT! ANY ADVICE FOR A BURGEONING YOUNG THERAPIST?
GET AN OFFICE. MAYBE ONE WITH A DIPLOMA ON THE WALL INSTEAD OF A LIQUOR LICENSE.
NO WAY. THE BOOZE LOOSENS POTENTIAL CLIENTS UP.
AND IT MAKES THEM ***TIP BETTER.***
SO IS THERAPY YOUR TRUE PASSION OR DID YOU FALL INTO IT?
NO, I-- GOD, THIS STILL SOUNDS SO STUPID--
I WANT TO BE AN ACTRESS.

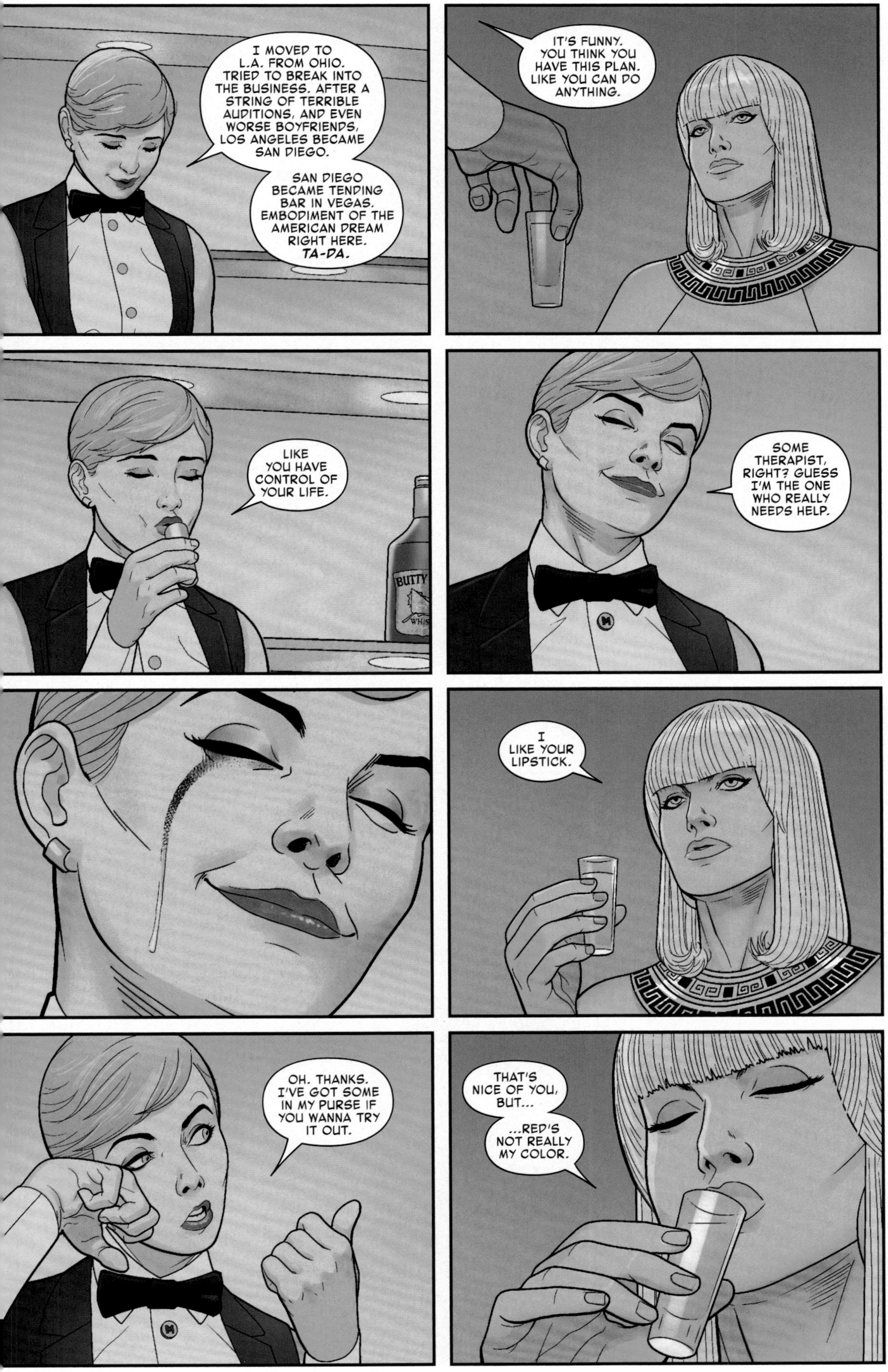
I MOVED TO L.A. FROM OHIO. TRIED TO BREAK INTO THE BUSINESS. AFTER A STRING OF TERRIBLE AUDITIONS, AND EVEN WORSE BOYFRIENDS, LOS ANGELES BECAME SAN DIEGO.
SAN DIEGO BECAME TENDING BAR IN VEGAS. EMBODIMENT OF THE AMERICAN DREAM RIGHT HERE. *TA-DA.*
IT'S FUNNY. YOU THINK YOU HAVE THIS PLAN. LIKE YOU CAN DO ANYTHING.
LIKE YOU HAVE CONTROL OF YOUR LIFE.
BUTTY
WHIS
SOME THERAPIST, RIGHT? GUESS I'M THE ONE WHO REALLY NEEDS HELP.
I LIKE YOUR LIPSTICK.
OH. THANKS. I'VE GOT SOME IN MY PURSE IF YOU WANNA TRY IT OUT.
THAT'S NICE OF YOU, BUT...
...RED'S NOT REALLY MY COLOR.

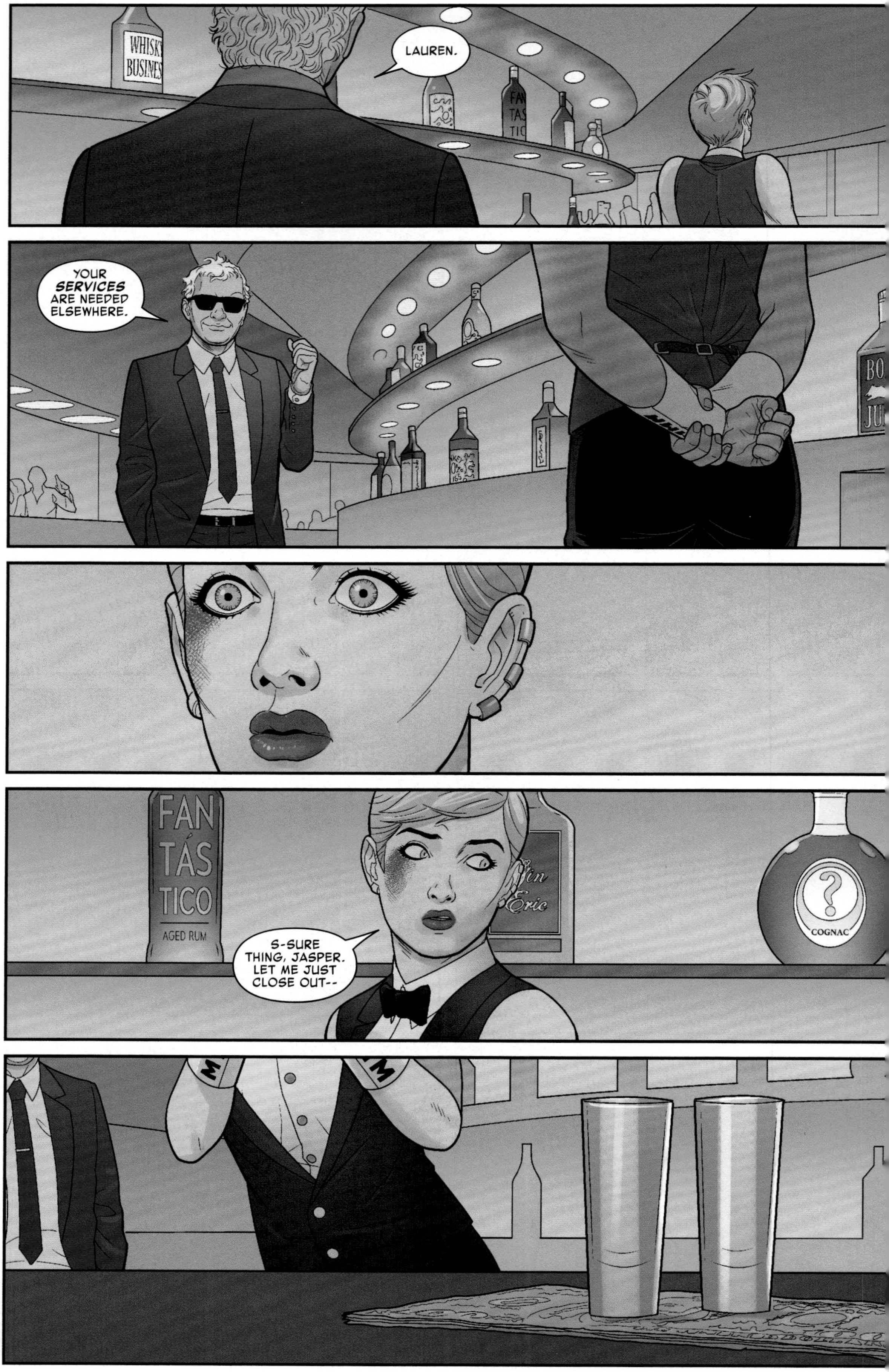

WHISKY BUSINES
LAUREN.
YOUR SERVICES ARE NEEDED ELSEWHERE.
FANTÁSTICO AGED RUM
COGNAC
S-SURE THING, JASPER. LET ME JUST CLOSE OUT--

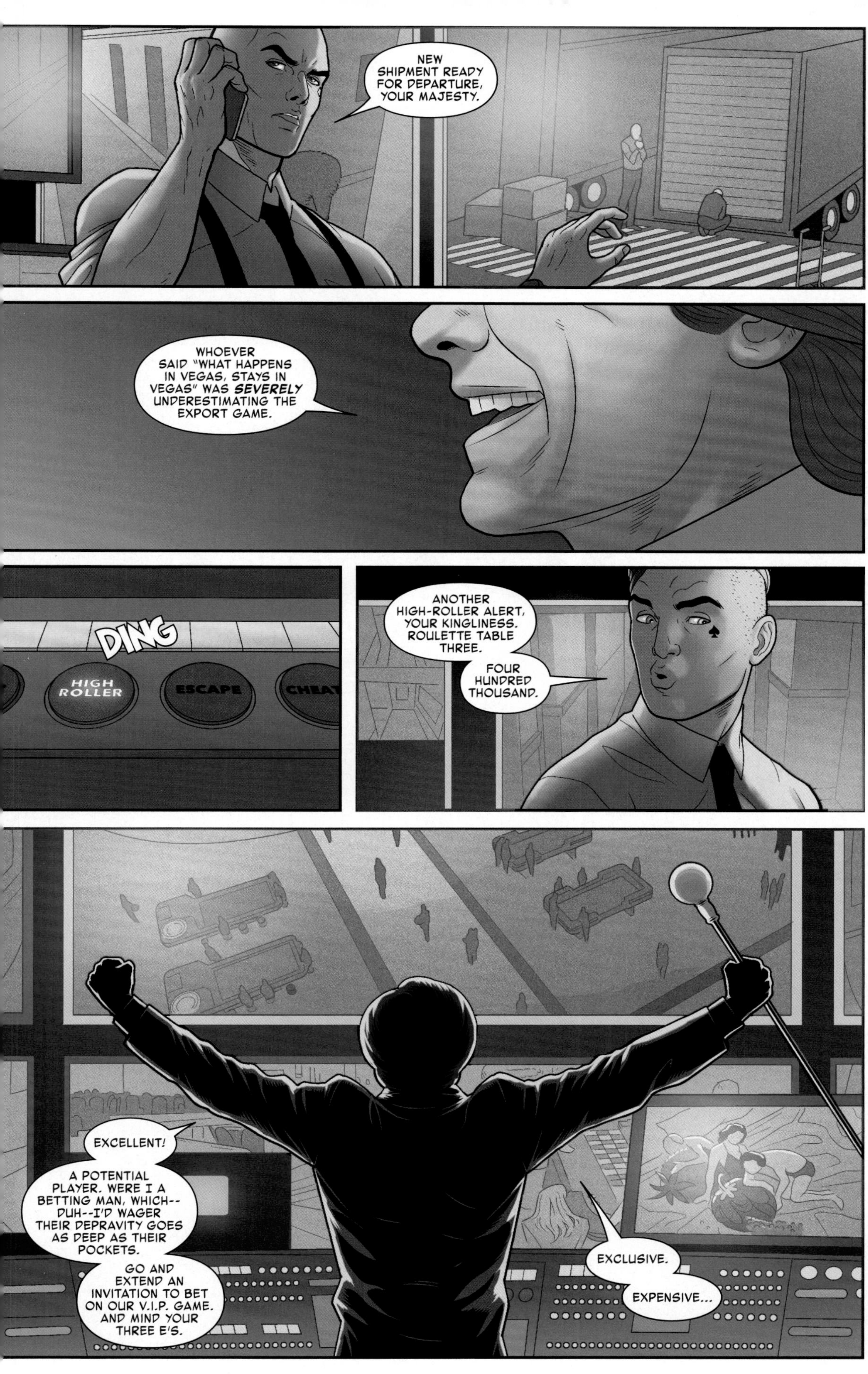
NEW SHIPMENT READY FOR DEPARTURE, YOUR MAJESTY.
WHOEVER SAID "WHAT HAPPENS IN VEGAS, STAYS IN VEGAS" WAS *SEVERELY* UNDERESTIMATING THE EXPORT GAME.
DING
HIGH ROLLER
ESCAPE
CHEAT
ANOTHER HIGH-ROLLER ALERT, YOUR KINGLINESS. ROULETTE TABLE THREE.
FOUR HUNDRED THOUSAND.
EXCELLENT!
A POTENTIAL PLAYER. WERE I A BETTING MAN, WHICH--DUH--I'D WAGER THEIR DEPRAVITY GOES AS DEEP AS THEIR POCKETS.
GO AND EXTEND AN INVITATION TO BET ON OUR V.I.P. GAME. AND MIND YOUR THREE E'S.
EXCLUSIVE.
EXPENSIVE...

"...AND *EXECUTION.*"

WINNER!

YOU SURE CLEANED UP.

JUST LUCKY, I GUESS.

PLACE YOUR BETS.

HOW'D YOU LIKE TO PLAY A MORE *HIGH-STAKES* GAME?

WORST. PICKUP LINE. EVER.

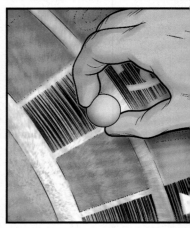

I MEAN NO DISRESPECT. I'M HERE TO OFFER YOU AN INVITATION. AN EXCLUSIVE CONTEST...

...FOR *SELECT* V.I.P. PLAYERS.

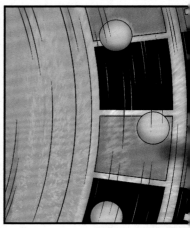

NOT INTERESTED.

WINNER!

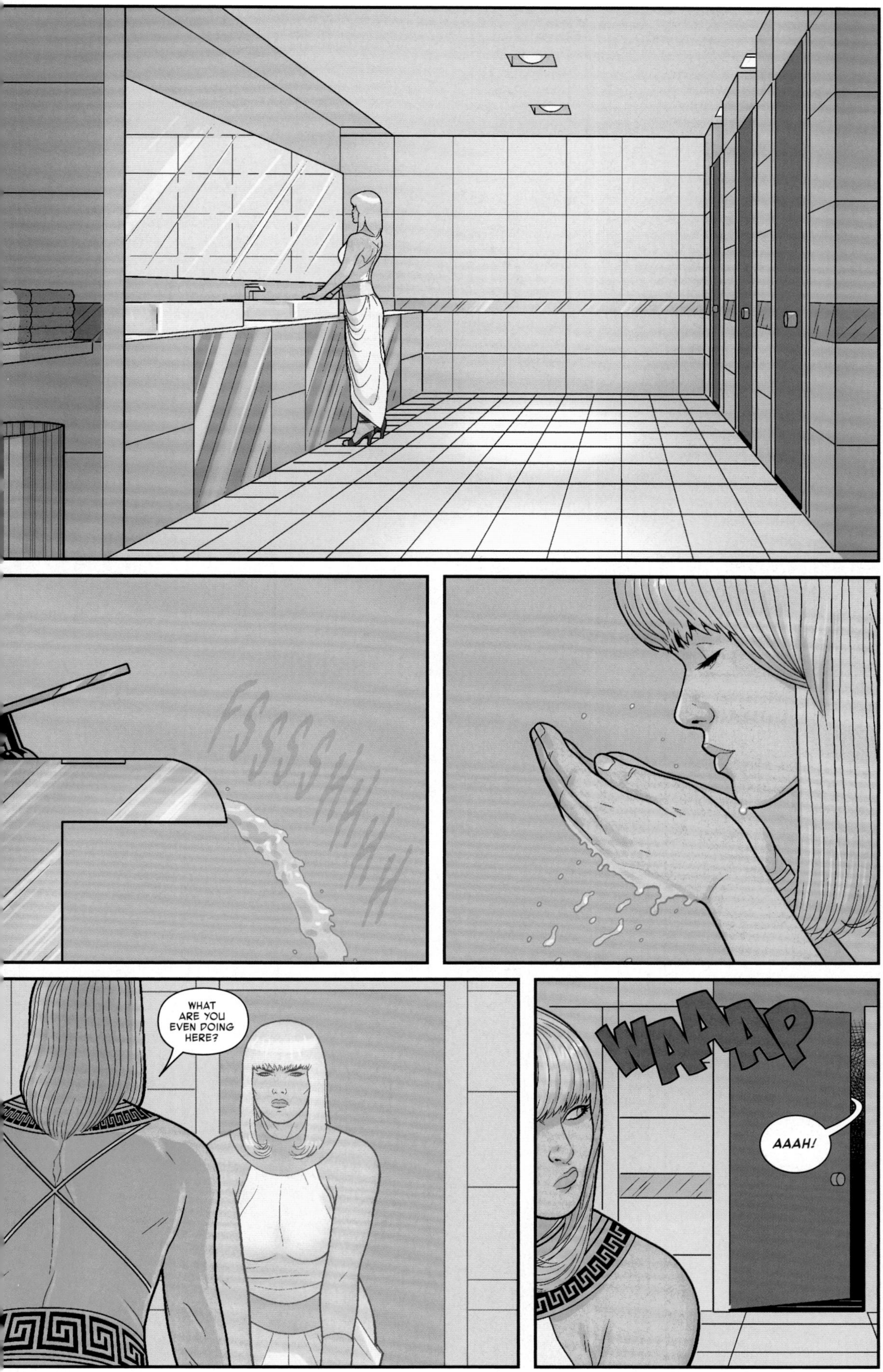

FSSSSHHHHH
WHAT ARE YOU EVEN DOING HERE?
WAAAP
AAAH!

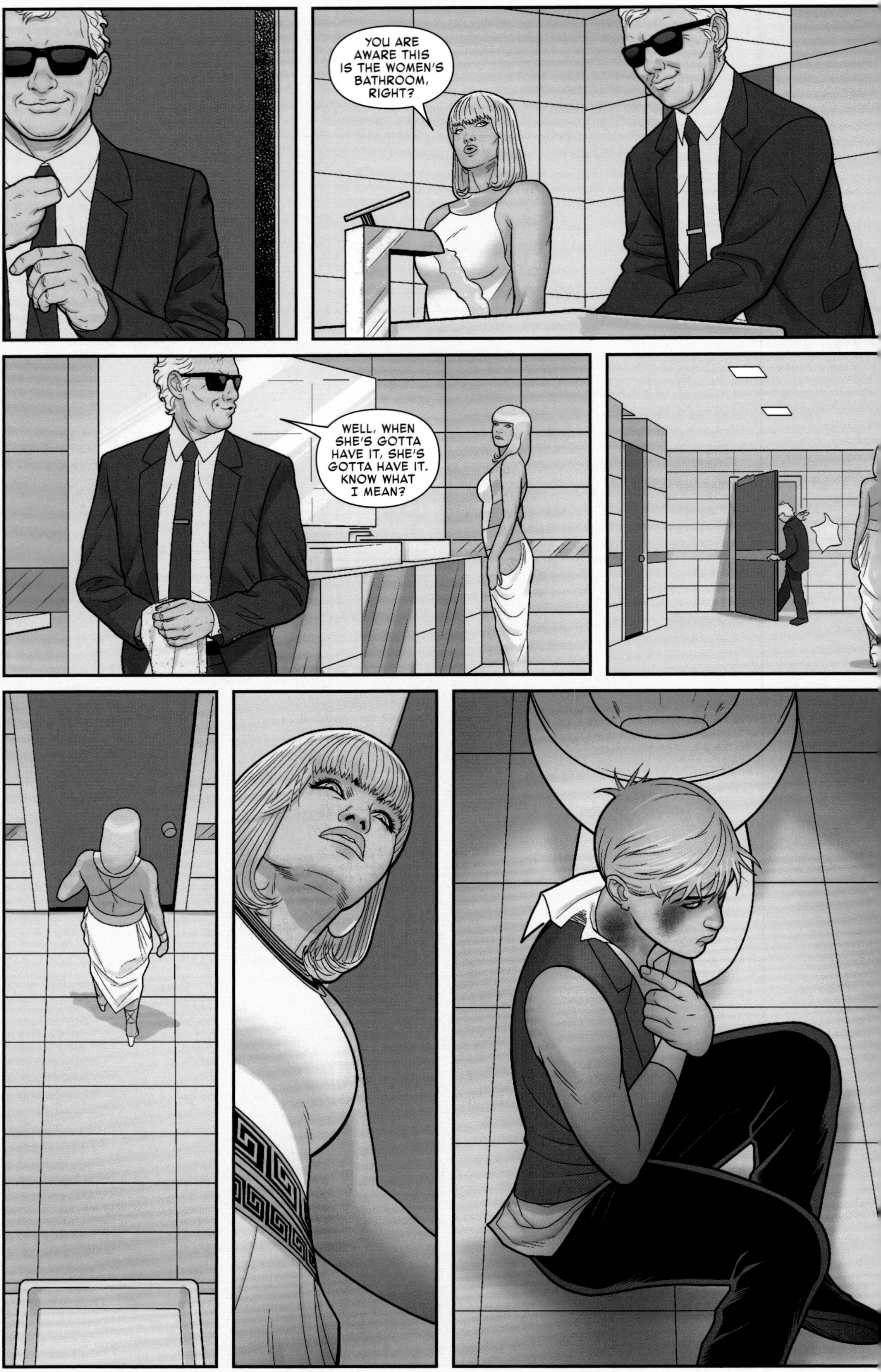
YOU ARE AWARE THIS IS THE WOMEN'S BATHROOM, RIGHT?
WELL, WHEN SHE'S GOTTA HAVE IT, SHE'S GOTTA HAVE IT. KNOW WHAT I MEAN?

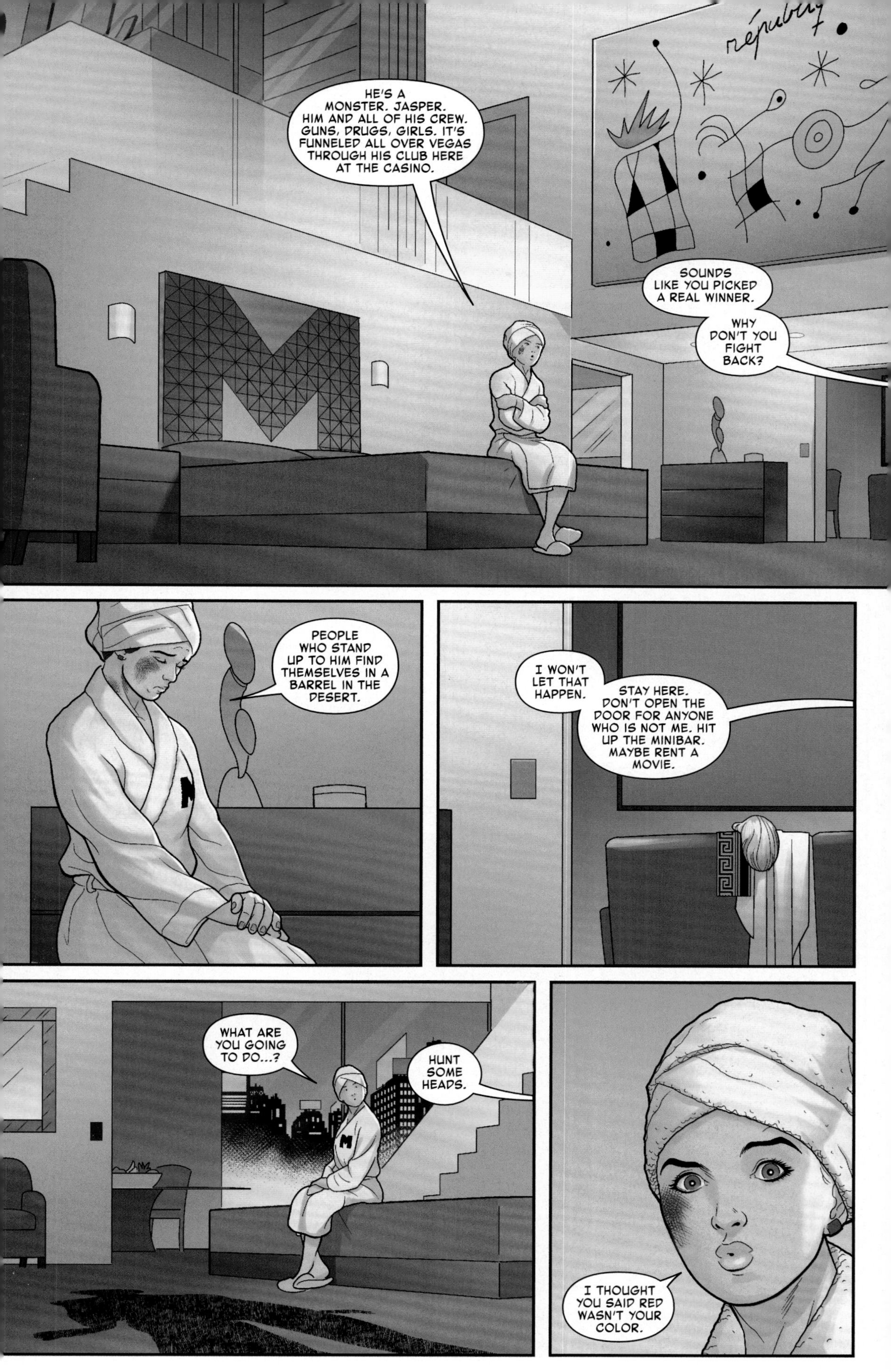
HE'S A MONSTER. JASPER. HIM AND ALL OF HIS CREW. GUNS, DRUGS, GIRLS. IT'S FUNNELED ALL OVER VEGAS THROUGH HIS CLUB HERE AT THE CASINO.
SOUNDS LIKE YOU PICKED A REAL WINNER.
WHY DON'T YOU FIGHT BACK?
PEOPLE WHO STAND UP TO HIM FIND THEMSELVES IN A BARREL IN THE DESERT.
I WON'T LET THAT HAPPEN.
STAY HERE. DON'T OPEN THE DOOR FOR ANYONE WHO IS NOT ME. HIT UP THE MINIBAR. MAYBE RENT A MOVIE.
WHAT ARE YOU GOING TO DO...?
HUNT SOME HEADS.
I THOUGHT YOU SAID RED WASN'T YOUR COLOR.

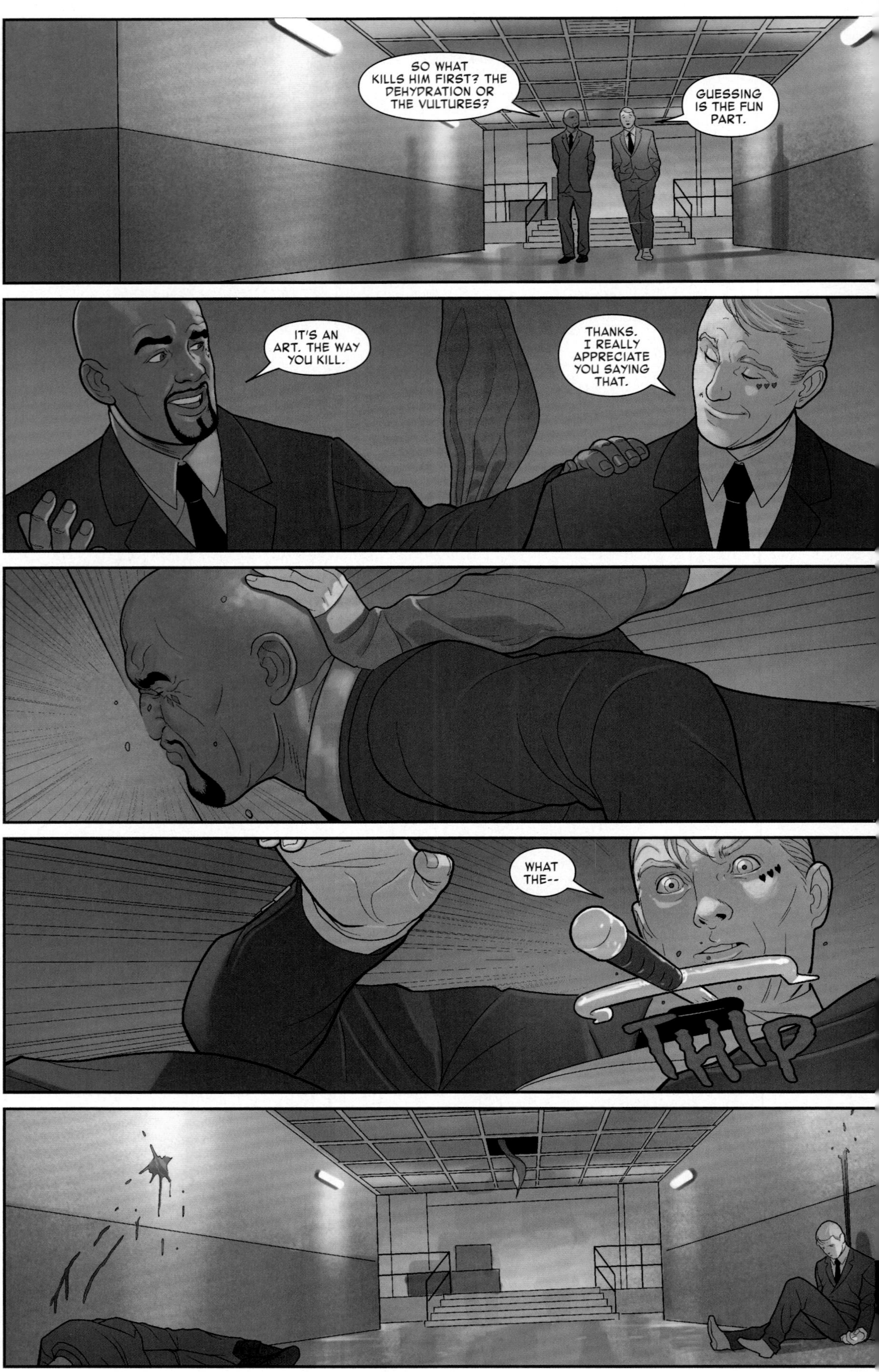
SO WHAT KILLS HIM FIRST? THE DEHYDRATION OR THE VULTURES?
GUESSING IS THE FUN PART.
IT'S AN ART. THE WAY YOU KILL.
THANKS. I REALLY APPRECIATE YOU SAYING THAT.
WHAT THE--
THIP

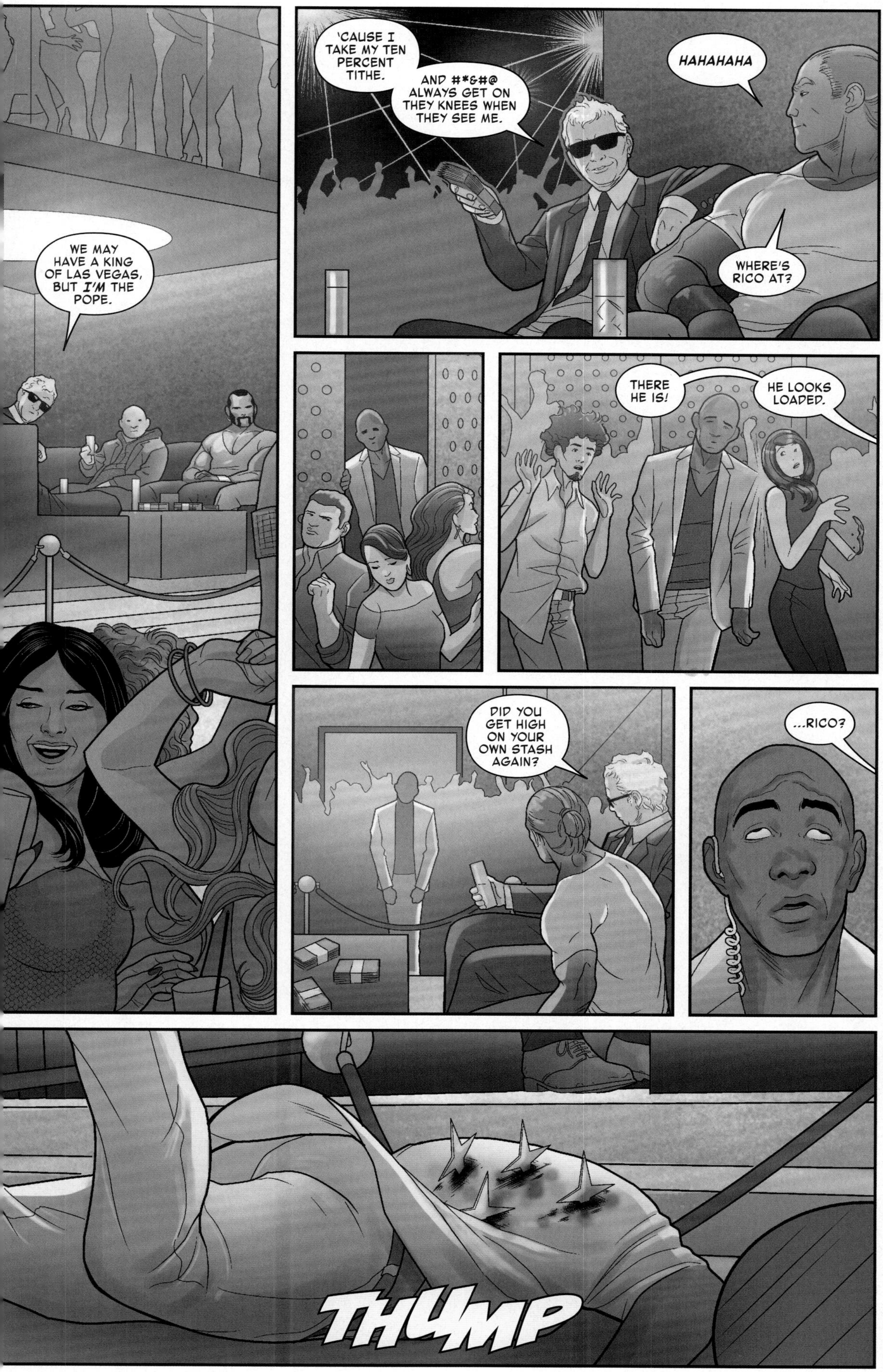
WE MAY HAVE A KING OF LAS VEGAS, BUT *I'M* THE POPE.
'CAUSE I TAKE MY TEN PERCENT TITHE.
AND #*&#@ ALWAYS GET ON THEY KNEES WHEN THEY SEE ME.
*HAHAHAHA*
WHERE'S RICO AT?
THERE HE IS!
HE LOOKS LOADED.
DID YOU GET HIGH ON YOUR OWN STASH AGAIN?
...RICO?
THUMP

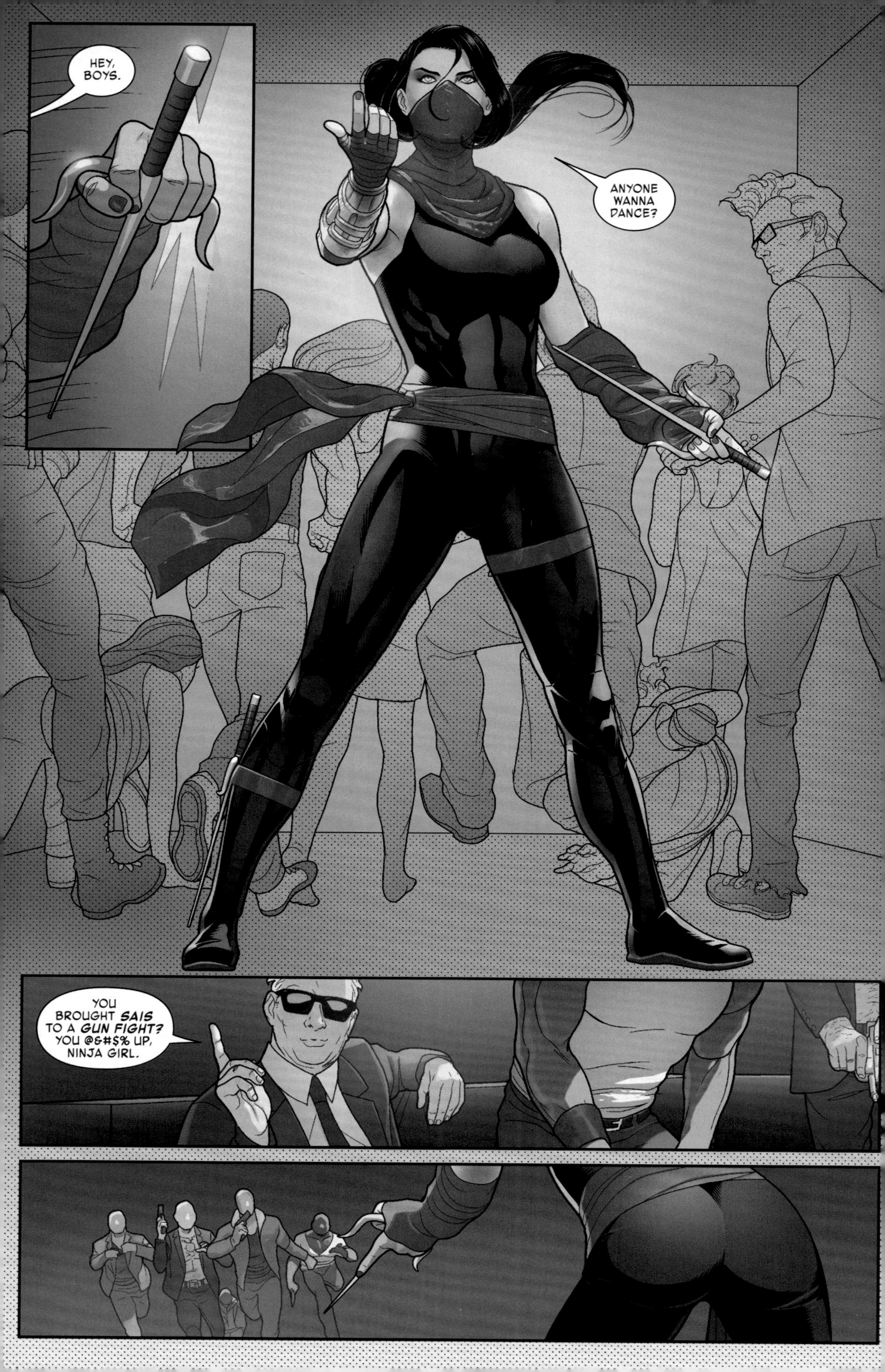
HEY, BOYS.
ANYONE WANNA DANCE?
YOU BROUGHT SAIS TO A GUN FIGHT? YOU @&#$% UP, NINJA GIRL.

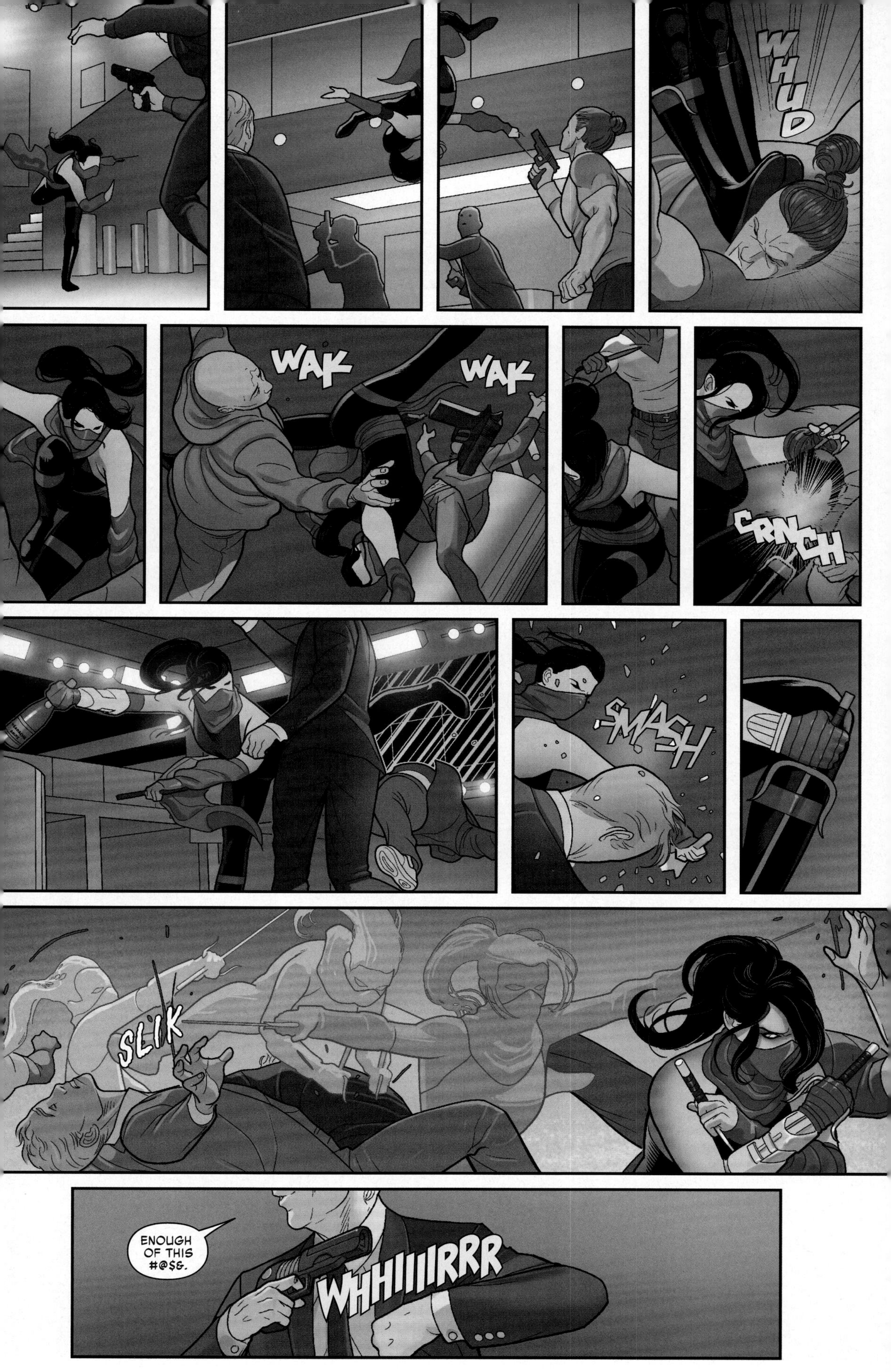
WHUD
WAK
WAK
CRNCH
SMASH
SLIK
ENOUGH OF THIS #@$&.
WHHIIIIRRR

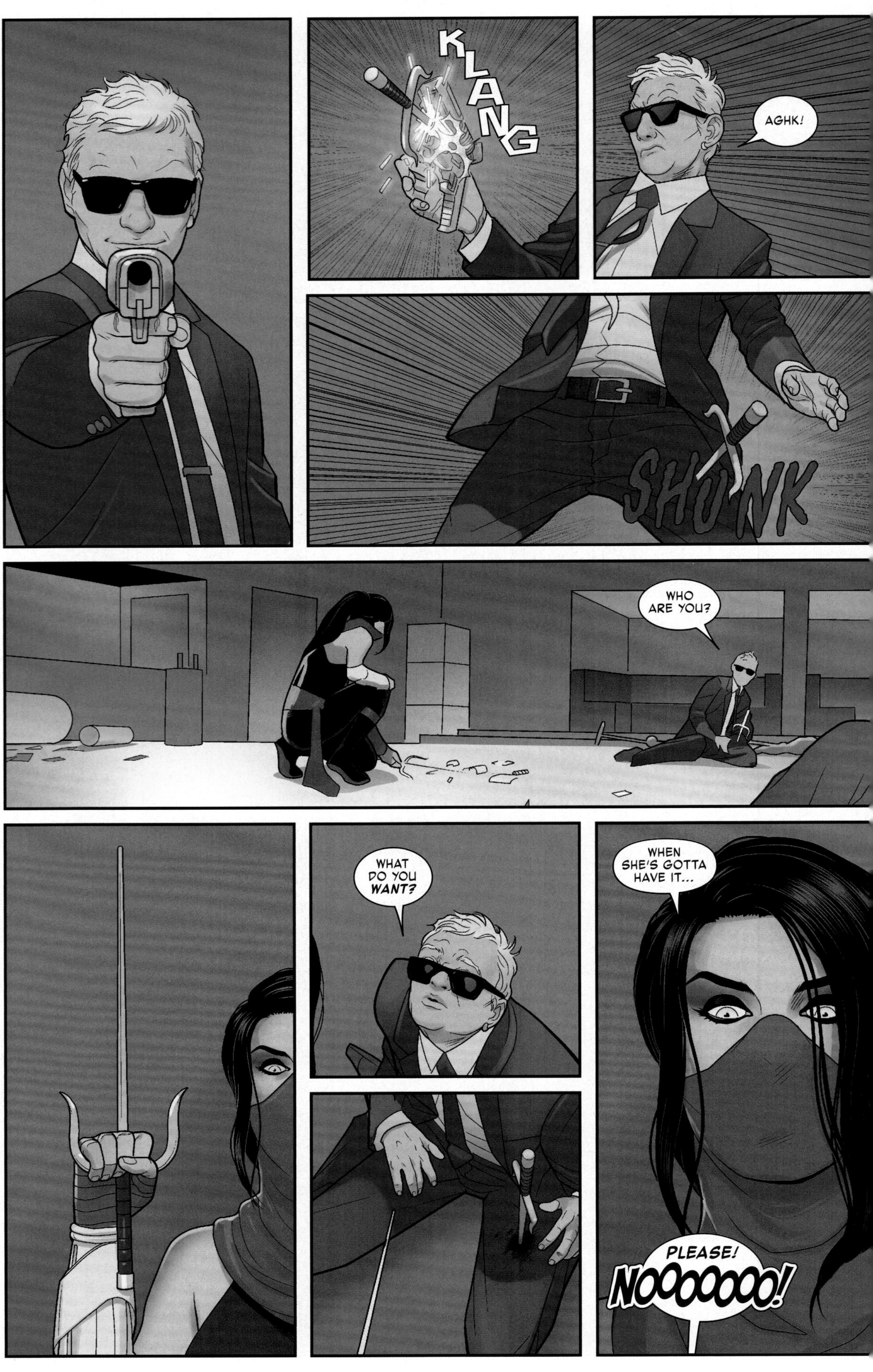
KLANG
AGHK!
SHUNK
WHO ARE YOU?
WHAT DO YOU WANT?
WHEN SHE'S GOTTA HAVE IT...
PLEASE!
NOOOOOOO!

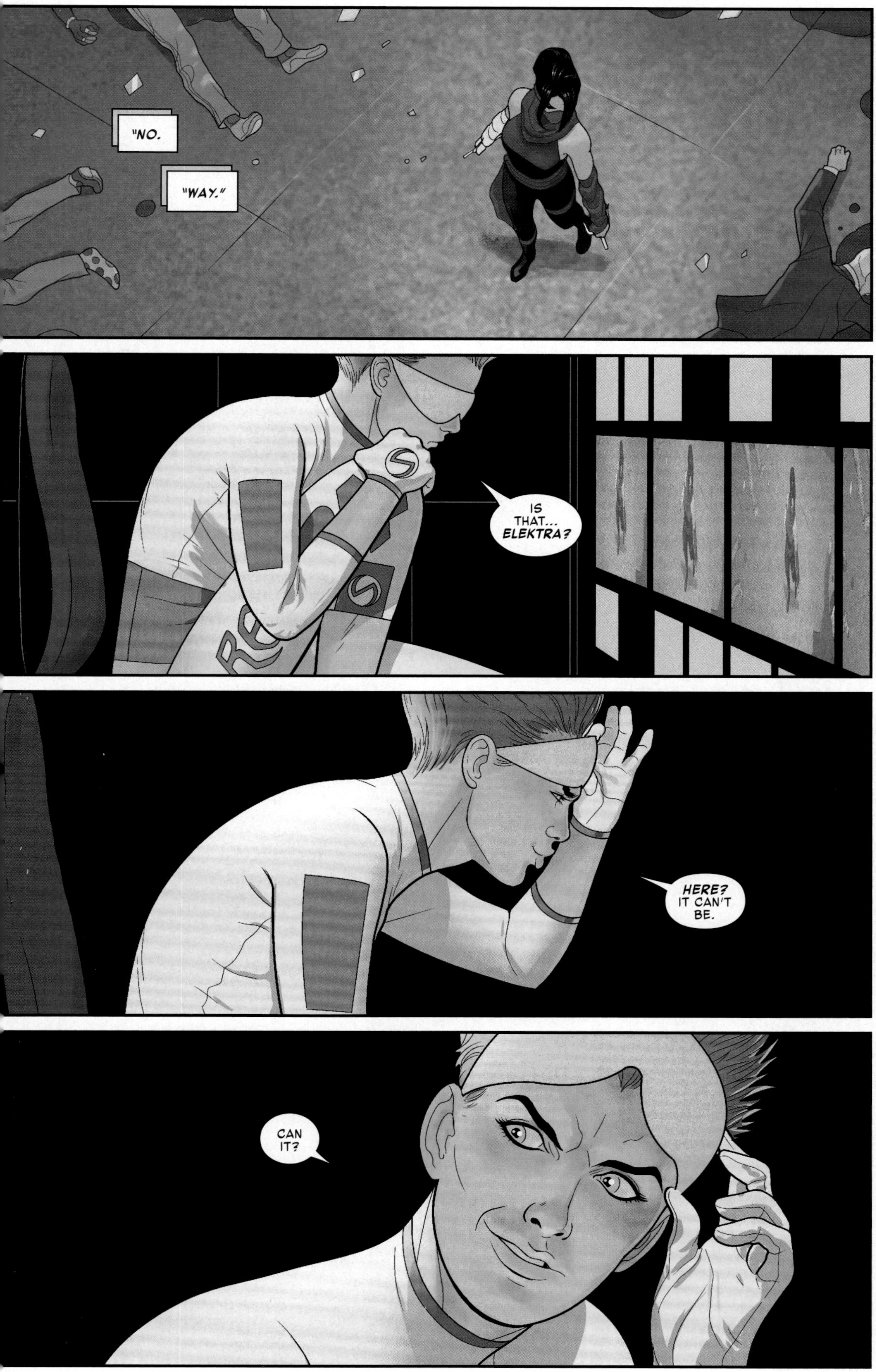
"NO.
"WAY."
IS THAT... ELEKTRA?
HERE? IT CAN'T BE.
CAN IT?

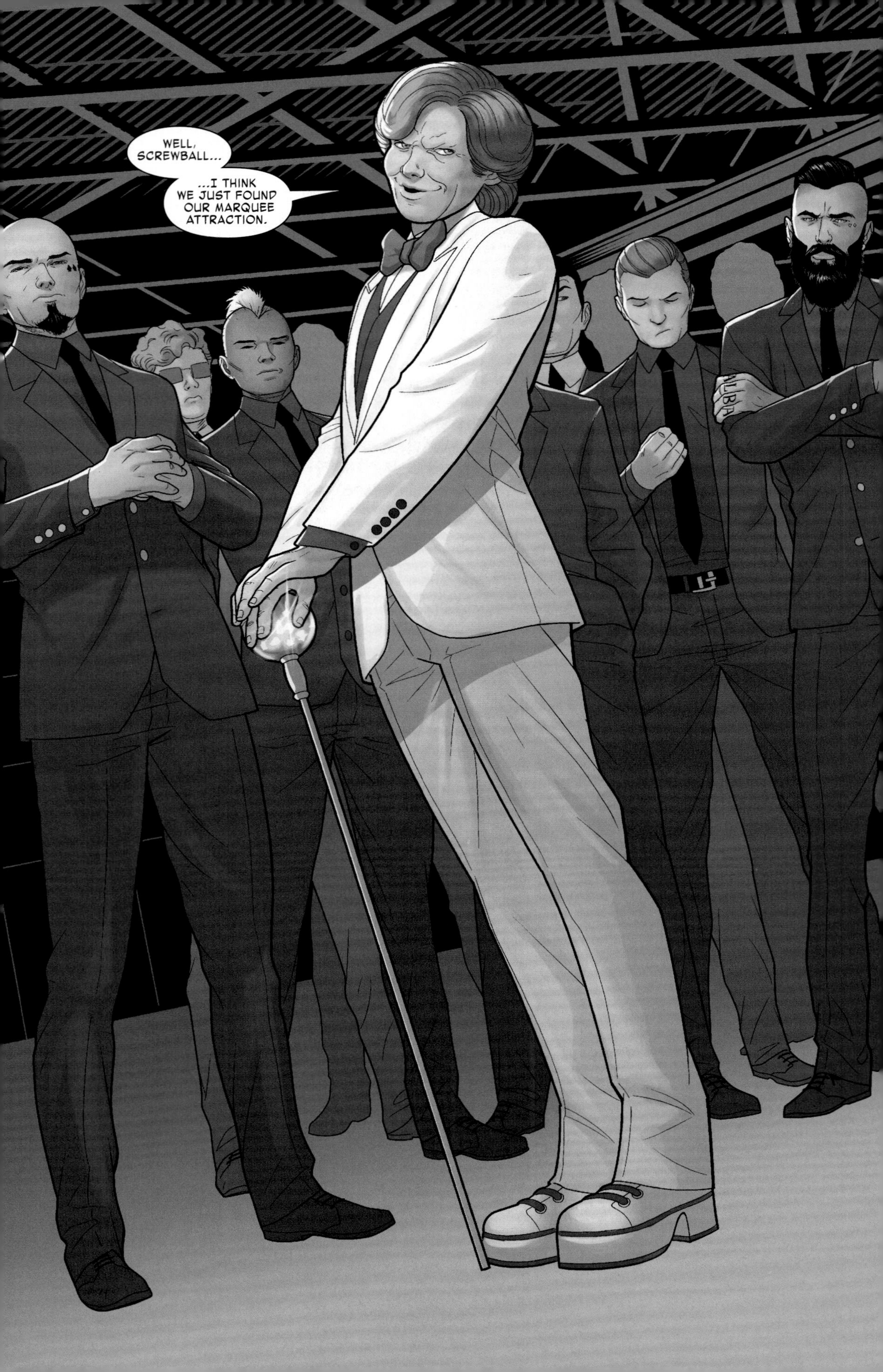
WELL, SCREWBALL...
...I THINK WE JUST FOUND OUR MARQUEE ATTRACTION.

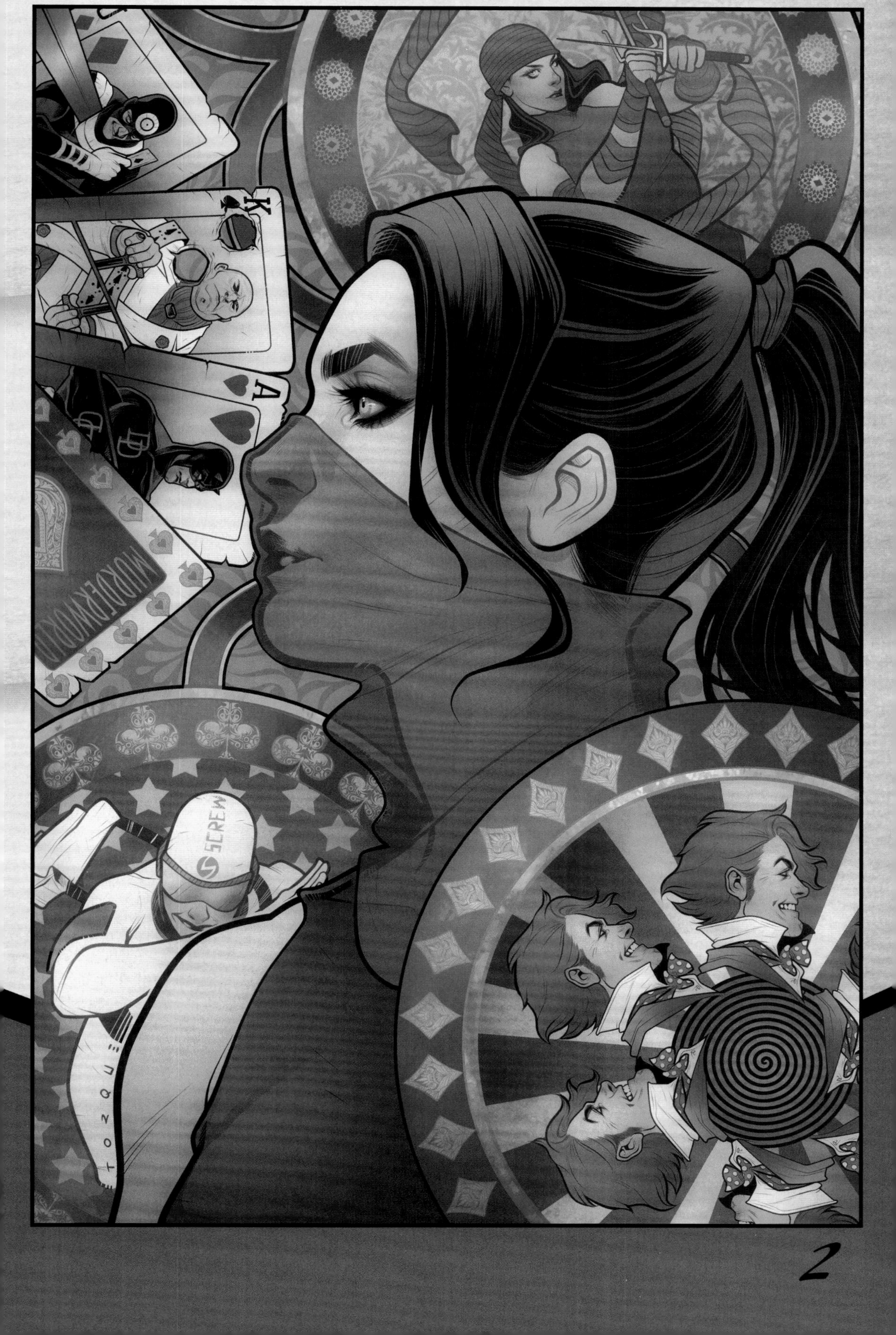
K
A
MURDERWORLD
SCREW

2

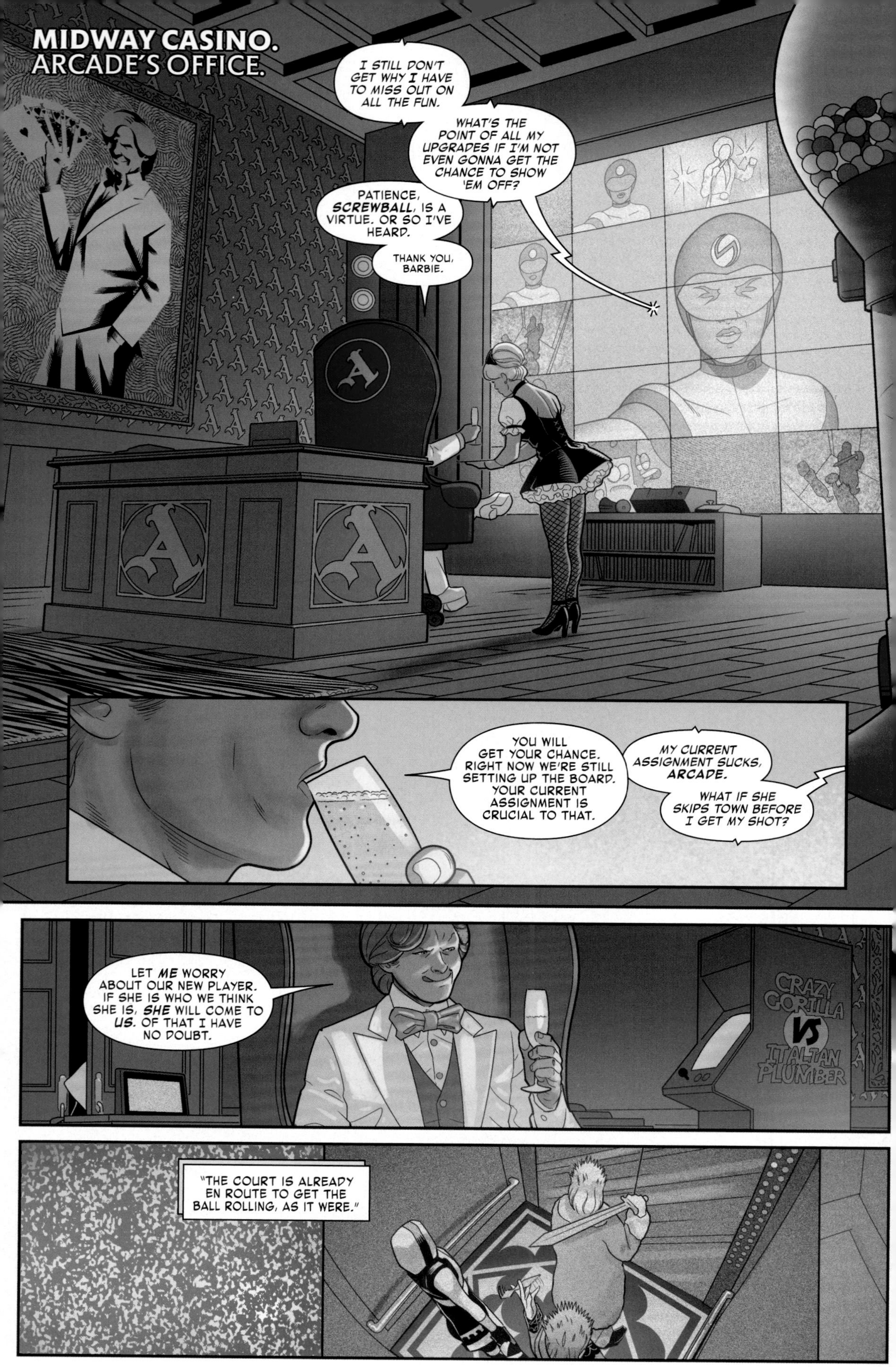
MIDWAY CASINO.
ARCADE'S OFFICE.
I STILL DON'T GET WHY I HAVE TO MISS OUT ON ALL THE FUN.
WHAT'S THE POINT OF ALL MY UPGRADES IF I'M NOT EVEN GONNA GET THE CHANCE TO SHOW 'EM OFF?
PATIENCE, SCREWBALL, IS A VIRTUE. OR SO I'VE HEARD.
THANK YOU, BARBIE.
YOU WILL GET YOUR CHANCE. RIGHT NOW WE'RE STILL SETTING UP THE BOARD. YOUR CURRENT ASSIGNMENT IS CRUCIAL TO THAT.
MY CURRENT ASSIGNMENT SUCKS, ARCADE.
WHAT IF SHE SKIPS TOWN BEFORE I GET MY SHOT?
LET ME WORRY ABOUT OUR NEW PLAYER. IF SHE IS WHO WE THINK SHE IS, SHE WILL COME TO US. OF THAT I HAVE NO DOUBT.
CRAZY GORILLA VS ITALIAN PLUMBER
"THE COURT IS ALREADY EN ROUTE TO GET THE BALL ROLLING, AS IT WERE."

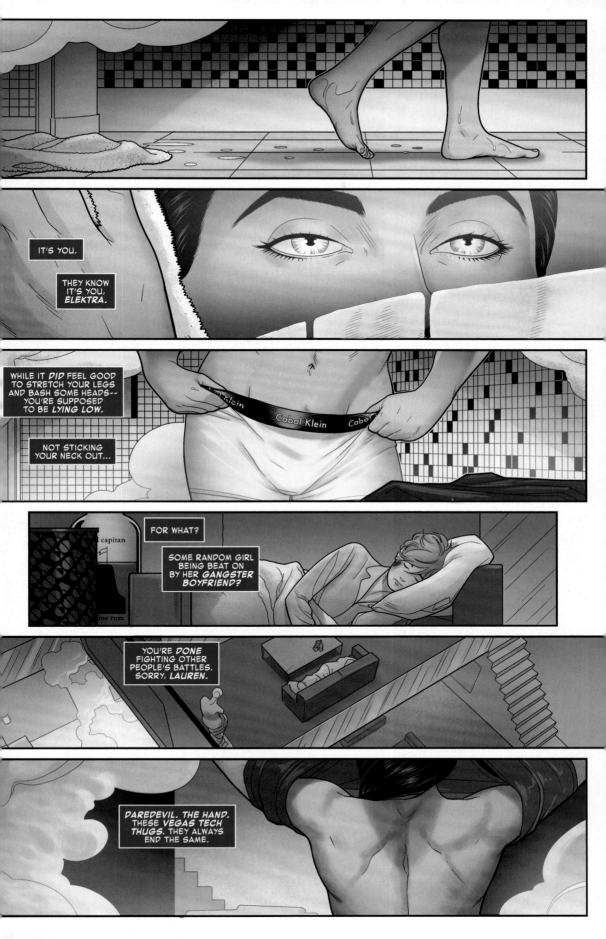

IT'S YOU.

THEY KNOW IT'S YOU, *ELEKTRA.*

WHILE IT *DID* FEEL GOOD TO STRETCH YOUR LEGS AND BASH SOME HEADS-- YOU'RE SUPPOSED TO BE *LYING LOW.*

NOT STICKING YOUR NECK OUT...

FOR WHAT?

SOME RANDOM GIRL BEING BEAT ON BY HER *GANGSTER BOYFRIEND?*

YOU'RE *DONE* FIGHTING OTHER PEOPLE'S BATTLES. SORRY, *LAUREN.*

*DAREDEVIL. THE HAND.* THESE *VEGAS TECH THUGS.* THEY ALWAYS END THE SAME.

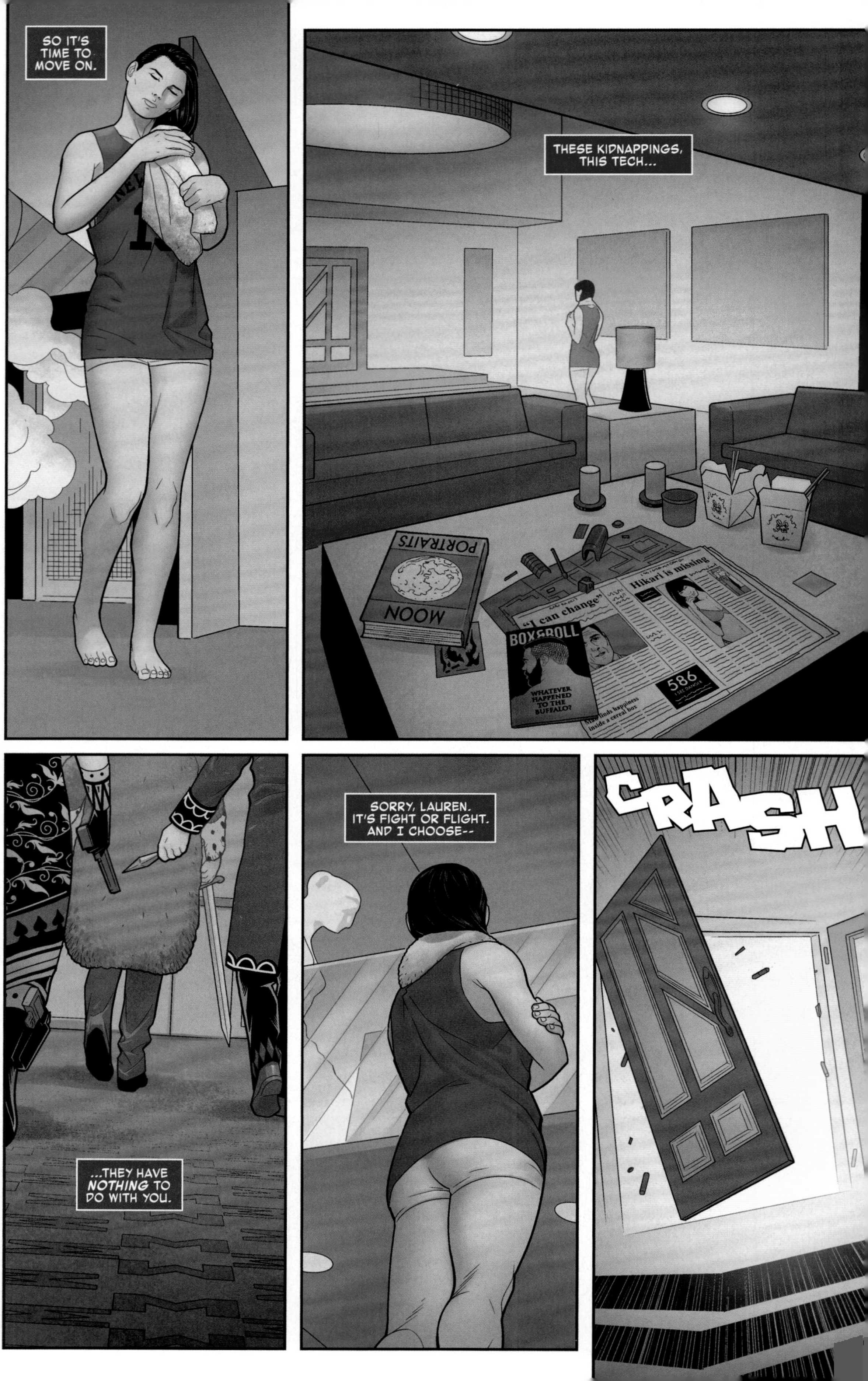
SO IT'S TIME TO MOVE ON.
THESE KIDNAPPINGS, THIS TECH...
PORTRAITS
MOON
"I can change"
Hikari is missing
BOX&ROLL
WHATEVER HAPPENED TO THE BUFFALO?
586
...THEY HAVE *NOTHING* TO DO WITH YOU.
SORRY, LAUREN. IT'S FIGHT OR FLIGHT. AND I CHOOSE--
CRASH

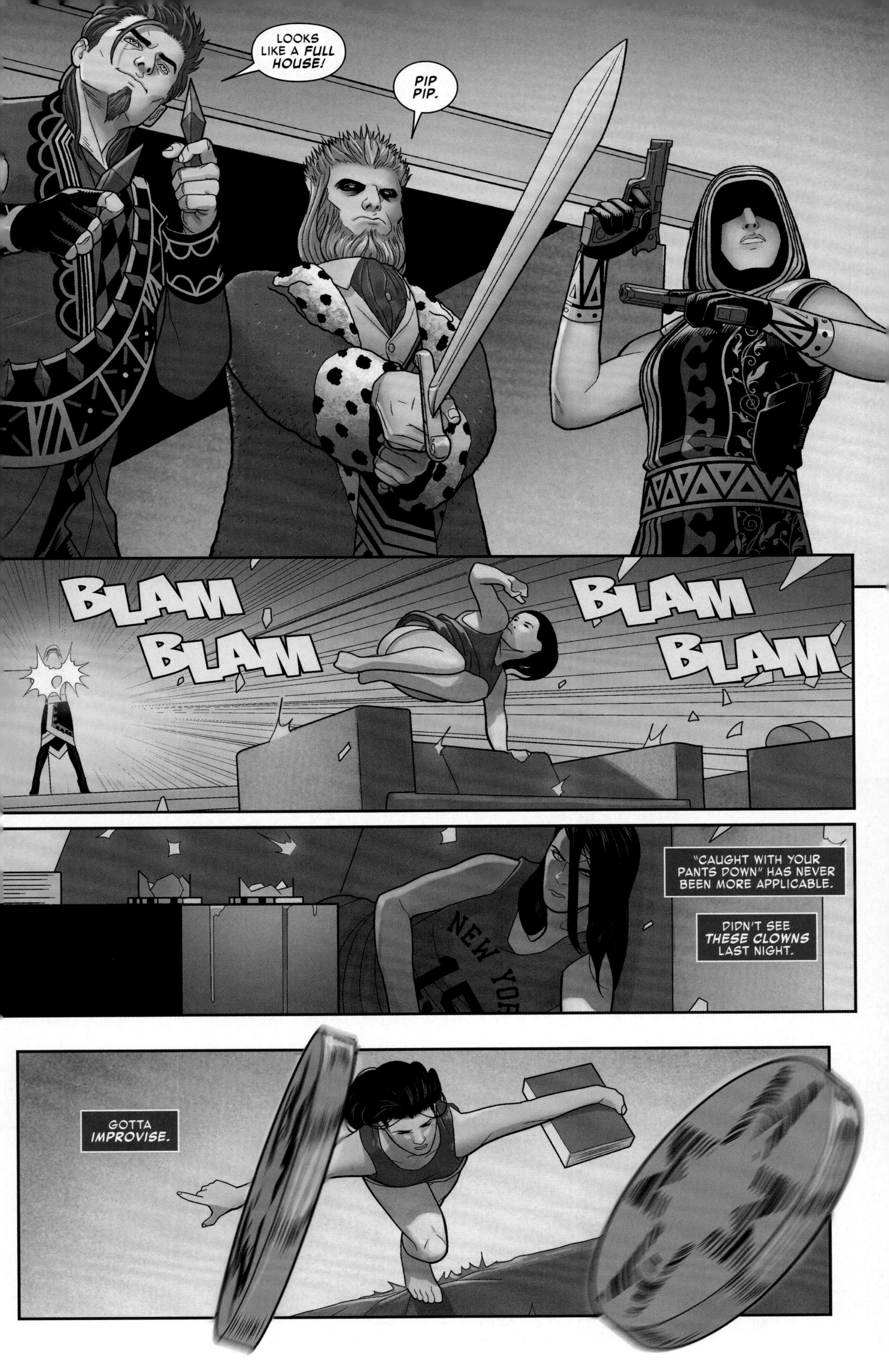
LOOKS LIKE A *FULL HOUSE!*
PIP PIP.
BLAM
BLAM
BLAM
BLAM
"CAUGHT WITH YOUR PANTS DOWN" HAS NEVER BEEN MORE APPLICABLE.
DIDN'T SEE *THESE CLOWNS* LAST NIGHT.
GOTTA *IMPROVISE.*

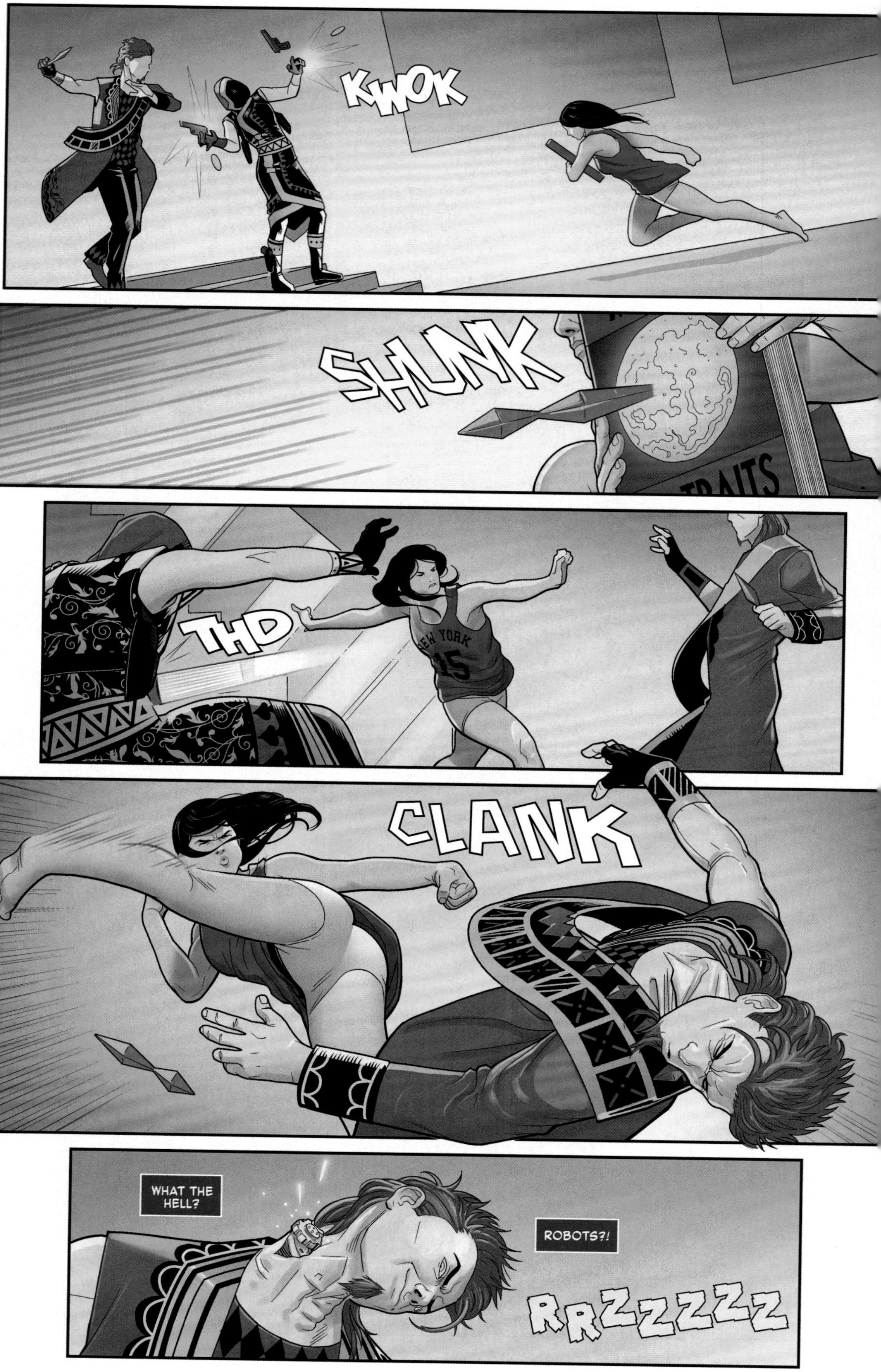
KWOK
SHUNK
TRAITS
THD
NEW YORK
15
CLANK
WHAT THE HELL?
ROBOTS?!
RRZZZZZZ

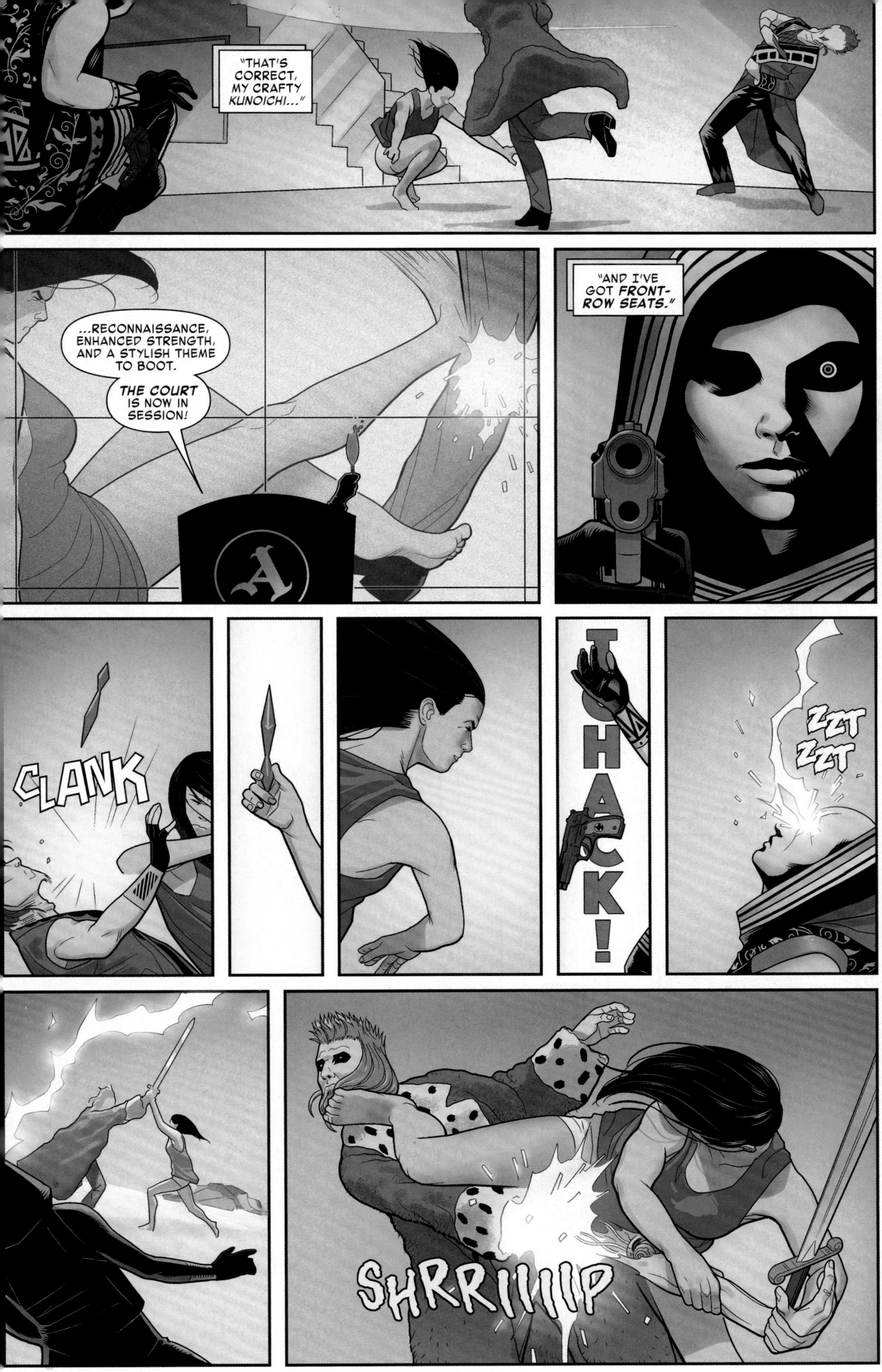
"THAT'S CORRECT, MY CRAFTY KUNOICHI..."
...RECONNAISSANCE, ENHANCED STRENGTH, AND A STYLISH THEME TO BOOT.
THE COURT IS NOW IN SESSION!
"AND I'VE GOT FRONT-ROW SEATS."
CLANK
THACK!
ZZZT ZZZT
SHRRIIIIP

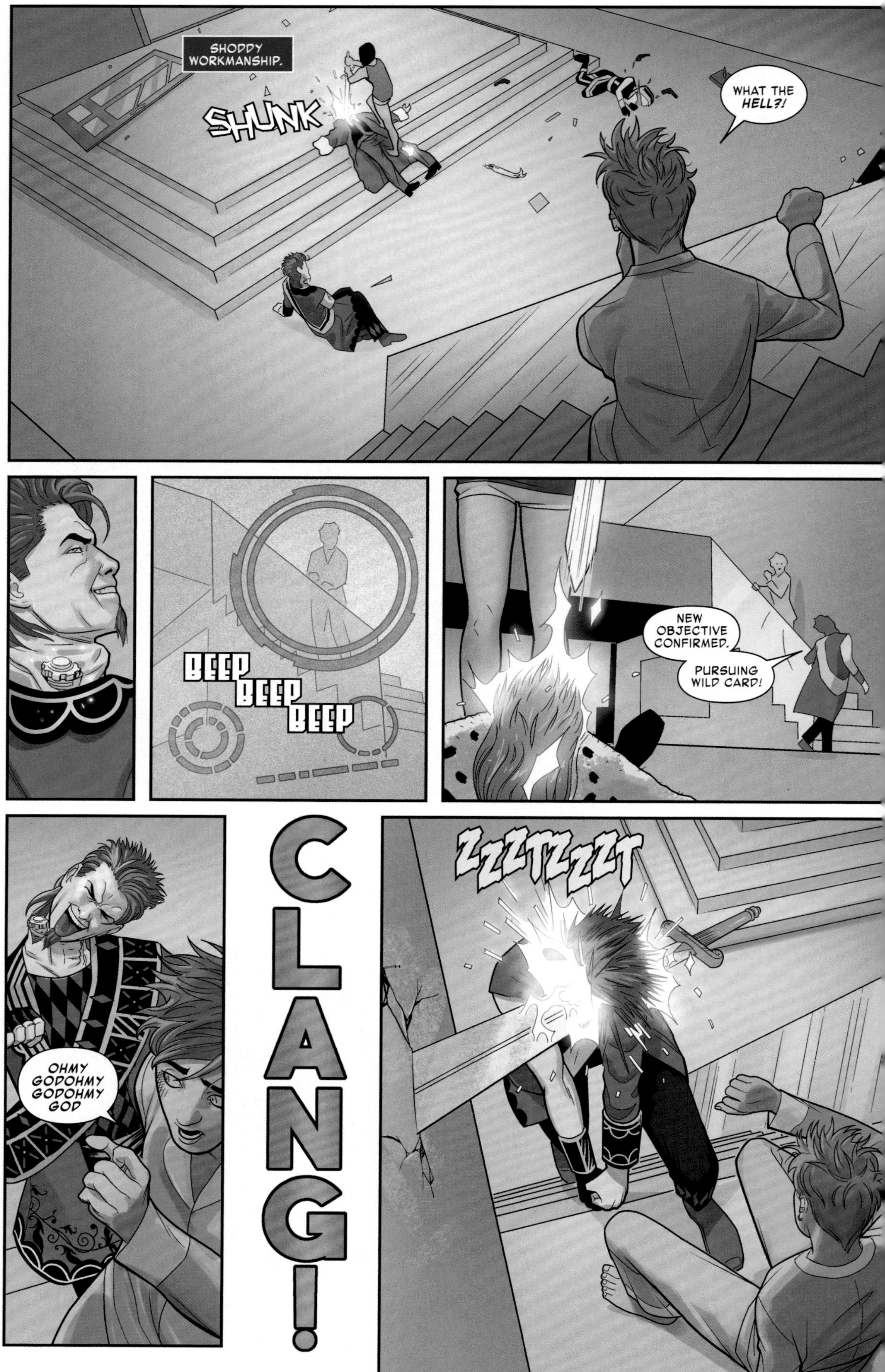
SHODDY WORKMANSHIP.
SHUNK
WHAT THE HELL?!
BEEP
BEEP
BEEP
NEW OBJECTIVE CONFIRMED.
PURSUING WILD CARD!
OHMY GODOHMY GODOHMY GOD
CLANG!
ZZZTZZZT

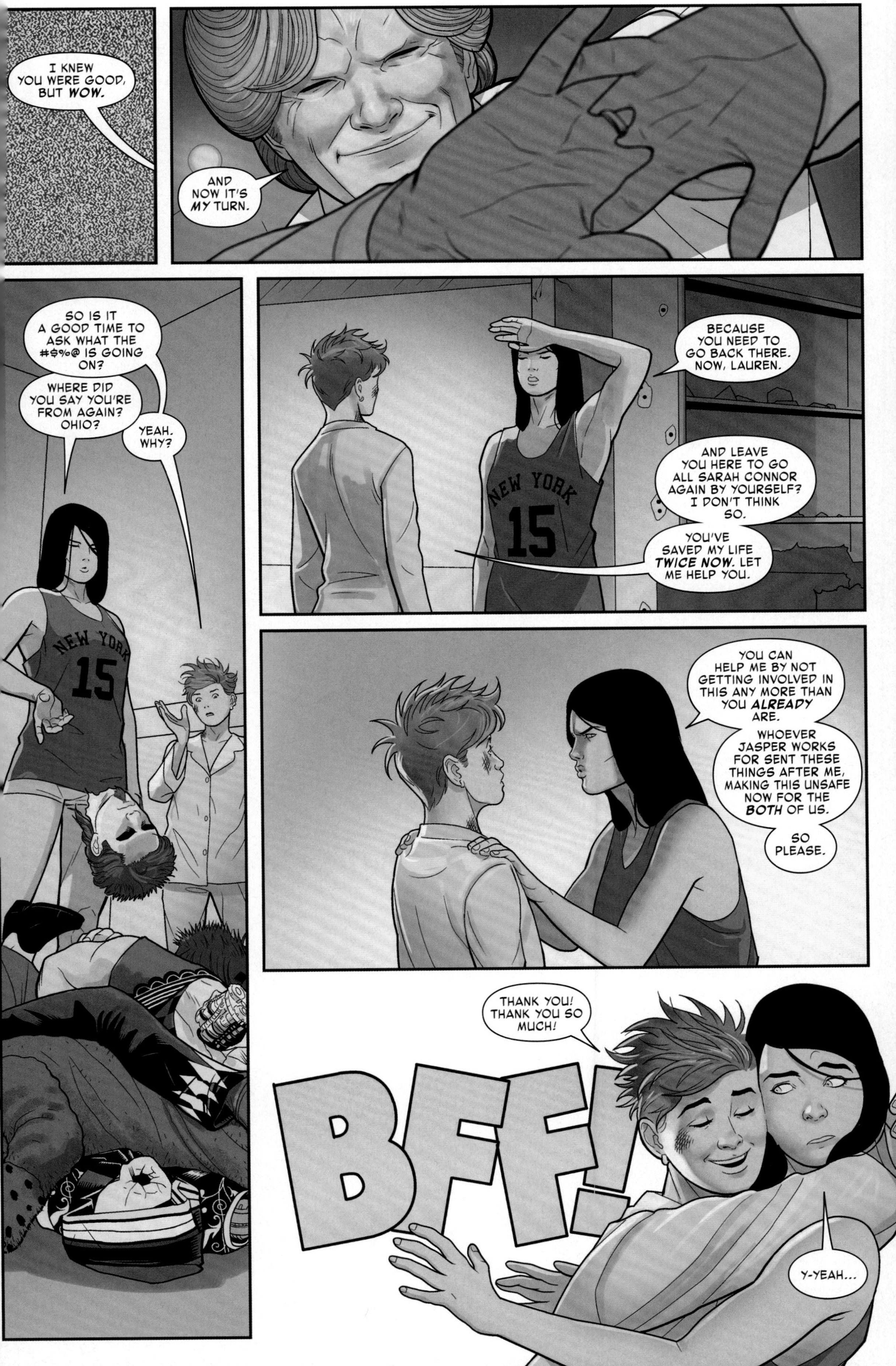
I KNEW YOU WERE GOOD, BUT *WOW.*
AND NOW IT'S *MY* TURN.
SO IS IT A GOOD TIME TO ASK WHAT THE #$%@ IS GOING ON?
WHERE DID YOU SAY YOU'RE FROM AGAIN? OHIO?
YEAH. WHY?
BECAUSE YOU NEED TO GO BACK THERE. NOW, LAUREN.
AND LEAVE YOU HERE TO GO ALL SARAH CONNOR AGAIN BY YOURSELF? I DON'T THINK SO.
YOU'VE SAVED MY LIFE ***TWICE NOW.*** LET ME HELP YOU.
YOU CAN HELP ME BY NOT GETTING INVOLVED IN THIS ANY MORE THAN YOU *ALREADY* ARE.
WHOEVER JASPER WORKS FOR SENT THESE THINGS AFTER ME, MAKING THIS UNSAFE NOW FOR THE *BOTH* OF US.
SO PLEASE.
THANK YOU! THANK YOU SO MUCH!
BFF!
Y-YEAH...

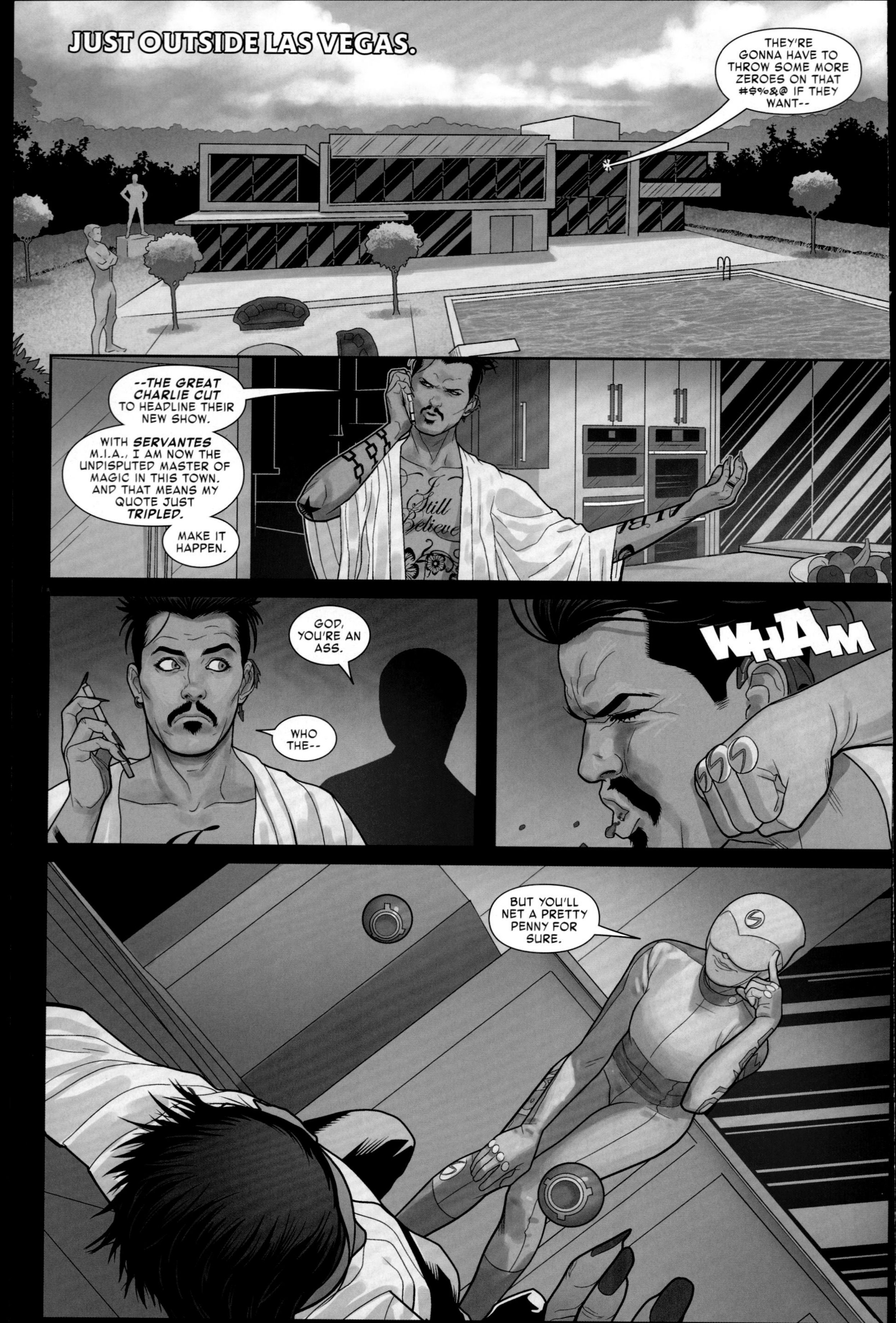
JUST OUTSIDE LAS VEGAS.
THEY'RE GONNA HAVE TO THROW SOME MORE ZEROES ON THAT #$%&@ IF THEY WANT--
--THE GREAT CHARLIE CUT TO HEADLINE THEIR NEW SHOW.
WITH SERVANTES M.I.A., I AM NOW THE UNDISPUTED MASTER OF MAGIC IN THIS TOWN. AND THAT MEANS MY QUOTE JUST TRIPLED.
MAKE IT HAPPEN.
I Still Believe
GOD, YOU'RE AN ASS.
WHO THE--
WHAM
BUT YOU'LL NET A PRETTY PENNY FOR SURE.

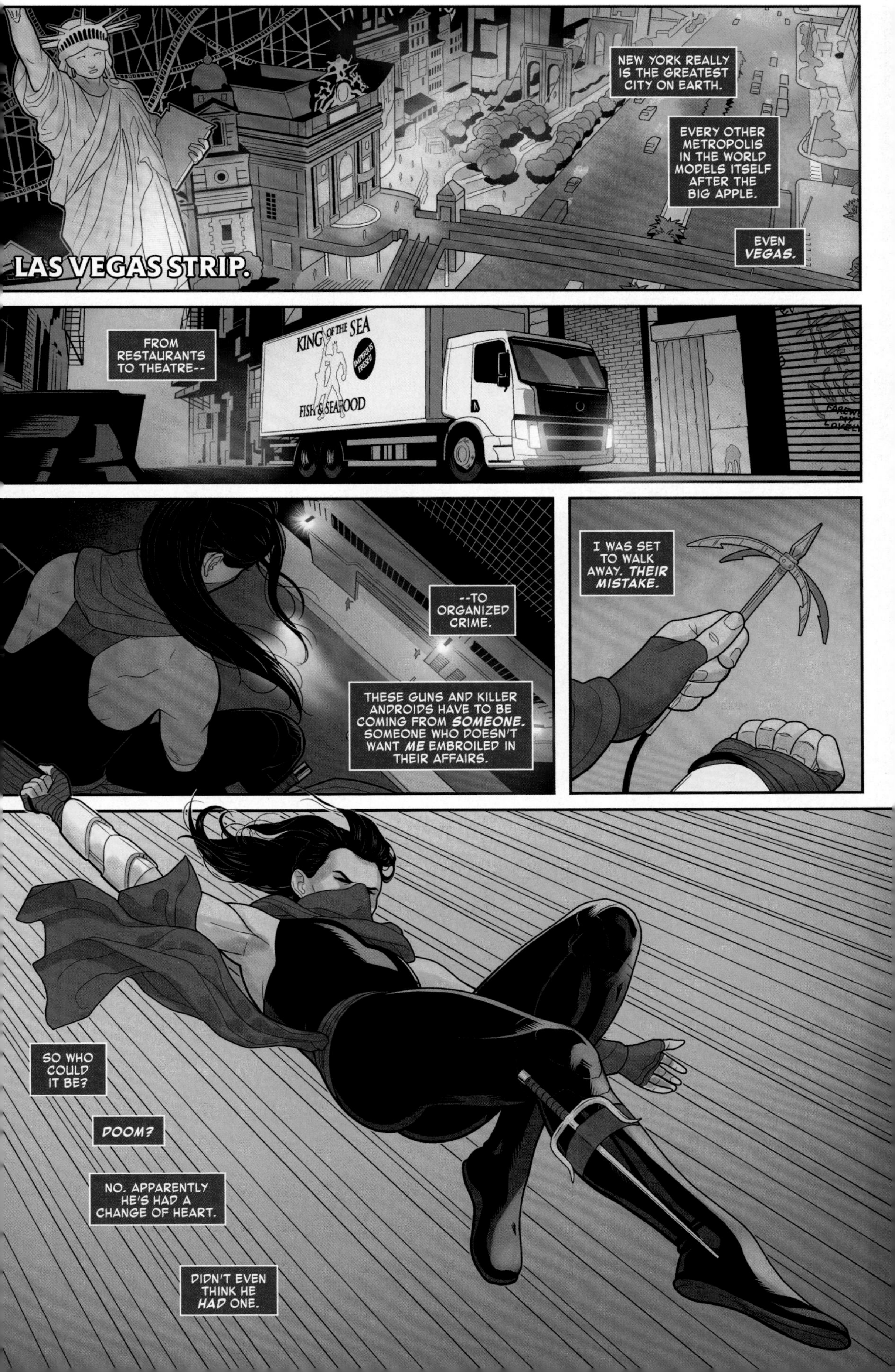
LAS VEGAS STRIP.
NEW YORK REALLY IS THE GREATEST CITY ON EARTH.
EVERY OTHER METROPOLIS IN THE WORLD MODELS ITSELF AFTER THE BIG APPLE.
EVEN *VEGAS.*
FROM RESTAURANTS TO THEATRE--
KING OF THE SEA
IMPERIUS FRESH!
FISH & SEAFOOD
--TO ORGANIZED CRIME.
THESE GUNS AND KILLER ANDROIDS HAVE TO BE COMING FROM *SOMEONE.* SOMEONE WHO DOESN'T WANT *ME* EMBROILED IN THEIR AFFAIRS.
I WAS SET TO WALK AWAY. *THEIR MISTAKE.*
SO WHO COULD IT BE?
*DOOM?*
NO. APPARENTLY HE'S HAD A CHANGE OF HEART.
DIDN'T EVEN THINK HE *HAD* ONE.

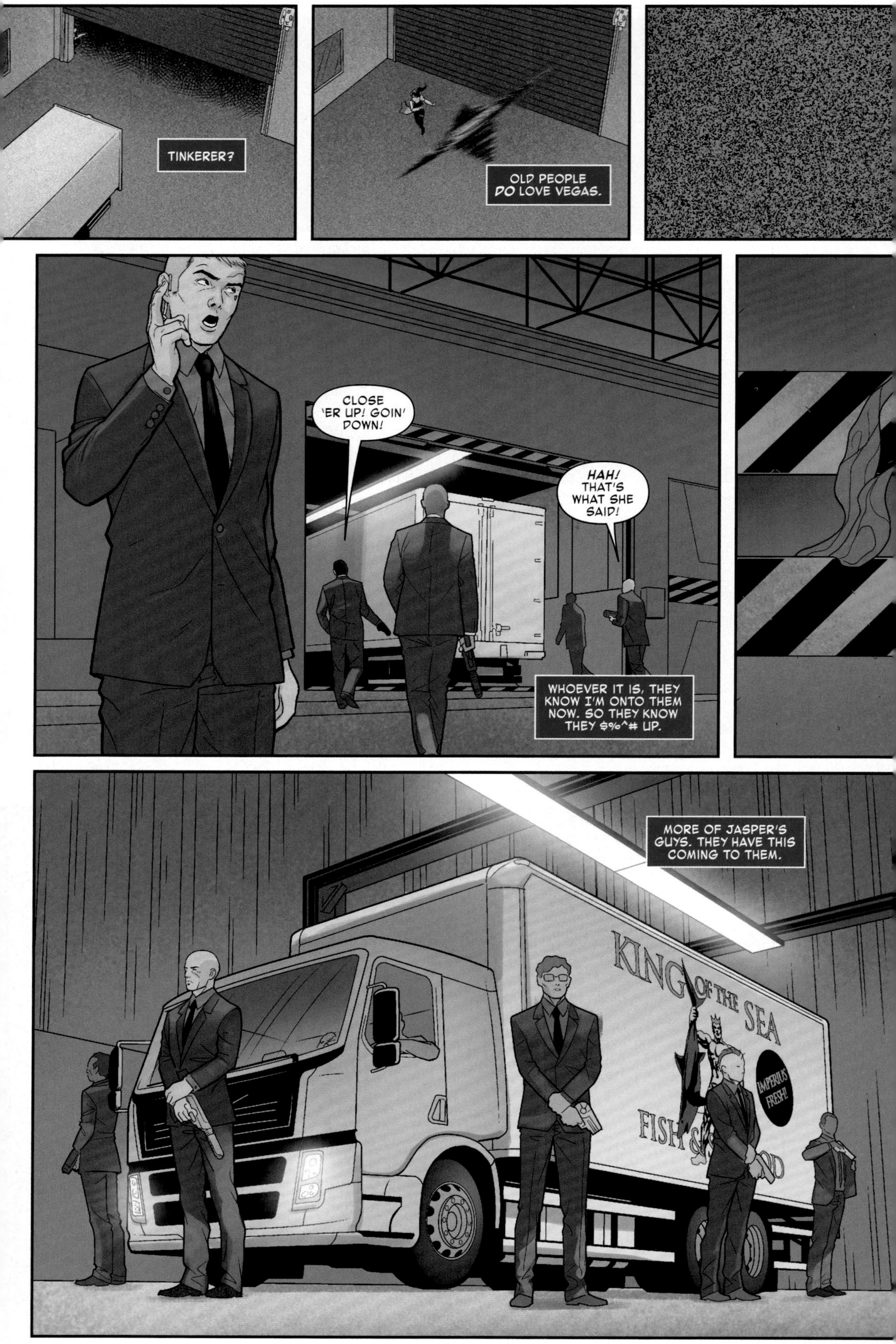
TINKERER?
OLD PEOPLE DO LOVE VEGAS.
CLOSE 'ER UP! GOIN' DOWN!
HAH! THAT'S WHAT SHE SAID!
WHOEVER IT IS, THEY KNOW I'M ONTO THEM NOW. SO THEY KNOW THEY $%^# UP.
MORE OF JASPER'S GUYS. THEY HAVE THIS COMING TO THEM.
KING OF THE SEA
IMPERIUS FRESH!
FISH &
OD

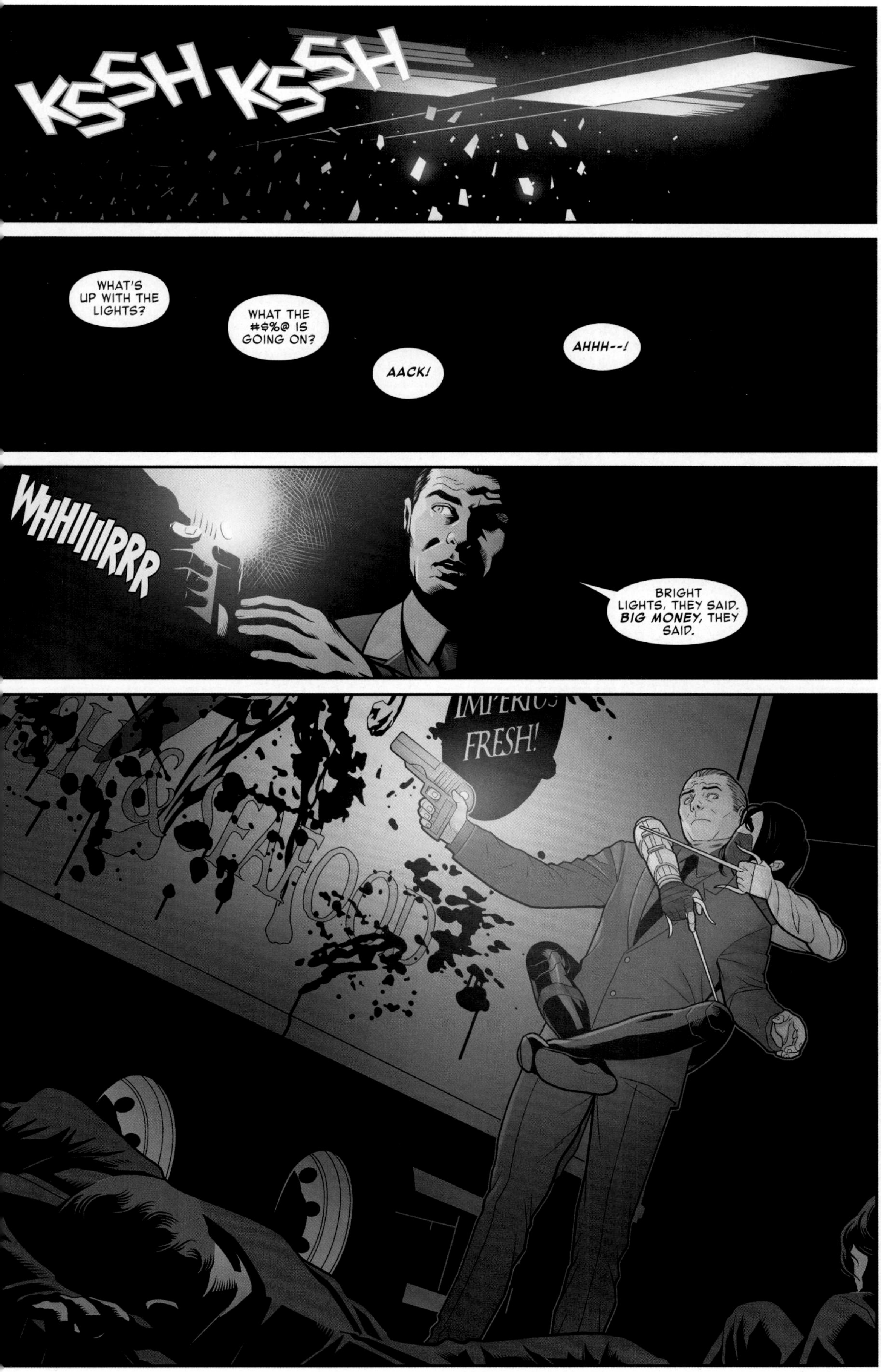
KSSH KSSH
WHAT'S UP WITH THE LIGHTS?
WHAT THE #$%@ IS GOING ON?
AACK!
AHHH--!
WHHIIIIIRRR
BRIGHT LIGHTS, THEY SAID. BIG MONEY, THEY SAID.
FRESH!

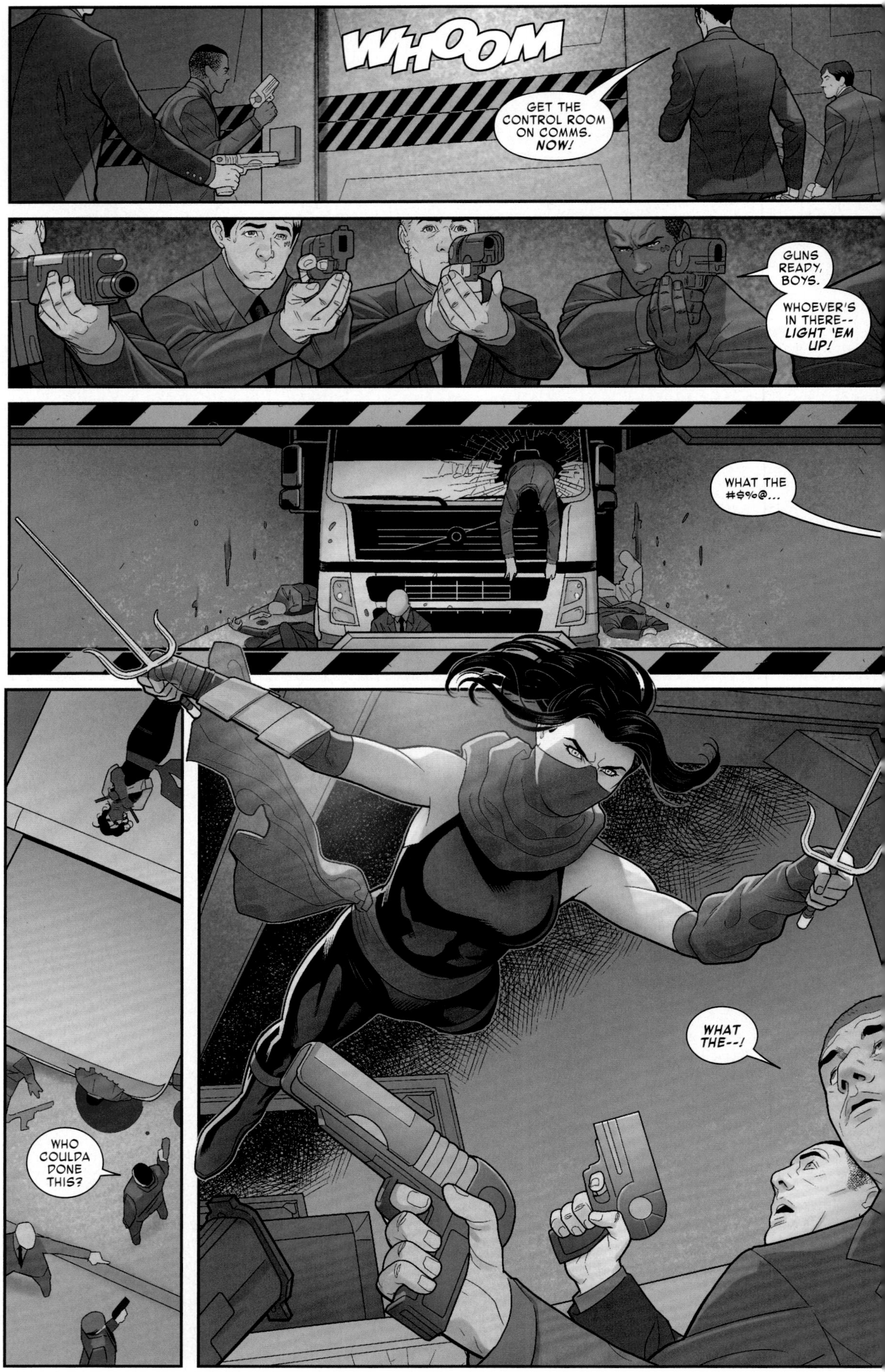
WHOOM
GET THE CONTROL ROOM ON COMMS. NOW!
GUNS READY, BOYS.
WHOEVER'S IN THERE-- LIGHT 'EM UP!
WHAT THE #$%@...
WHAT THE--!
WHO COULDA DONE THIS?

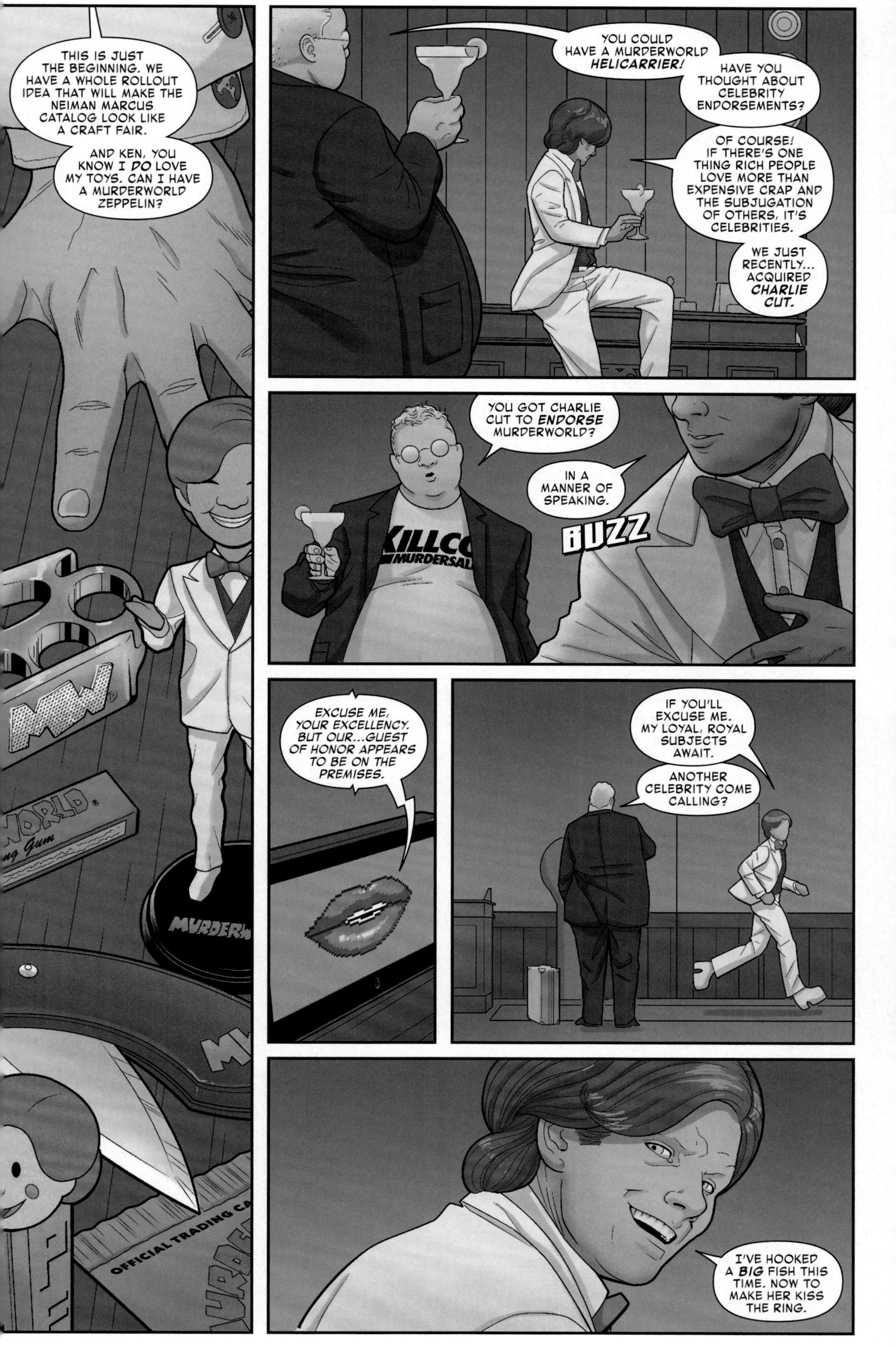

THIS IS JUST THE BEGINNING. WE HAVE A WHOLE ROLLOUT IDEA THAT WILL MAKE THE NEIMAN MARCUS CATALOG LOOK LIKE A CRAFT FAIR.
AND KEN, YOU KNOW I *DO* LOVE MY TOYS. CAN I HAVE A MURDERWORLD ZEPPELIN?
YOU COULD HAVE A MURDERWORLD ***HELICARRIER!***
HAVE YOU THOUGHT ABOUT CELEBRITY ENDORSEMENTS?
OF COURSE! IF THERE'S ONE THING RICH PEOPLE LOVE MORE THAN EXPENSIVE CRAP AND THE SUBJUGATION OF OTHERS, IT'S CELEBRITIES.
WE JUST RECENTLY... ACQUIRED ***CHARLIE CUT.***
YOU GOT CHARLIE CUT TO ***ENDORSE*** MURDERWORLD?
IN A MANNER OF SPEAKING.
BUZZ
*EXCUSE ME, YOUR EXCELLENCY. BUT OUR...GUEST OF HONOR APPEARS TO BE ON THE PREMISES.*
IF YOU'LL EXCUSE ME. MY LOYAL, ROYAL SUBJECTS AWAIT.
ANOTHER CELEBRITY COME CALLING?
I'VE HOOKED A ***BIG*** FISH THIS TIME. NOW TO MAKE HER KISS THE RING.

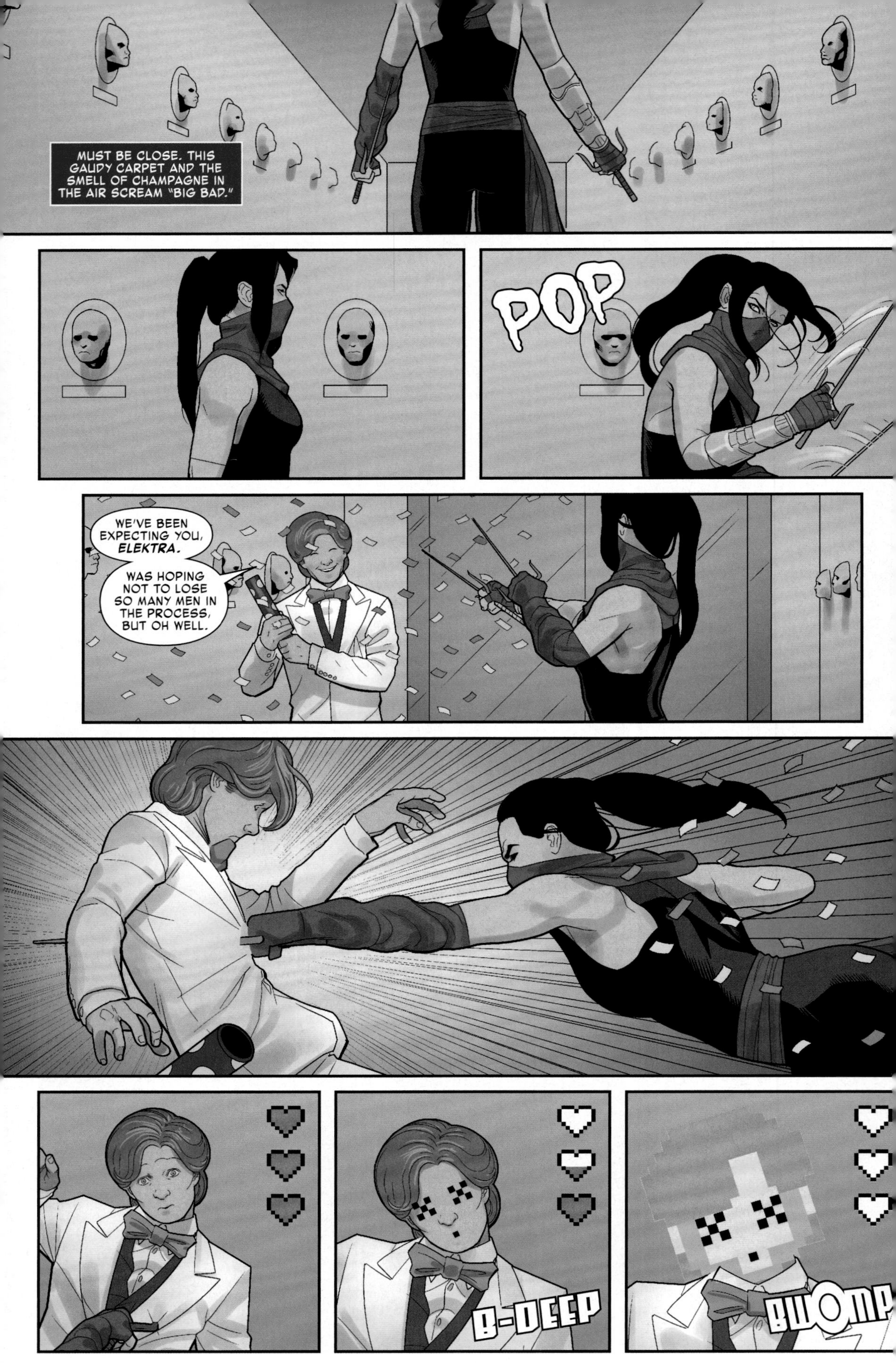
MUST BE CLOSE. THIS GAUDY CARPET AND THE SMELL OF CHAMPAGNE IN THE AIR SCREAM "BIG BAD."
POP
WE'VE BEEN EXPECTING YOU, ELEKTRA.
WAS HOPING NOT TO LOSE SO MANY MEN IN THE PROCESS, BUT OH WELL.
B-DEEP
BWOMP

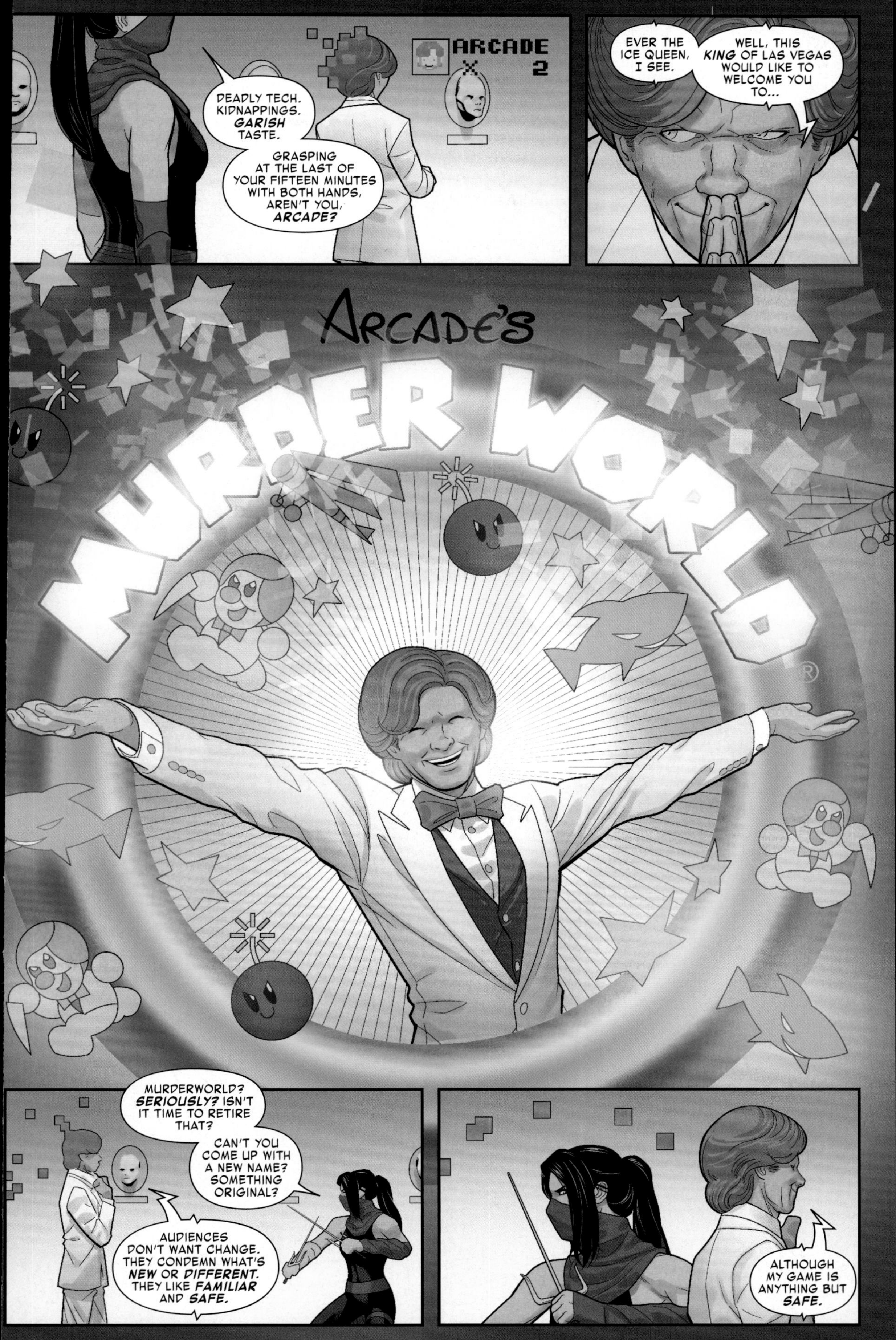
ARCADE
X 2
DEADLY TECH. KIDNAPPINGS. GARISH TASTE.
GRASPING AT THE LAST OF YOUR FIFTEEN MINUTES WITH BOTH HANDS, AREN'T YOU, ARCADE?
EVER THE ICE QUEEN, I SEE.
WELL, THIS KING OF LAS VEGAS WOULD LIKE TO WELCOME YOU TO...
ARCADE'S
MURDER WORLD®
MURDERWORLD? SERIOUSLY? ISN'T IT TIME TO RETIRE THAT?
CAN'T YOU COME UP WITH A NEW NAME? SOMETHING ORIGINAL?
AUDIENCES DON'T WANT CHANGE. THEY CONDEMN WHAT'S NEW OR DIFFERENT. THEY LIKE FAMILIAR AND SAFE.
ALTHOUGH MY GAME IS ANYTHING BUT SAFE.

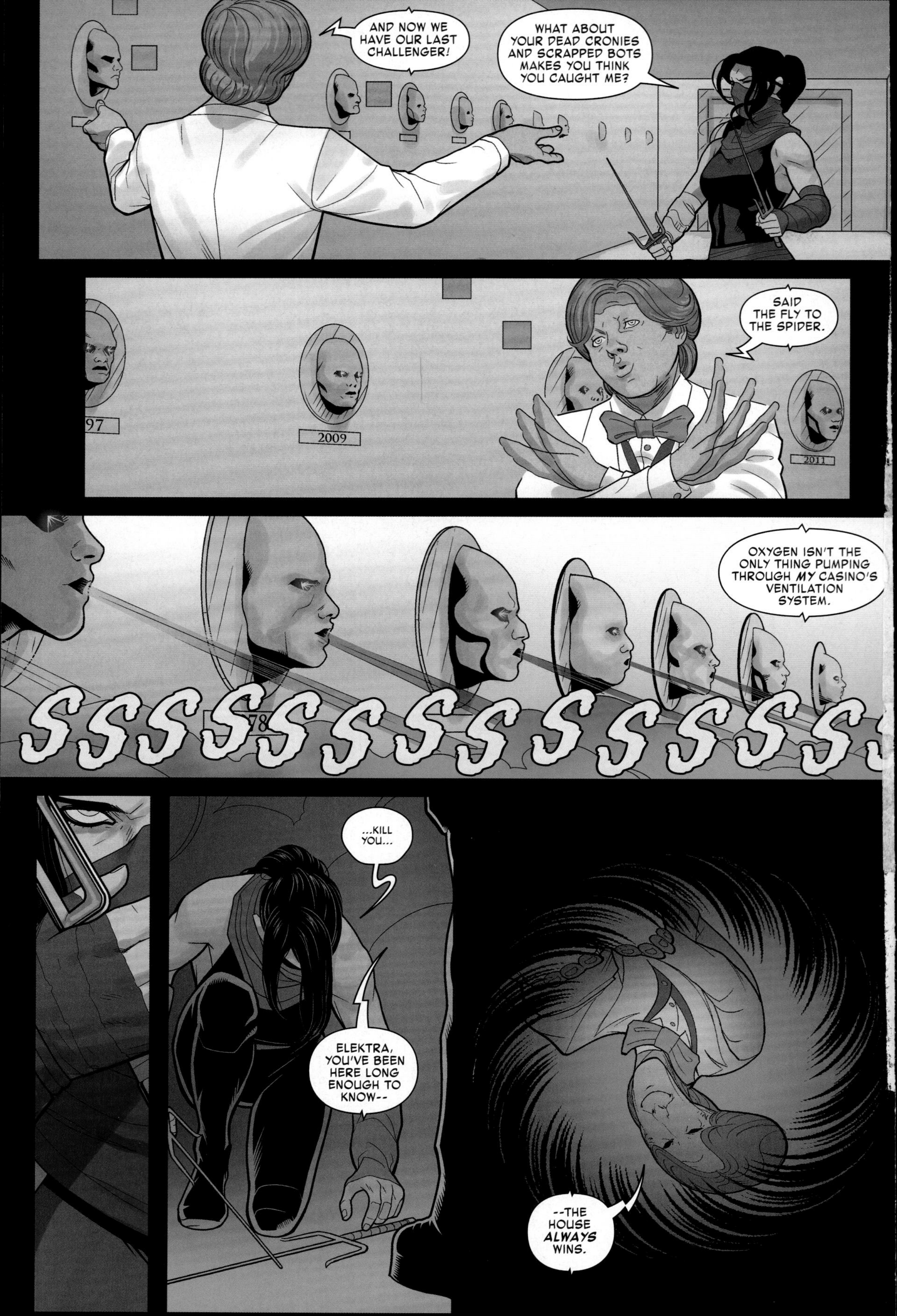
AND NOW WE HAVE OUR LAST CHALLENGER!
WHAT ABOUT YOUR DEAD CRONIES AND SCRAPPED BOTS MAKES YOU THINK YOU CAUGHT ME?
97
2009
2011
SAID THE FLY TO THE SPIDER.
OXYGEN ISN'T THE ONLY THING PUMPING THROUGH *MY* CASINO'S VENTILATION SYSTEM.
SSSSSSSSSSSS
...KILL YOU...
ELEKTRA, YOU'VE BEEN HERE LONG ENOUGH TO KNOW--
--THE HOUSE *ALWAYS* WINS.

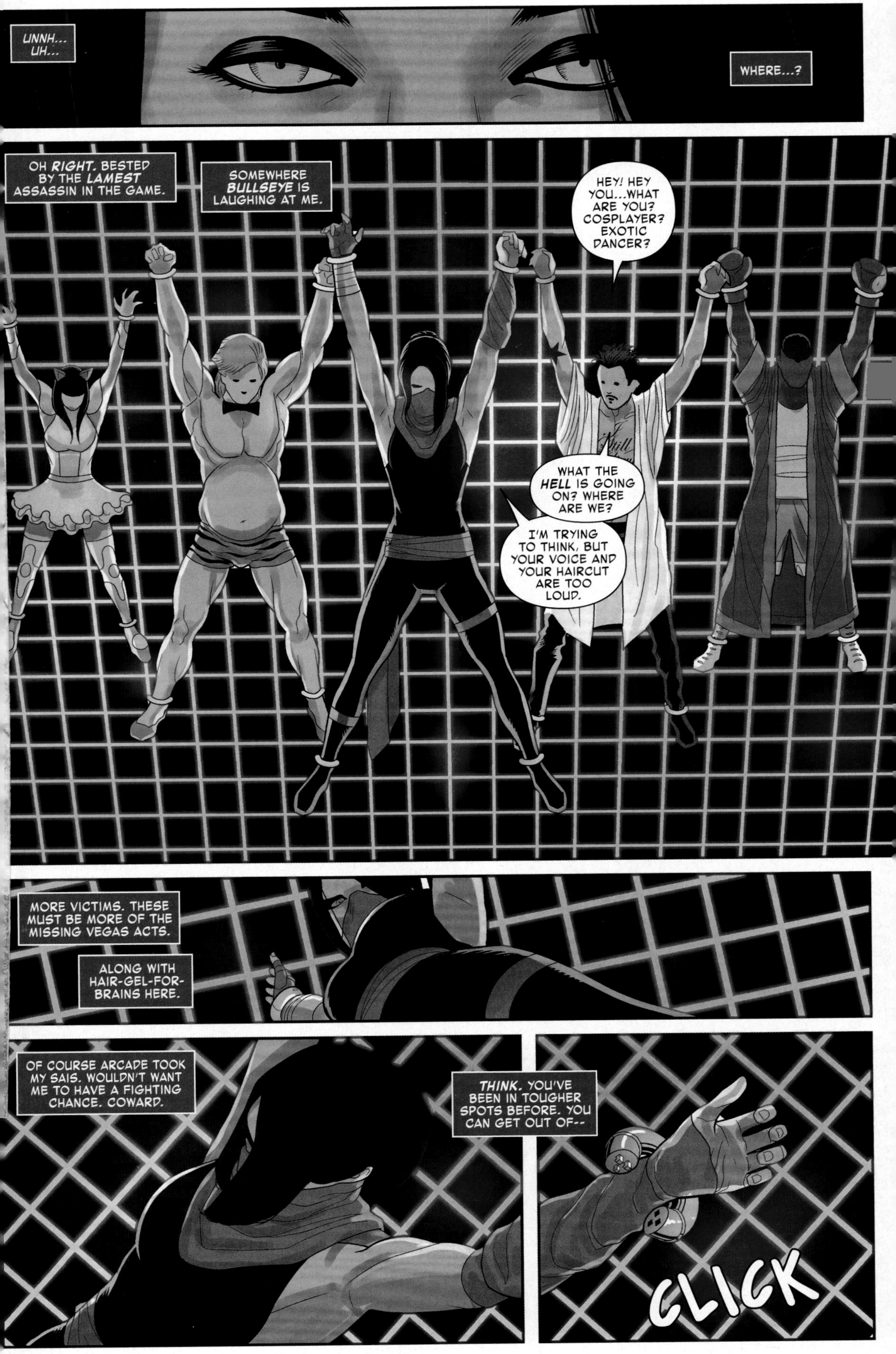
UNNH... UH...
WHERE...?
OH RIGHT. BESTED BY THE LAMEST ASSASSIN IN THE GAME.
SOMEWHERE BULLSEYE IS LAUGHING AT ME.
HEY! HEY YOU...WHAT ARE YOU? COSPLAYER? EXOTIC DANCER?
WHAT THE HELL IS GOING ON? WHERE ARE WE?
I'M TRYING TO THINK, BUT YOUR VOICE AND YOUR HAIRCUT ARE TOO LOUD.
MORE VICTIMS. THESE MUST BE MORE OF THE MISSING VEGAS ACTS.
ALONG WITH HAIR-GEL-FOR-BRAINS HERE.
OF COURSE ARCADE TOOK MY SAIS. WOULDN'T WANT ME TO HAVE A FIGHTING CHANCE. COWARD.
THINK. YOU'VE BEEN IN TOUGHER SPOTS BEFORE. YOU CAN GET OUT OF--
CLICK

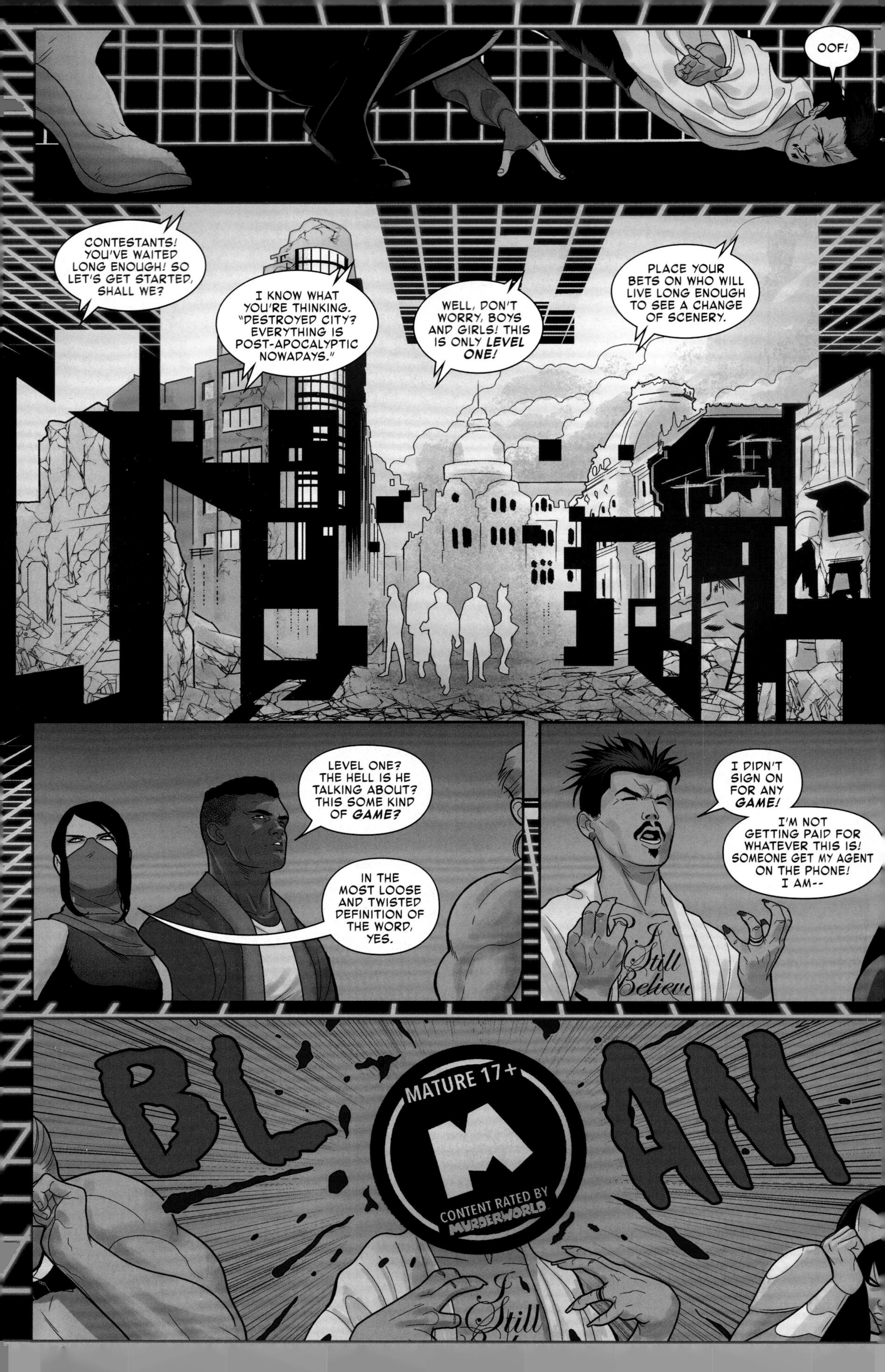
OOF!
CONTESTANTS! YOU'VE WAITED LONG ENOUGH! SO LET'S GET STARTED, SHALL WE?
I KNOW WHAT YOU'RE THINKING. "DESTROYED CITY? EVERYTHING IS POST-APOCALYPTIC NOWADAYS."
WELL, DON'T WORRY, BOYS AND GIRLS! THIS IS ONLY *LEVEL ONE!*
PLACE YOUR BETS ON WHO WILL LIVE LONG ENOUGH TO SEE A CHANGE OF SCENERY.
LEVEL ONE? THE HELL IS HE TALKING ABOUT? THIS SOME KIND OF *GAME?*
IN THE MOST LOOSE AND TWISTED DEFINITION OF THE WORD, YES.
I DIDN'T SIGN ON FOR ANY *GAME!*
I'M NOT GETTING PAID FOR WHATEVER THIS IS! SOMEONE GET MY AGENT ON THE PHONE! I AM--
I Still Believe
BL AM
MATURE 17+
M
CONTENT RATED BY MURDERWORLD
I Still

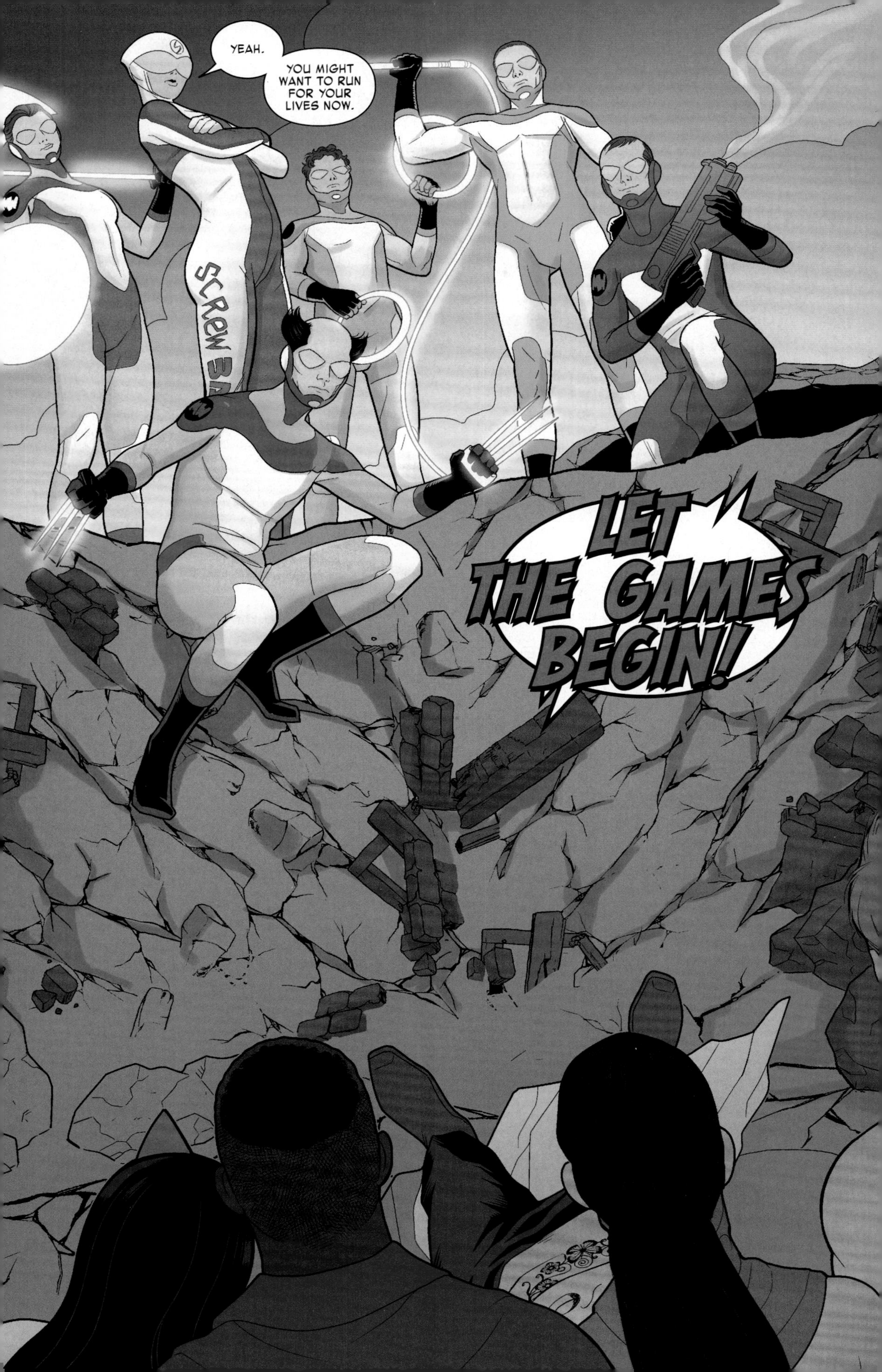
YEAH.
YOU MIGHT WANT TO RUN FOR YOUR LIVES NOW.
SCREW
LET THE GAMES BEGIN!

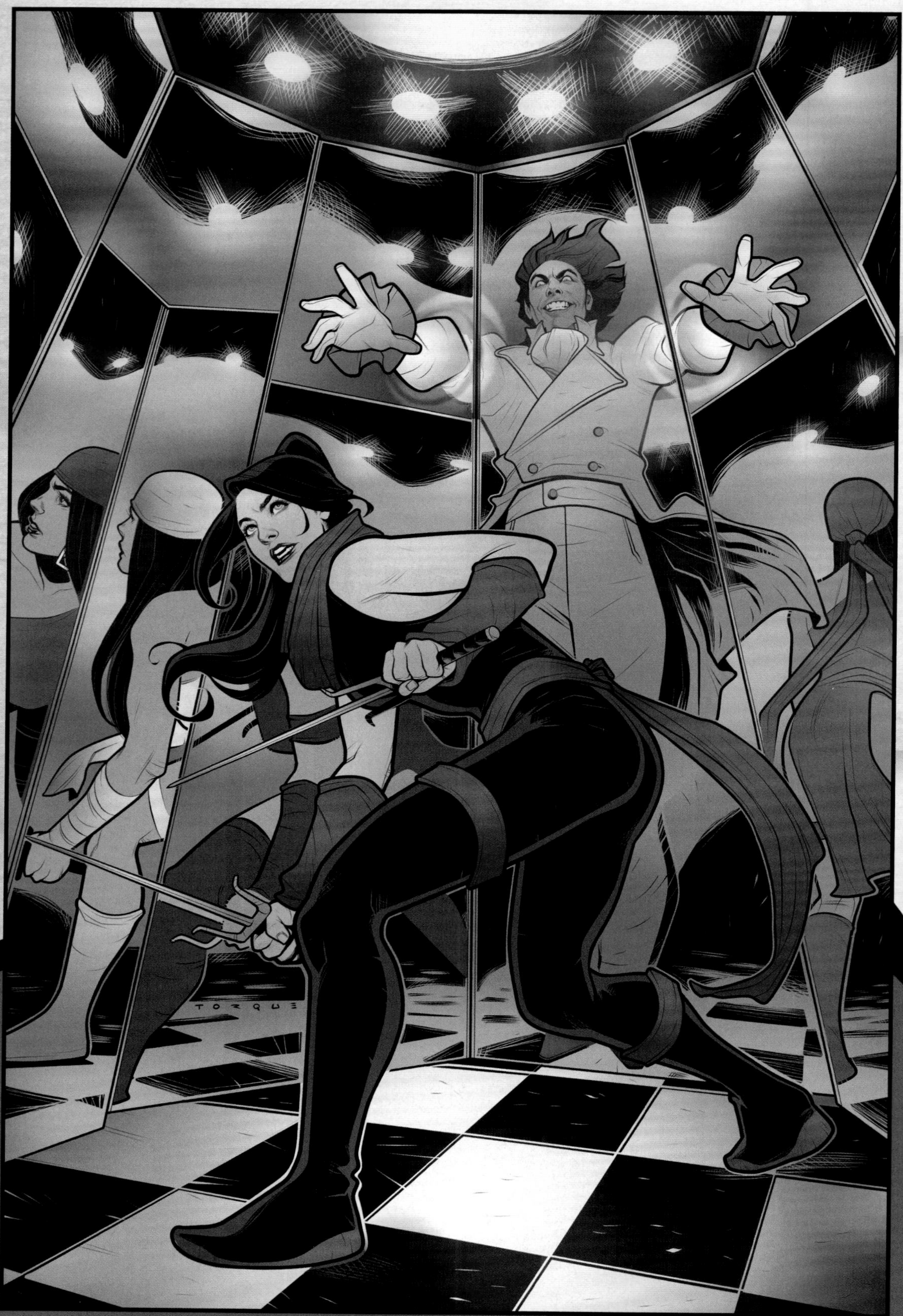
TORQUE

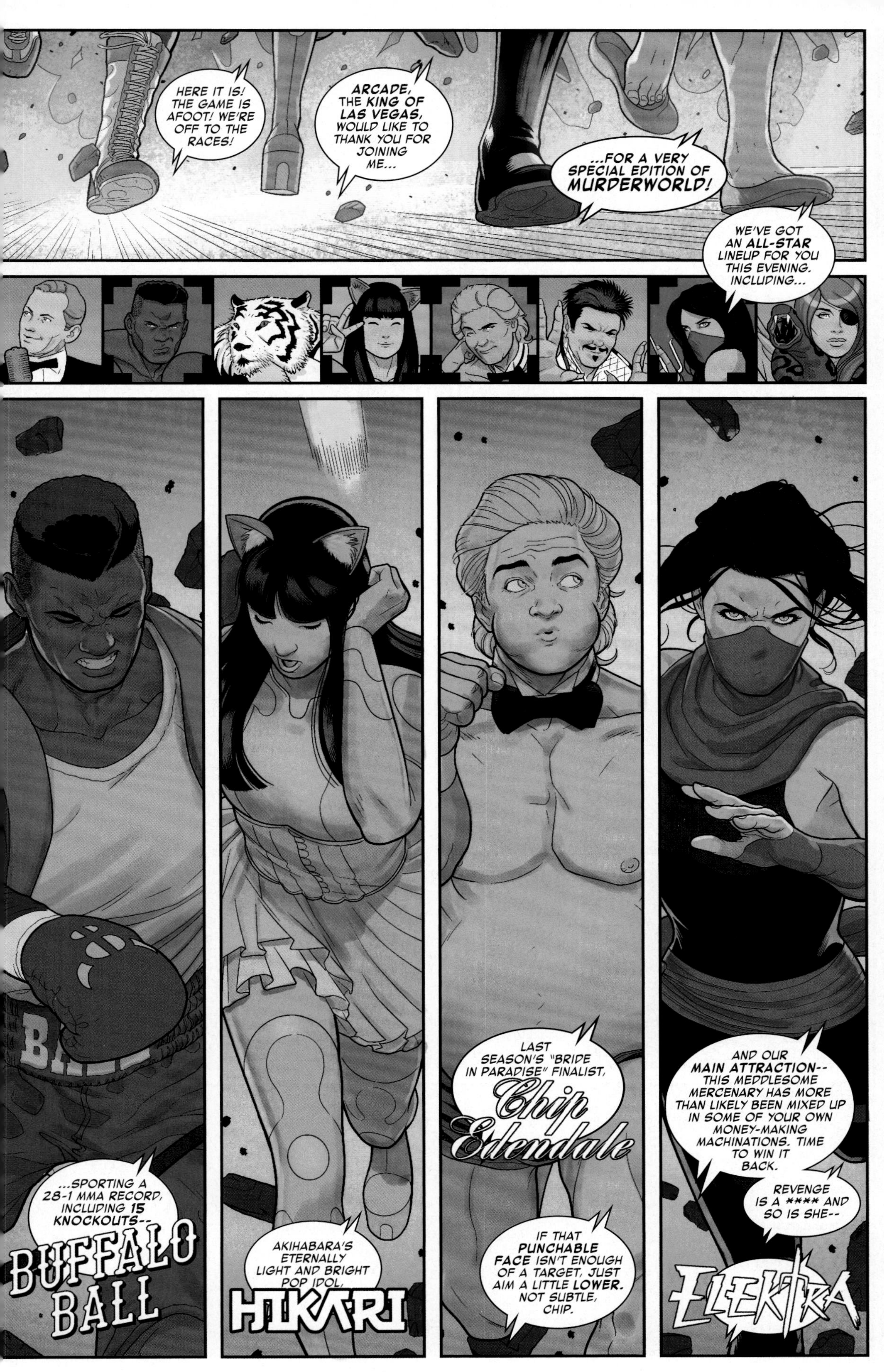

HERE IT IS! THE GAME IS AFOOT! WE'RE OFF TO THE RACES!
ARCADE, THE KING OF LAS VEGAS, WOULD LIKE TO THANK YOU FOR JOINING ME...
...FOR A VERY SPECIAL EDITION OF MURDERWORLD!
WE'VE GOT AN ALL-STAR LINEUP FOR YOU THIS EVENING. INCLUDING...
...SPORTING A 28-1 MMA RECORD, INCLUDING 15 KNOCKOUTS--
BUFFALO BALL
AKIHABARA'S ETERNALLY LIGHT AND BRIGHT POP IDOL,
HIKARI
LAST SEASON'S "BRIDE IN PARADISE" FINALIST,
Chip Edendale
IF THAT PUNCHABLE FACE ISN'T ENOUGH OF A TARGET, JUST AIM A LITTLE LOWER. NOT SUBTLE, CHIP.
AND OUR MAIN ATTRACTION-- THIS MEDDLESOME MERCENARY HAS MORE THAN LIKELY BEEN MIXED UP IN SOME OF YOUR OWN MONEY-MAKING MACHINATIONS. TIME TO WIN IT BACK.
REVENGE IS A **** AND SO IS SHE--
ELEKTRA

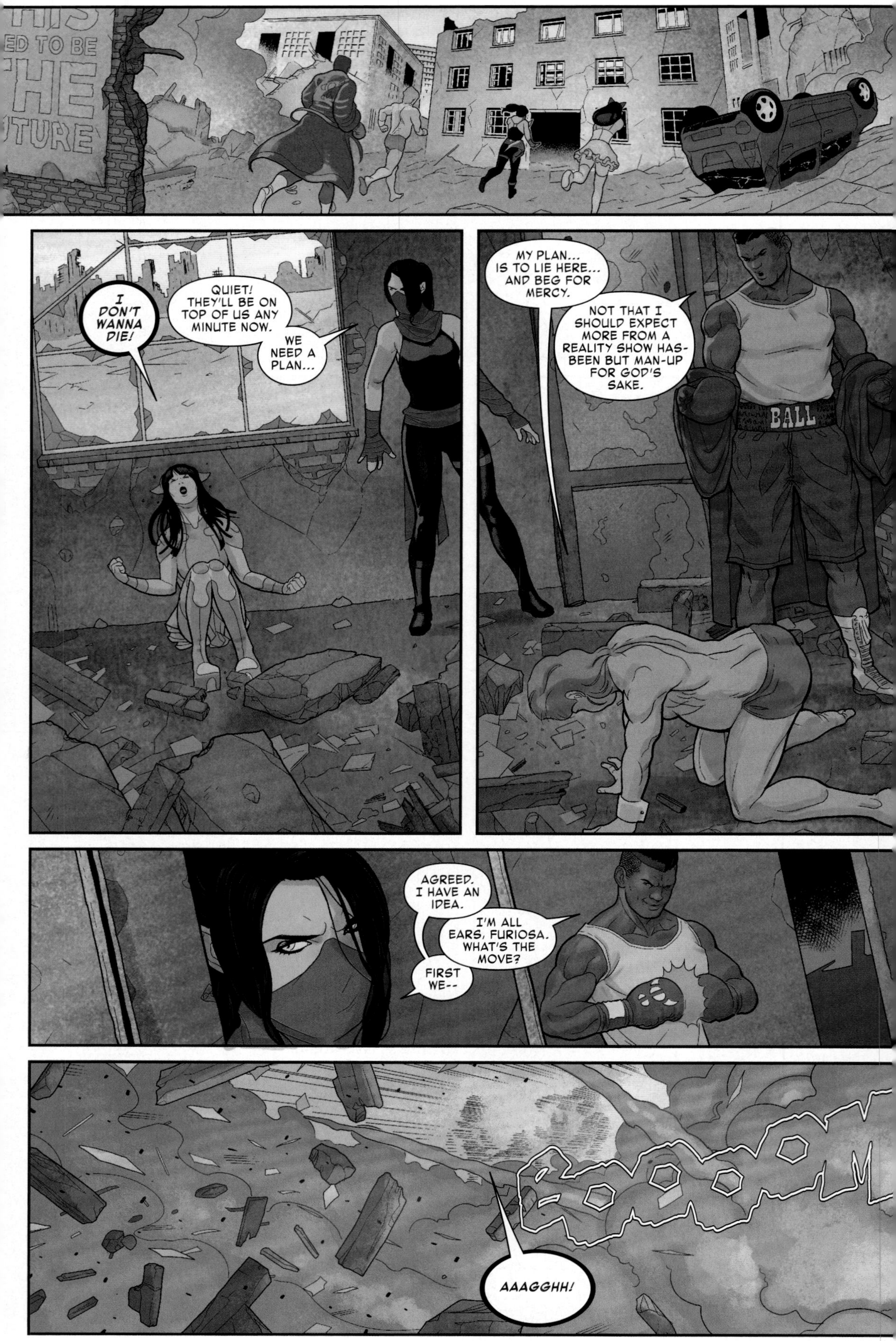

...ED TO BE ...HE ...UTURE
I DON'T WANNA DIE!
QUIET! THEY'LL BE ON TOP OF US ANY MINUTE NOW.
WE NEED A PLAN...
MY PLAN... IS TO LIE HERE... AND BEG FOR MERCY.
NOT THAT I SHOULD EXPECT MORE FROM A REALITY SHOW HAS-BEEN BUT MAN-UP FOR GOD'S SAKE.
BALL
AGREED. I HAVE AN IDEA.
I'M ALL EARS, FURIOSA. WHAT'S THE MOVE?
FIRST WE--
AAAGGHH!

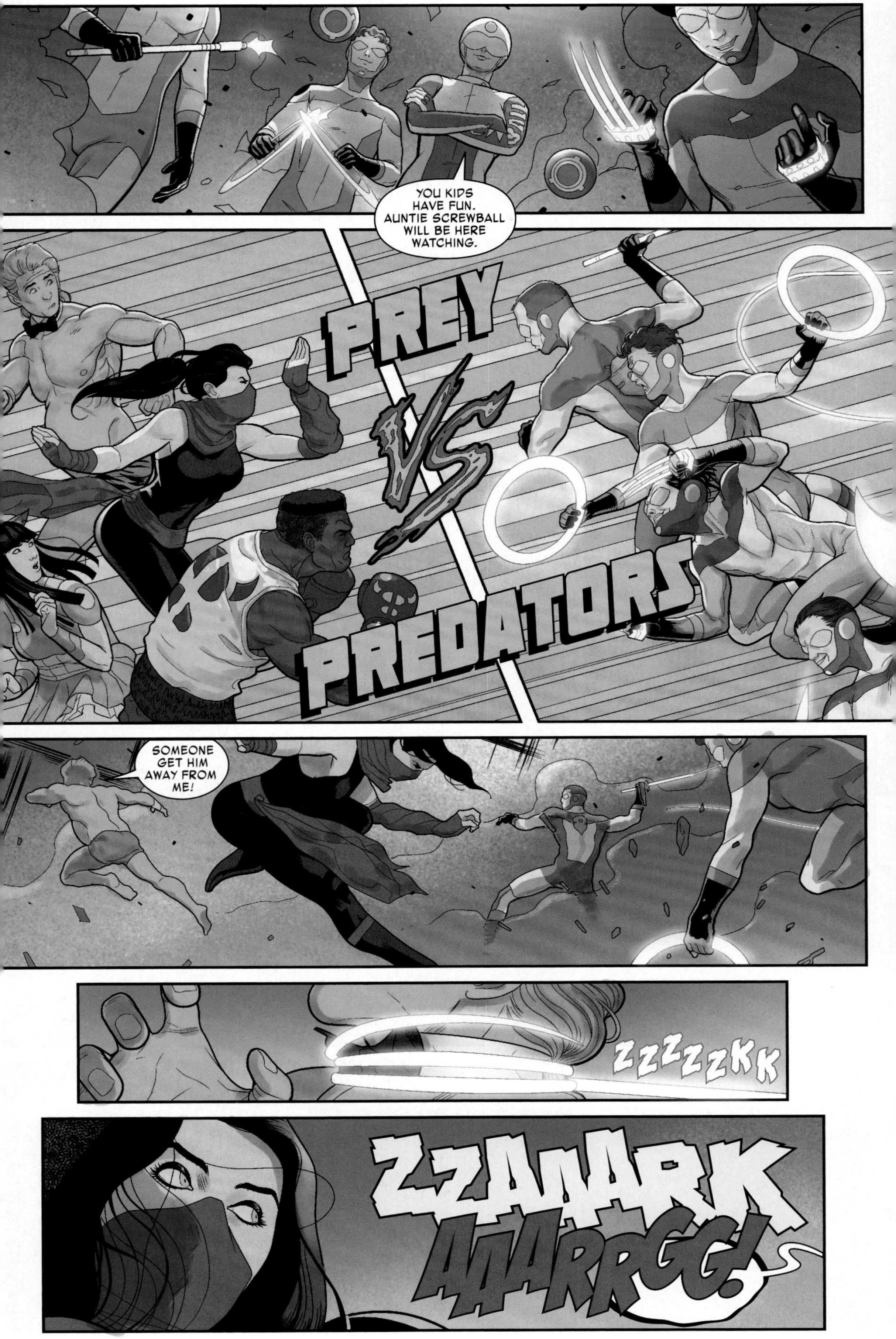
YOU KIDS HAVE FUN. AUNTIE SCREWBALL WILL BE HERE WATCHING.
PREY VS PREDATORS
SOMEONE GET HIM AWAY FROM ME!
ZZZZZKK
ZZAAARK
AAARRGG!

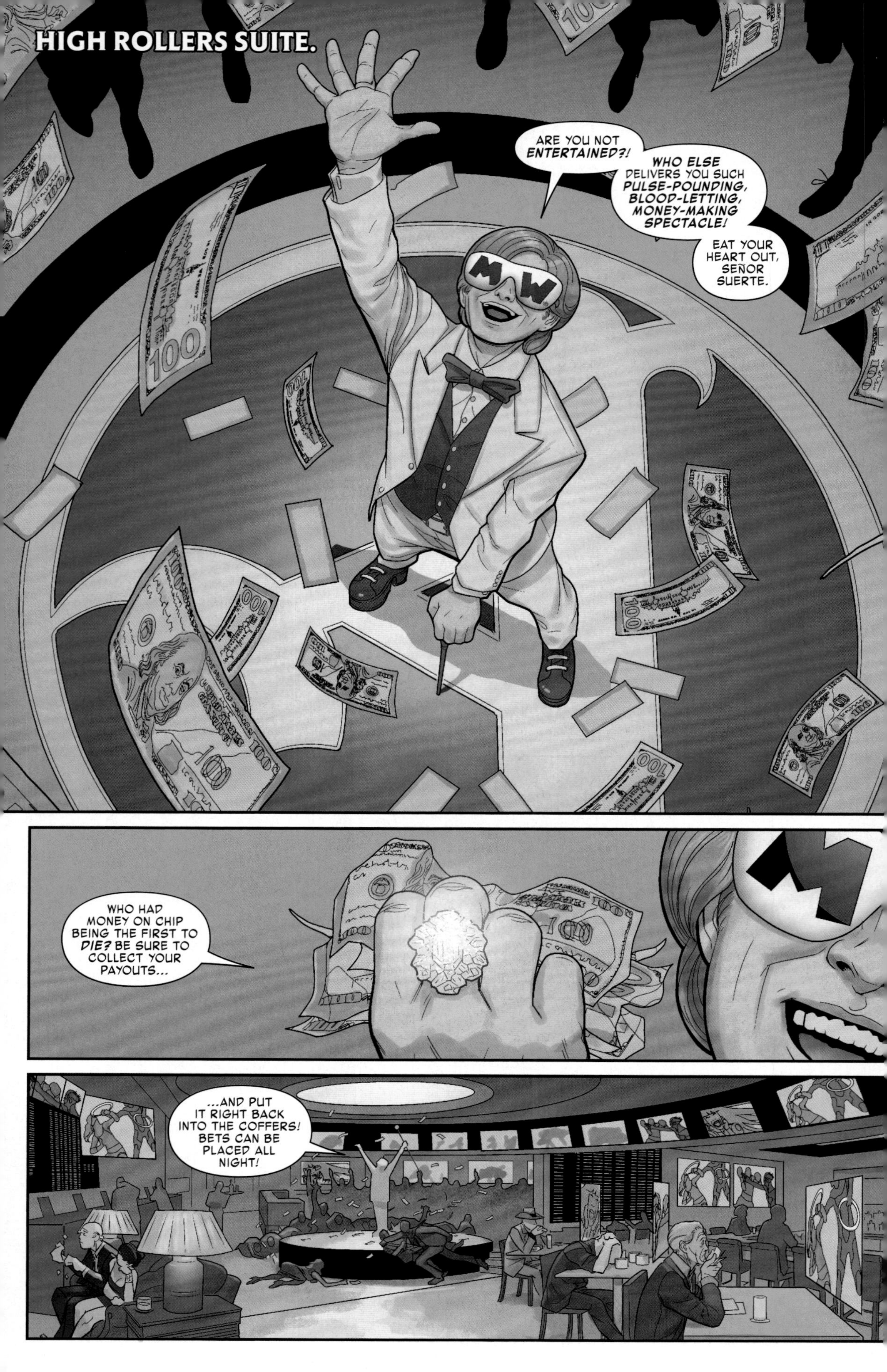
HIGH ROLLERS SUITE.
ARE YOU NOT ENTERTAINED?!
WHO ELSE DELIVERS YOU SUCH PULSE-POUNDING, BLOOD-LETTING, MONEY-MAKING SPECTACLE!
EAT YOUR HEART OUT, SEÑOR SUERTE.
WHO HAD MONEY ON CHIP BEING THE FIRST TO DIE? BE SURE TO COLLECT YOUR PAYOUTS...
...AND PUT IT RIGHT BACK INTO THE COFFERS! BETS CAN BE PLACED ALL NIGHT!

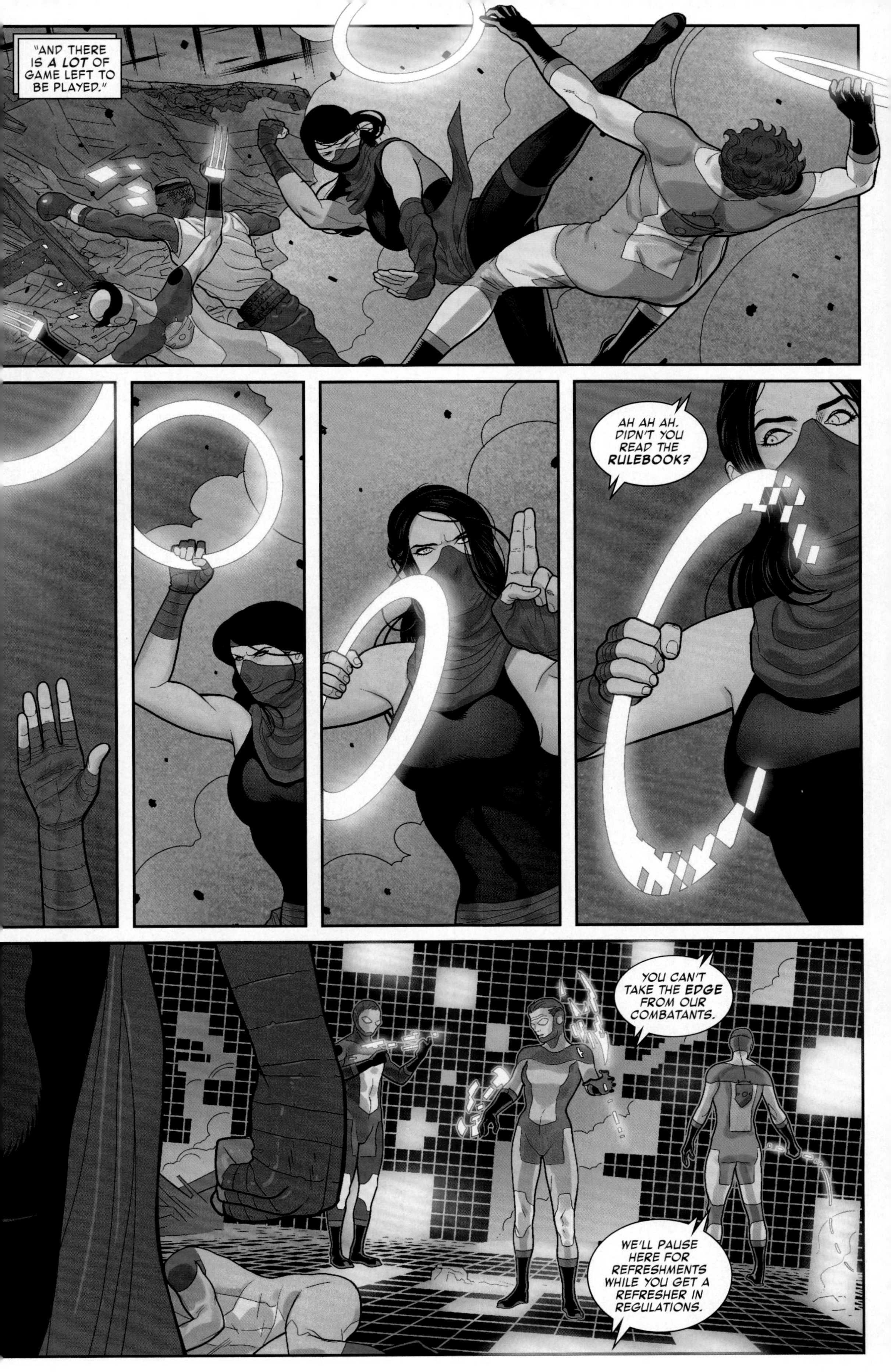
"AND THERE IS A LOT OF GAME LEFT TO BE PLAYED."
AH AH AH. DIDN'T YOU READ THE RULEBOOK?
YOU CAN'T TAKE THE EDGE FROM OUR COMBATANTS.
WE'LL PAUSE HERE FOR REFRESHMENTS WHILE YOU GET A REFRESHER IN REGULATIONS.

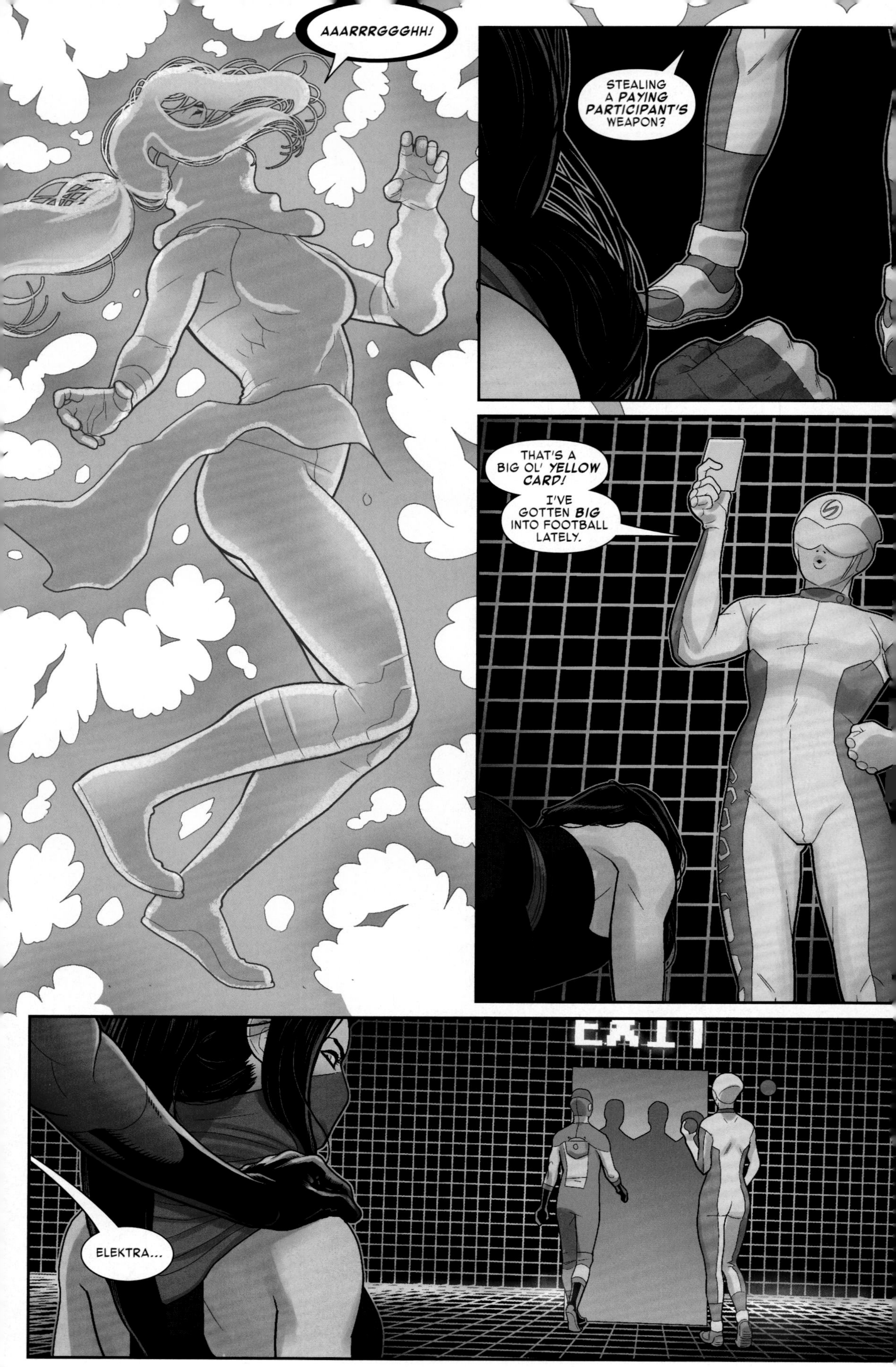
AAARRRGGGHH!
STEALING A PAYING PARTICIPANT'S WEAPON?
THAT'S A BIG OL' YELLOW CARD!
I'VE GOTTEN BIG INTO FOOTBALL LATELY.
ELEKTRA...

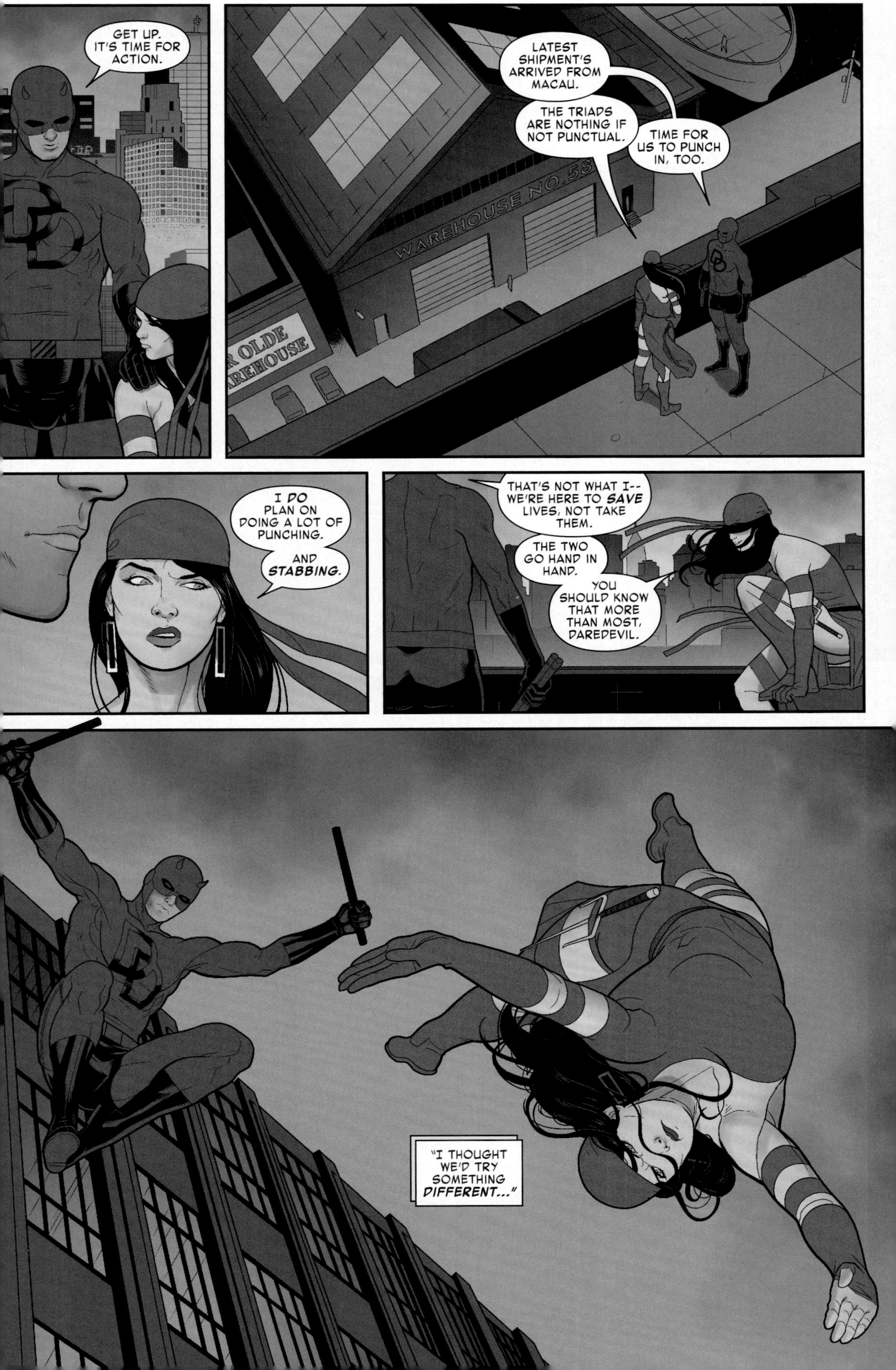
GET UP. IT'S TIME FOR ACTION.
LATEST SHIPMENT'S ARRIVED FROM MACAU.
THE TRIADS ARE NOTHING IF NOT PUNCTUAL.
TIME FOR US TO PUNCH IN, TOO.
WAREHOUSE NO.58
R OLDE AREHOUSE
I DO PLAN ON DOING A LOT OF PUNCHING.
AND STABBING.
THAT'S NOT WHAT I-- WE'RE HERE TO SAVE LIVES, NOT TAKE THEM.
THE TWO GO HAND IN HAND.
YOU SHOULD KNOW THAT MORE THAN MOST, DAREDEVIL.
"I THOUGHT WE'D TRY SOMETHING DIFFERENT..."

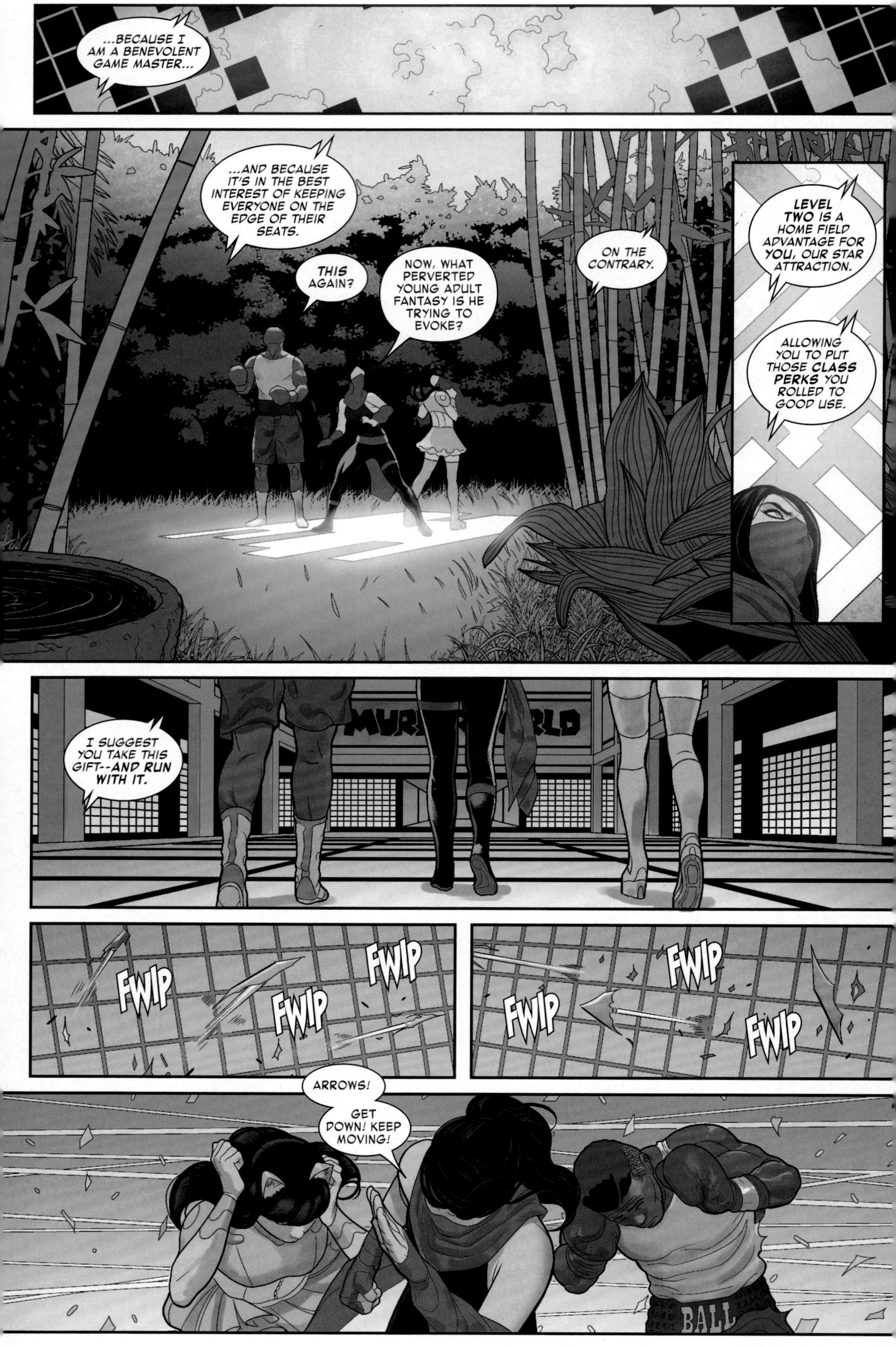

...BECAUSE I AM A BENEVOLENT GAME MASTER...
...AND BECAUSE IT'S IN THE BEST INTEREST OF KEEPING EVERYONE ON THE EDGE OF THEIR SEATS.
THIS AGAIN?
NOW, WHAT PERVERTED YOUNG ADULT FANTASY IS HE TRYING TO EVOKE?
ON THE CONTRARY.
LEVEL TWO IS A HOME FIELD ADVANTAGE FOR YOU, OUR STAR ATTRACTION.
ALLOWING YOU TO PUT THOSE CLASS PERKS YOU ROLLED TO GOOD USE.
I SUGGEST YOU TAKE THIS GIFT--AND RUN WITH IT.
FWIP
FWIP
FWIP
FWIP
FWIP
FWIP
ARROWS!
GET DOWN! KEEP MOVING!
BALL

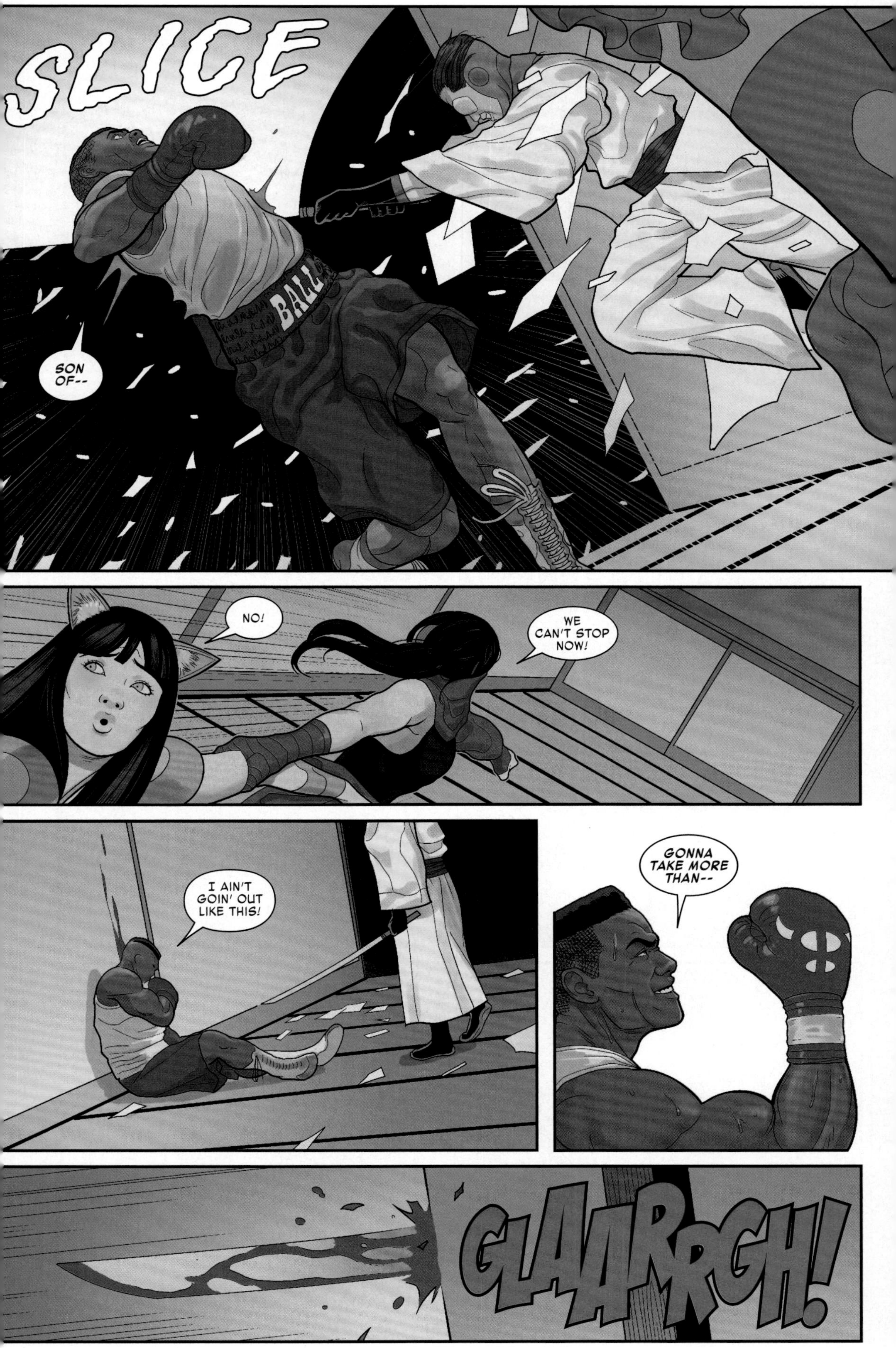
SLICE
BALL
SON OF--
NO!
WE CAN'T STOP NOW!
I AIN'T GOIN' OUT LIKE THIS!
GONNA TAKE MORE THAN--
GLAARRGH!

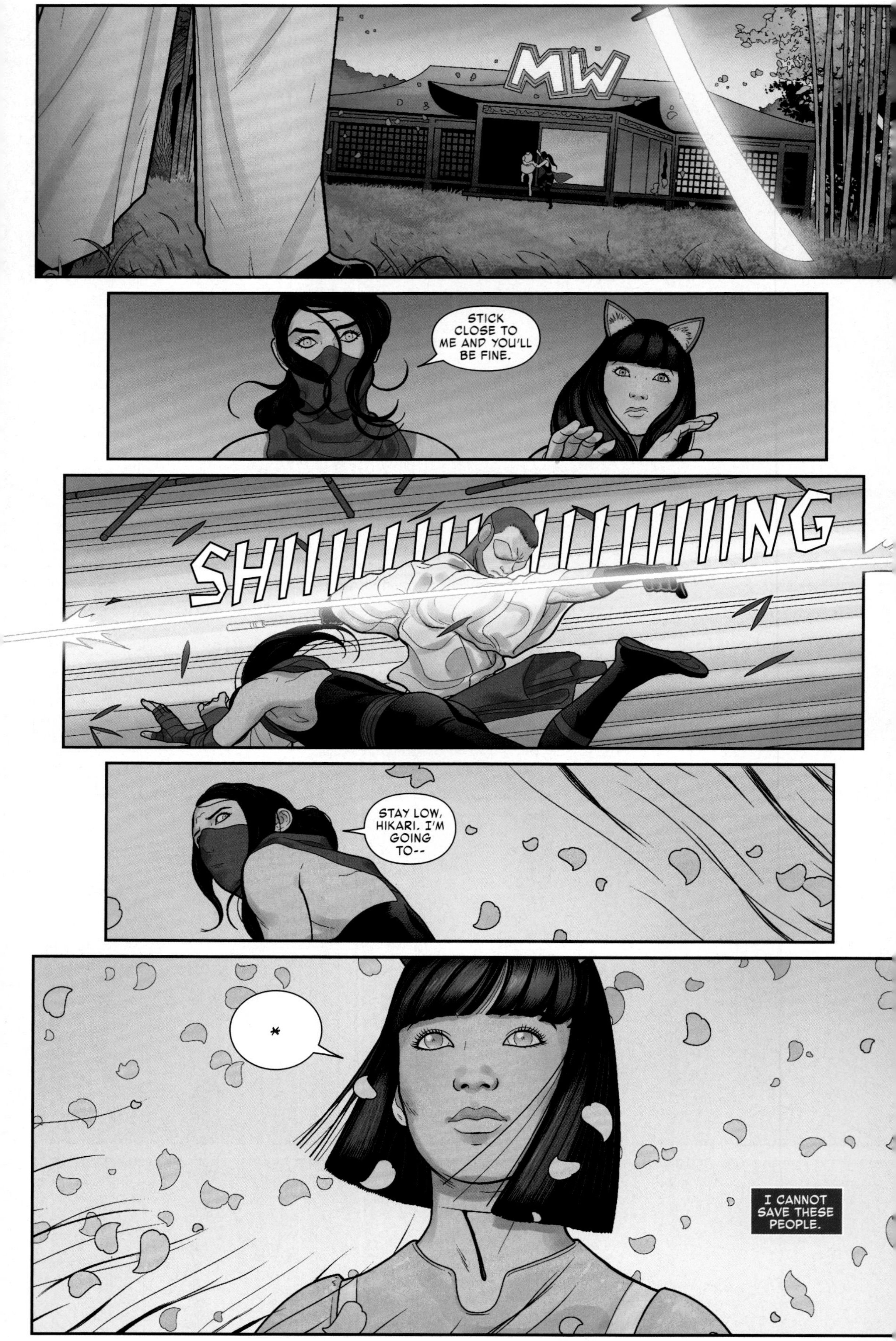
MW
STICK CLOSE TO ME AND YOU'LL BE FINE.
SHIIIIIIIIIIIIIIIING
STAY LOW, HIKARI. I'M GOING TO--
*
I CANNOT SAVE THESE PEOPLE.

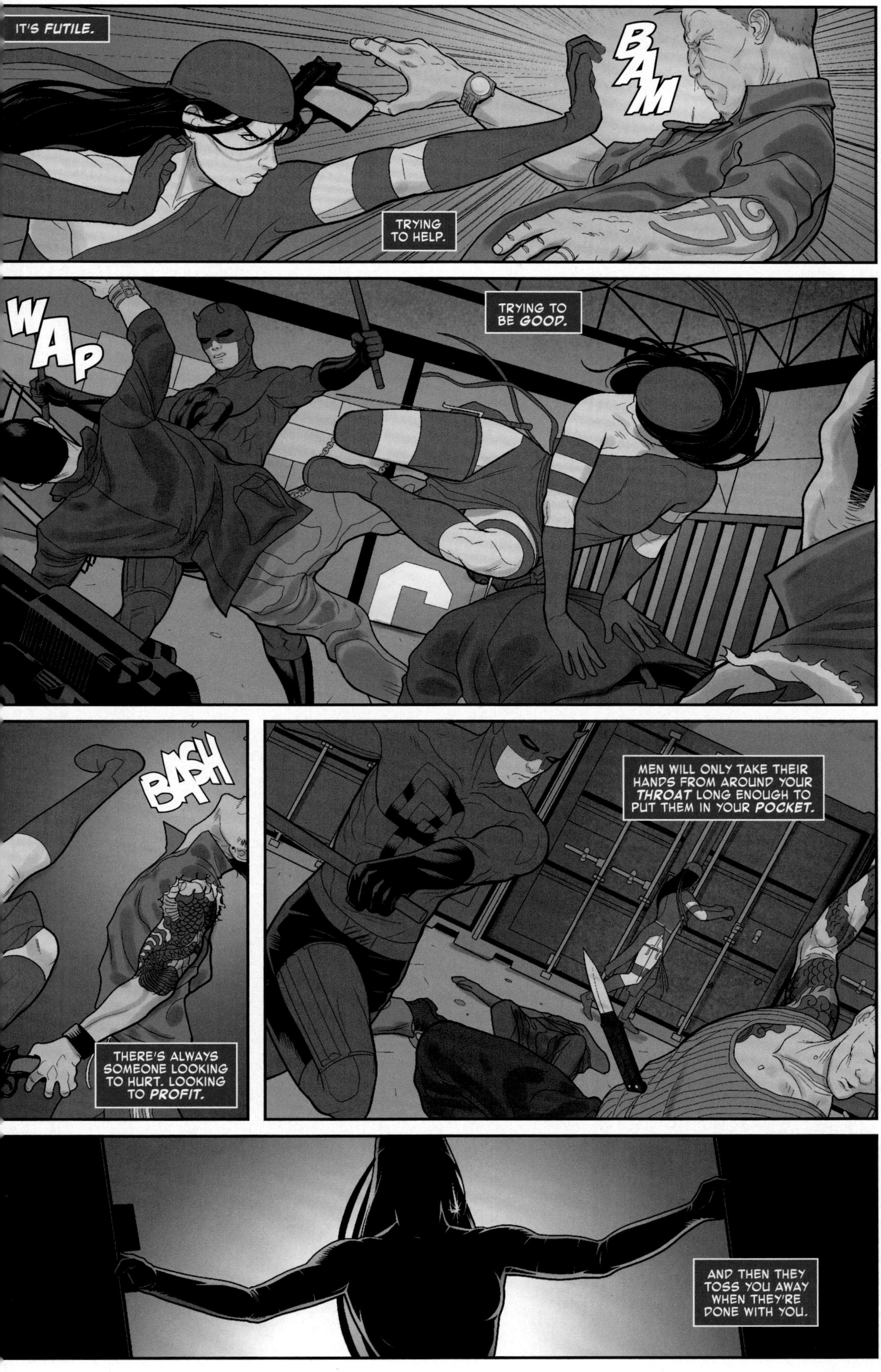
IT'S FUTILE.
BAM
TRYING TO HELP.
WAP
TRYING TO BE GOOD.
BASH
THERE'S ALWAYS SOMEONE LOOKING TO HURT. LOOKING TO PROFIT.
MEN WILL ONLY TAKE THEIR HANDS FROM AROUND YOUR THROAT LONG ENOUGH TO PUT THEM IN YOUR POCKET.
AND THEN THEY TOSS YOU AWAY WHEN THEY'RE DONE WITH YOU.

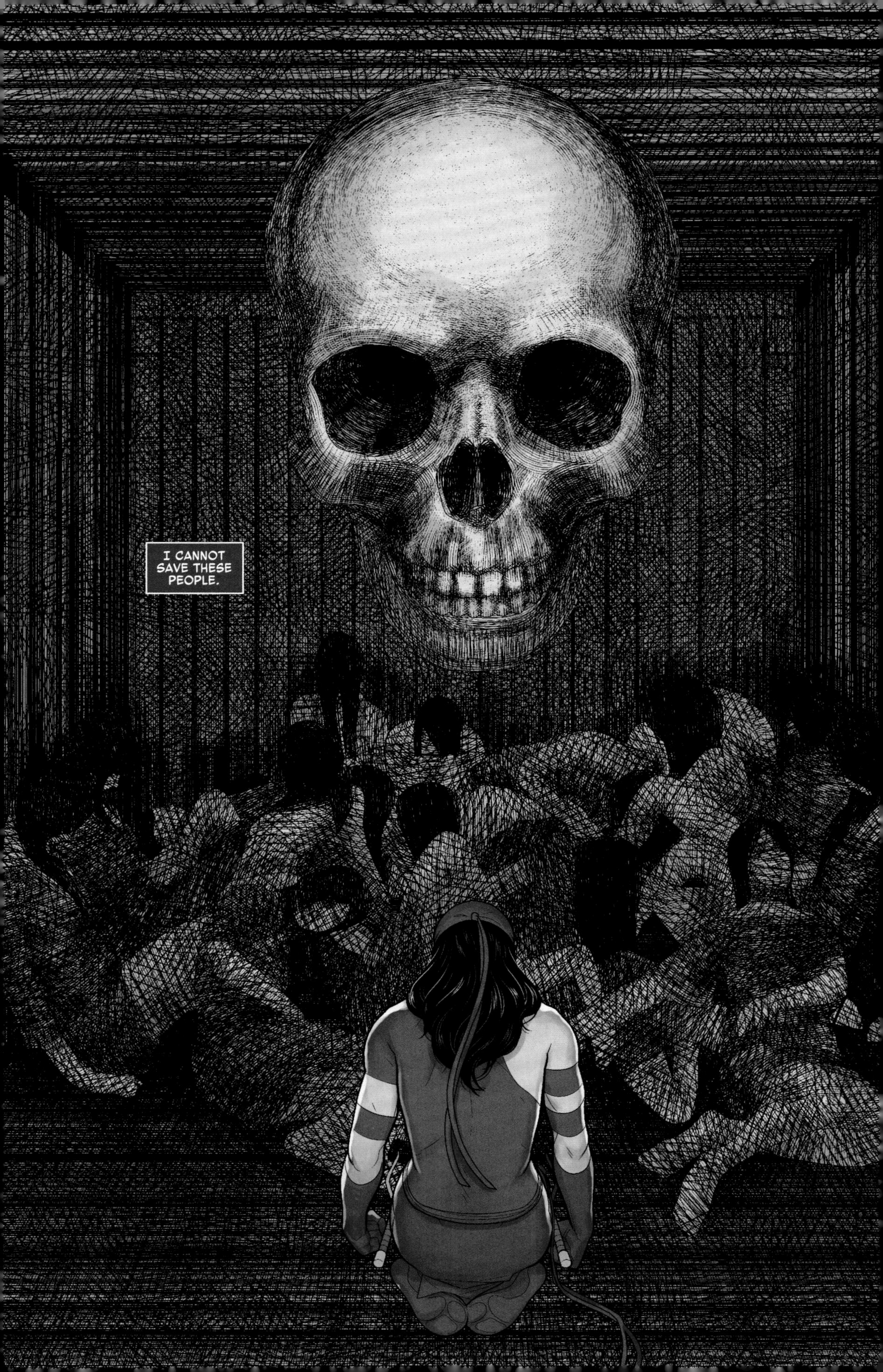
I CANNOT SAVE THESE PEOPLE.

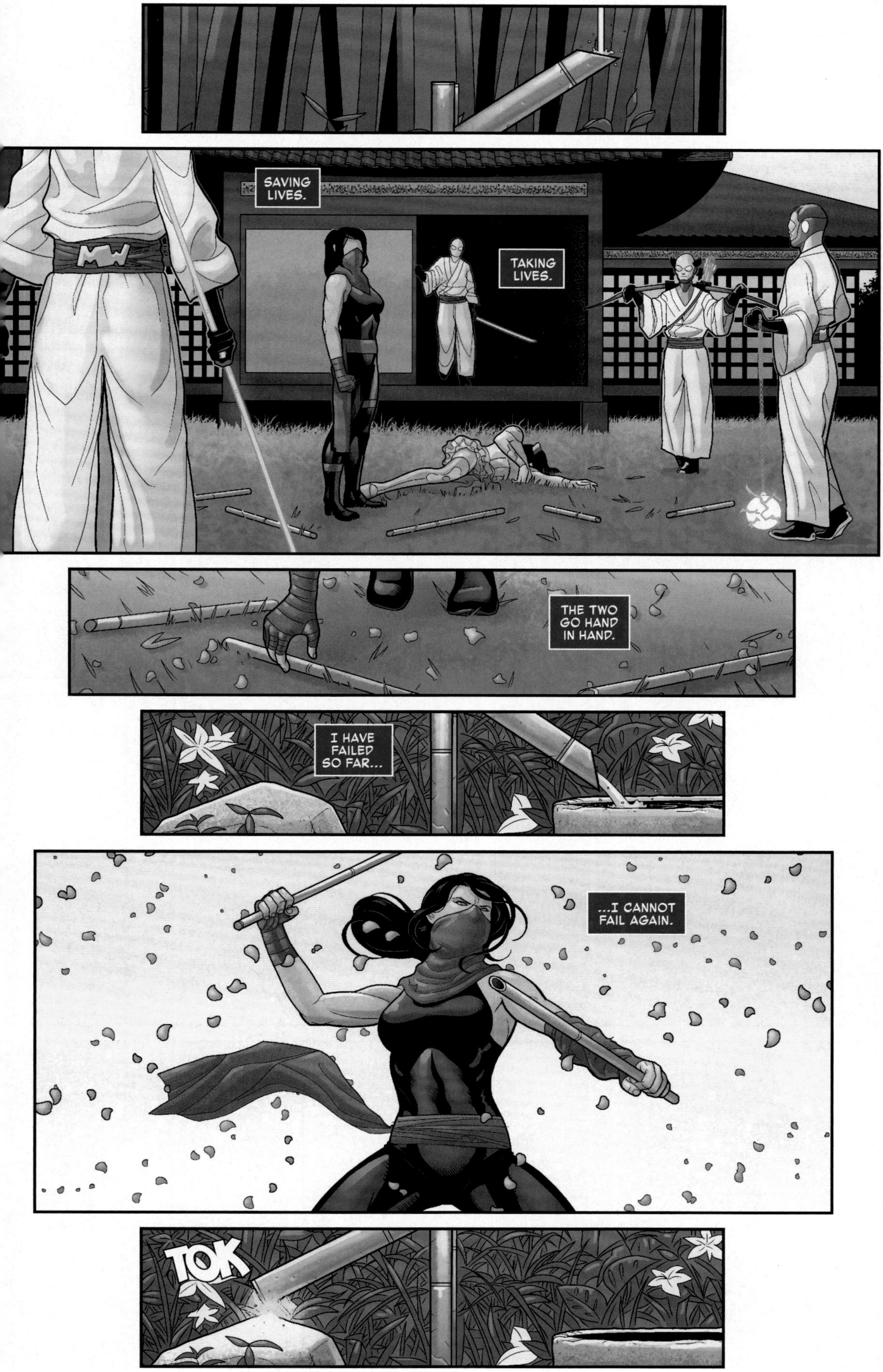
SAVING LIVES.
TAKING LIVES.
THE TWO GO HAND IN HAND.
I HAVE FAILED SO FAR...
...I CANNOT FAIL AGAIN.
TOK

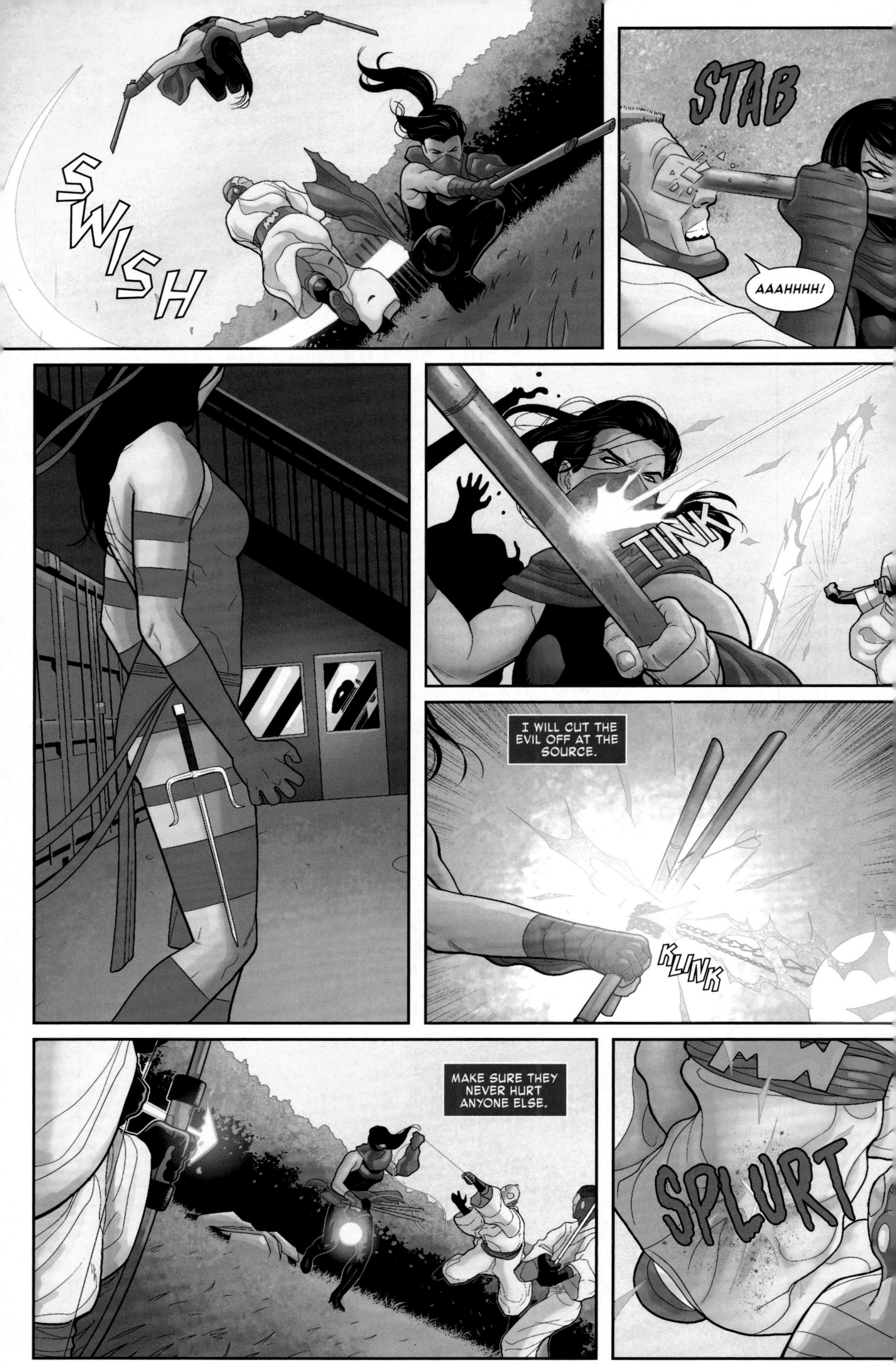
SWISH
STAB
AAAHHHH!
TINK
I WILL CUT THE EVIL OFF AT THE SOURCE.
KLINK
MAKE SURE THEY NEVER HURT ANYONE ELSE.
SPLURT

SO ALL THE SICK **** WATCHING ME NOW...

...IF THEY EVEN BREATHE A HINT OF *ARCADE'S* NAME...

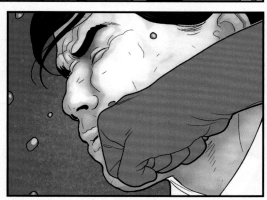

...*I* WILL BE THE ONE DOING THE HUNTING.

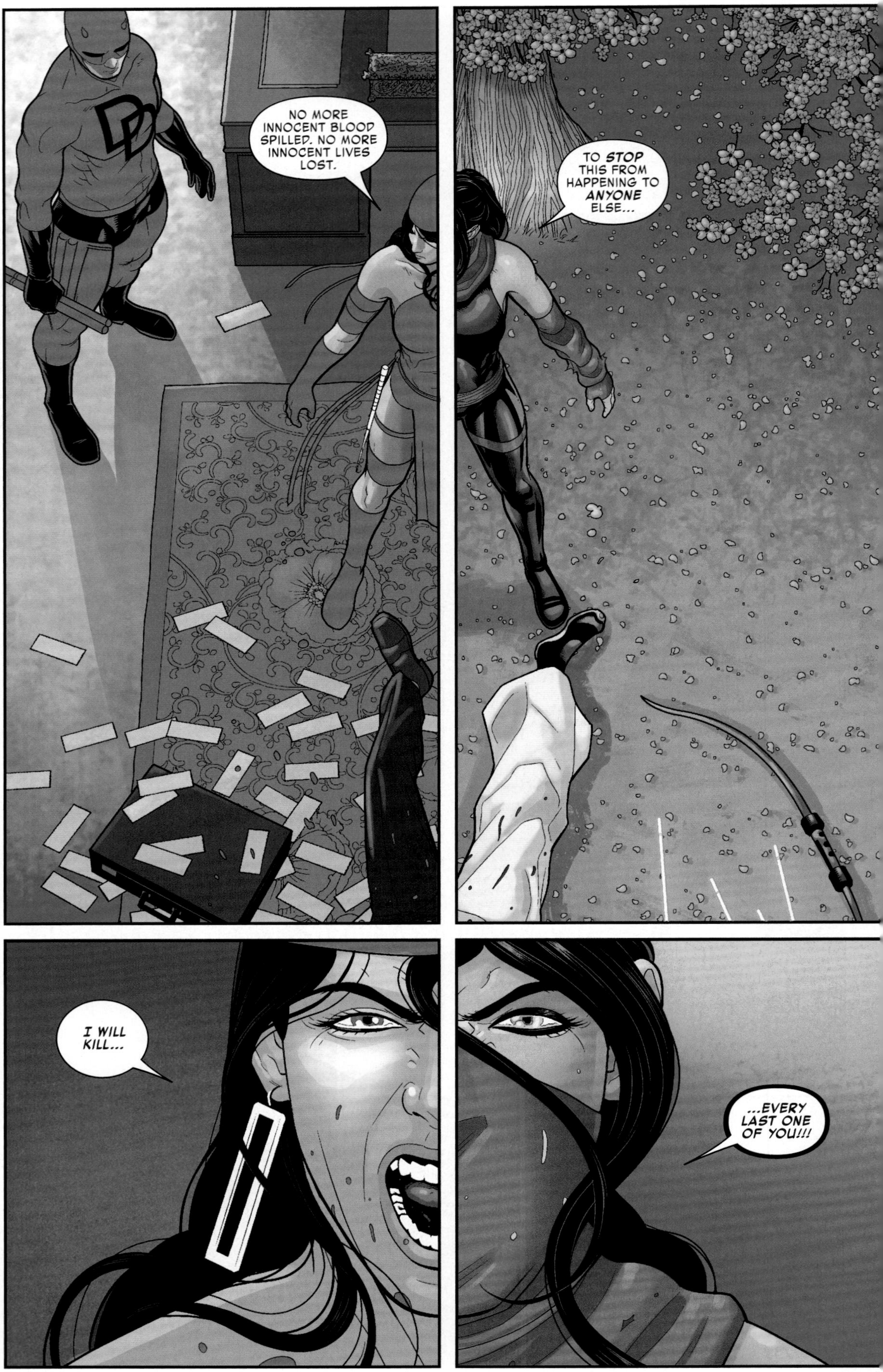
NO MORE INNOCENT BLOOD SPILLED. NO MORE INNOCENT LIVES LOST.
TO *STOP* THIS FROM HAPPENING TO *ANYONE* ELSE...
*I WILL KILL...*
*...EVERY LAST ONE OF YOU!!!*

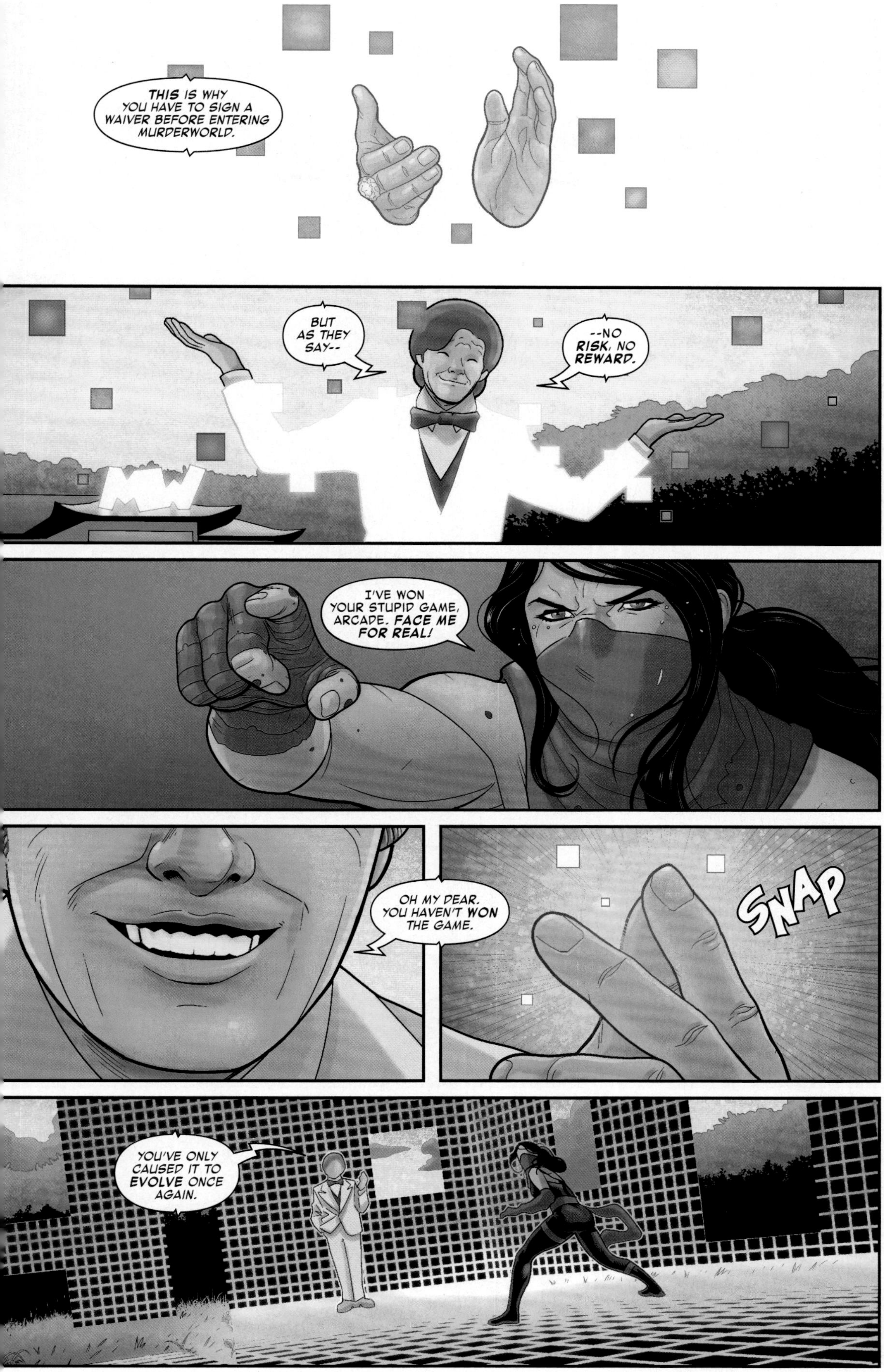

THIS IS WHY YOU HAVE TO SIGN A WAIVER BEFORE ENTERING MURDERWORLD.
BUT AS THEY SAY--
--NO RISK, NO REWARD.
I'VE WON YOUR STUPID GAME, ARCADE. FACE ME FOR REAL!
OH MY DEAR. YOU HAVEN'T WON THE GAME.
SNAP
YOU'VE ONLY CAUSED IT TO EVOLVE ONCE AGAIN.

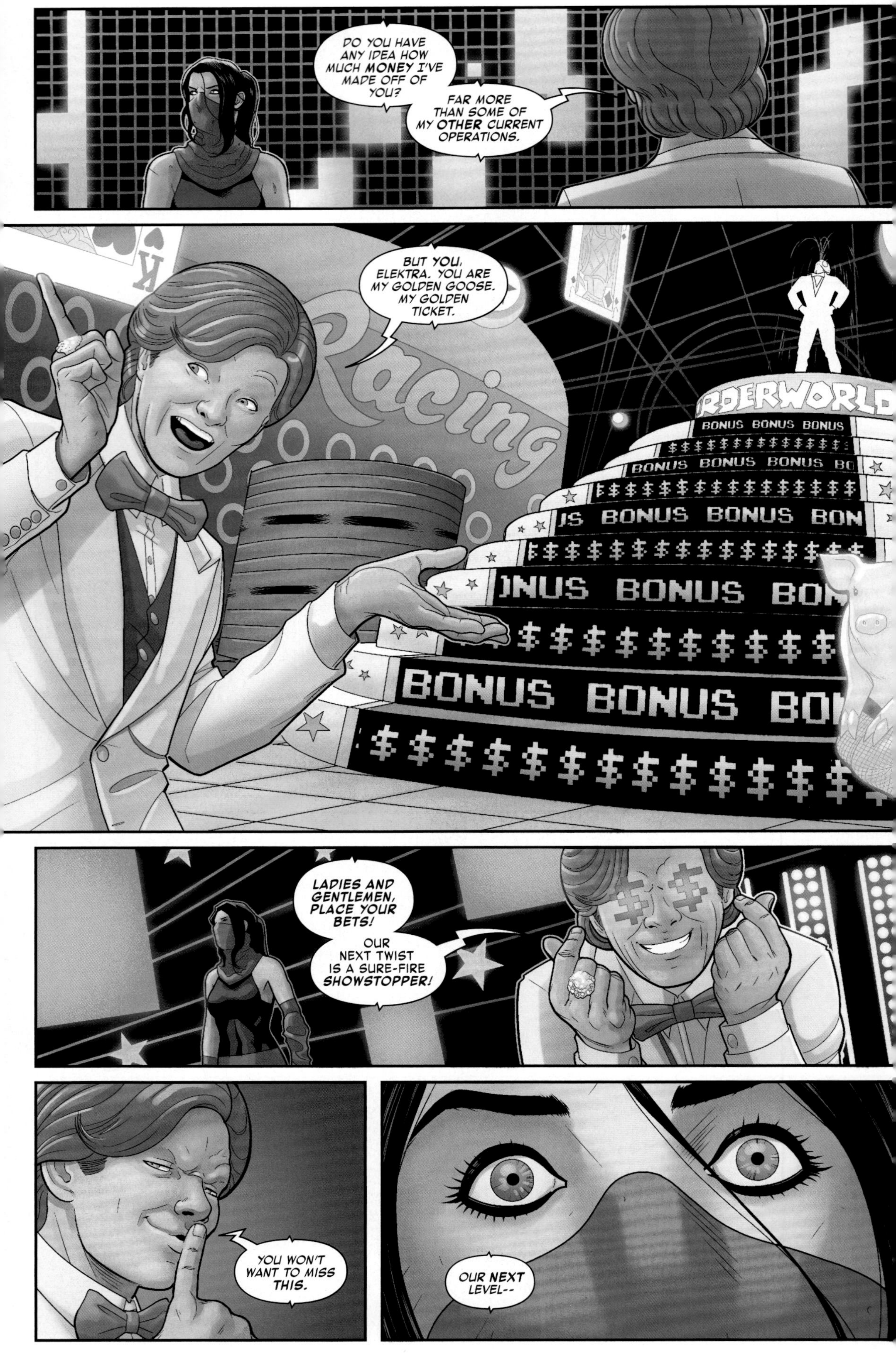

DO YOU HAVE ANY IDEA HOW MUCH MONEY I'VE MADE OFF OF YOU?
FAR MORE THAN SOME OF MY OTHER CURRENT OPERATIONS.
BUT YOU, ELEKTRA. YOU ARE MY GOLDEN GOOSE. MY GOLDEN TICKET.
Racing
RDERWORLD
BONUS BONUS BONUS
LADIES AND GENTLEMEN, PLACE YOUR BETS!
OUR NEXT TWIST IS A SURE-FIRE SHOWSTOPPER!
YOU WON'T WANT TO MISS THIS.
OUR NEXT LEVEL--

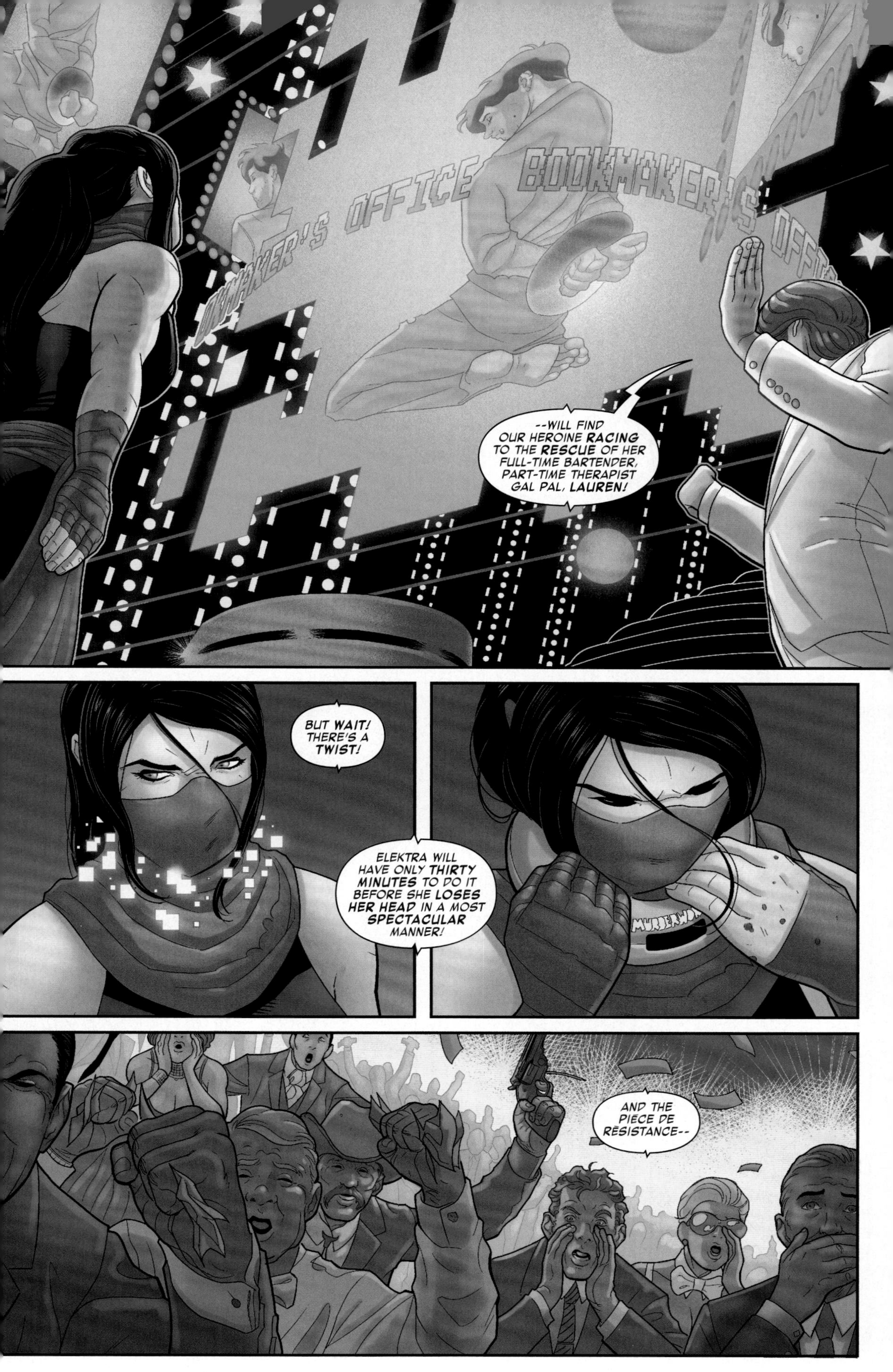
BOOKMAKER'S OFFICE
--WILL FIND OUR HEROINE RACING TO THE RESCUE OF HER FULL-TIME BARTENDER, PART-TIME THERAPIST GAL PAL, LAUREN!
BUT WAIT! THERE'S A TWIST!
ELEKTRA WILL HAVE ONLY THIRTY MINUTES TO DO IT BEFORE SHE LOSES HER HEAD IN A MOST SPECTACULAR MANNER!
AND THE PIÈCE DE RÉSISTANCE--

BEWARE, BEWARE, ELEKTRA! ELEKTRA! ELEK BEWARE! BEWAR A NEW A NEW NEW LAYER PLAYER PLAYE RED HAS ENTERED ME THE GAME THE GA

--A NEW CHALLENGER APPROACHES! READY TO MIX IT UP IN THE METAPHORICAL OCTAGON.

IT'S *SCREWBALL!*

SCREWBA

STUP

LIGHTS!

CAMERA!

KONG

ACTION!

29:59

MURDERWORLD

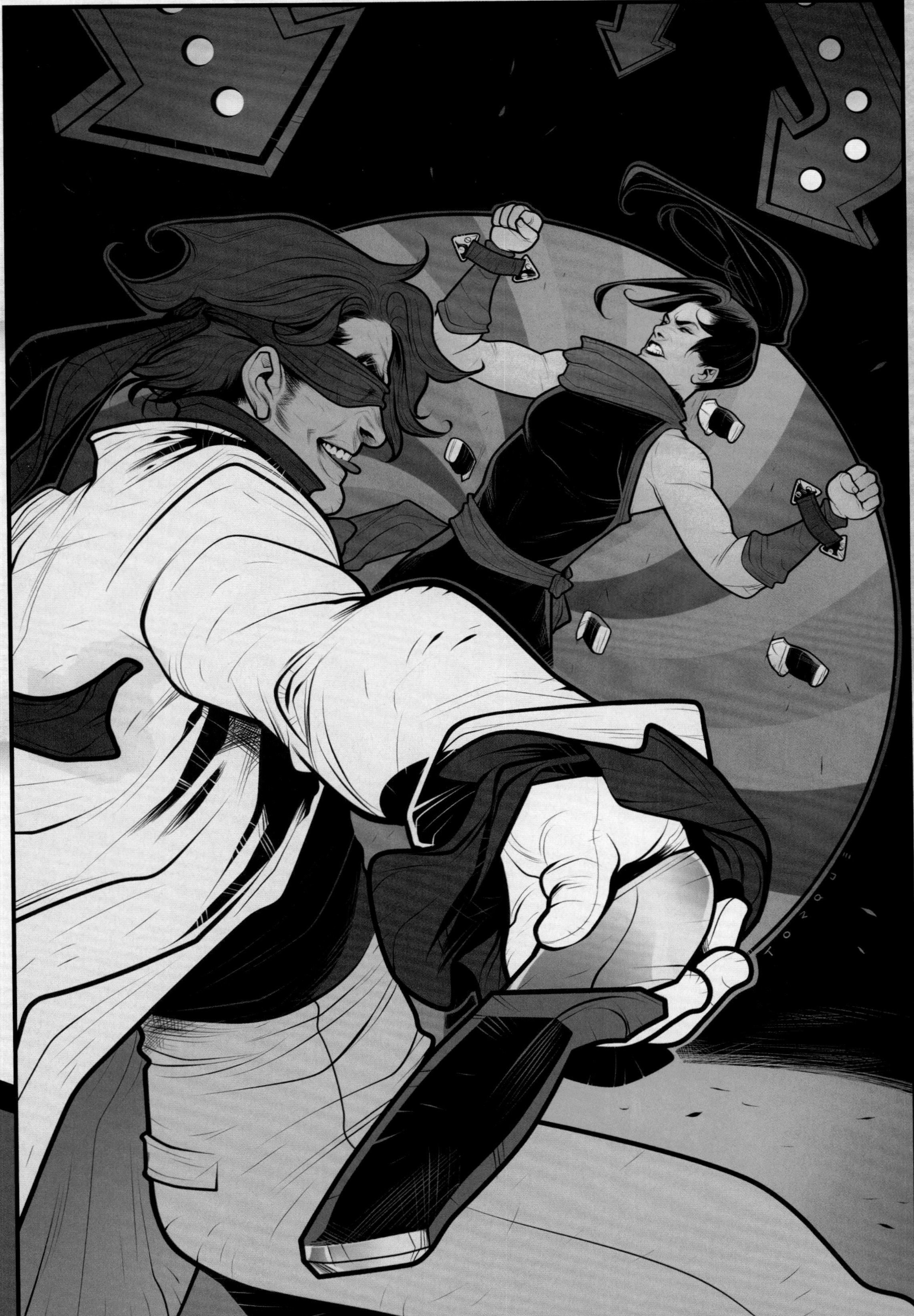

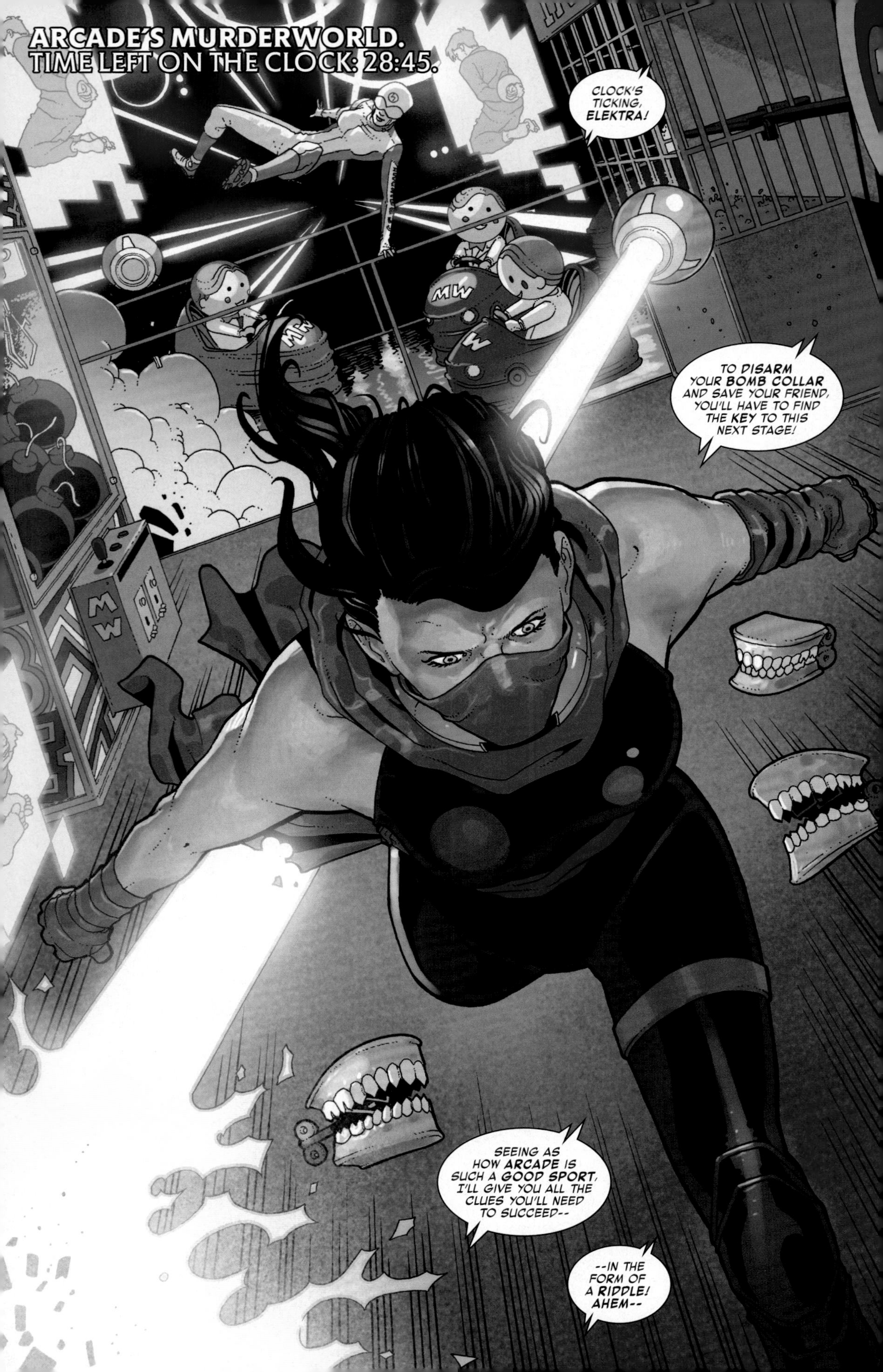
ARCADE'S MURDERWORLD.
TIME LEFT ON THE CLOCK: 28:45.
CLOCK'S TICKING, ELEKTRA!
TO DISARM YOUR BOMB COLLAR AND SAVE YOUR FRIEND, YOU'LL HAVE TO FIND THE KEY TO THIS NEXT STAGE!
SEEING AS HOW ARCADE IS SUCH A GOOD SPORT, I'LL GIVE YOU ALL THE CLUES YOU'LL NEED TO SUCCEED--
--IN THE FORM OF A RIDDLE! AHEM--

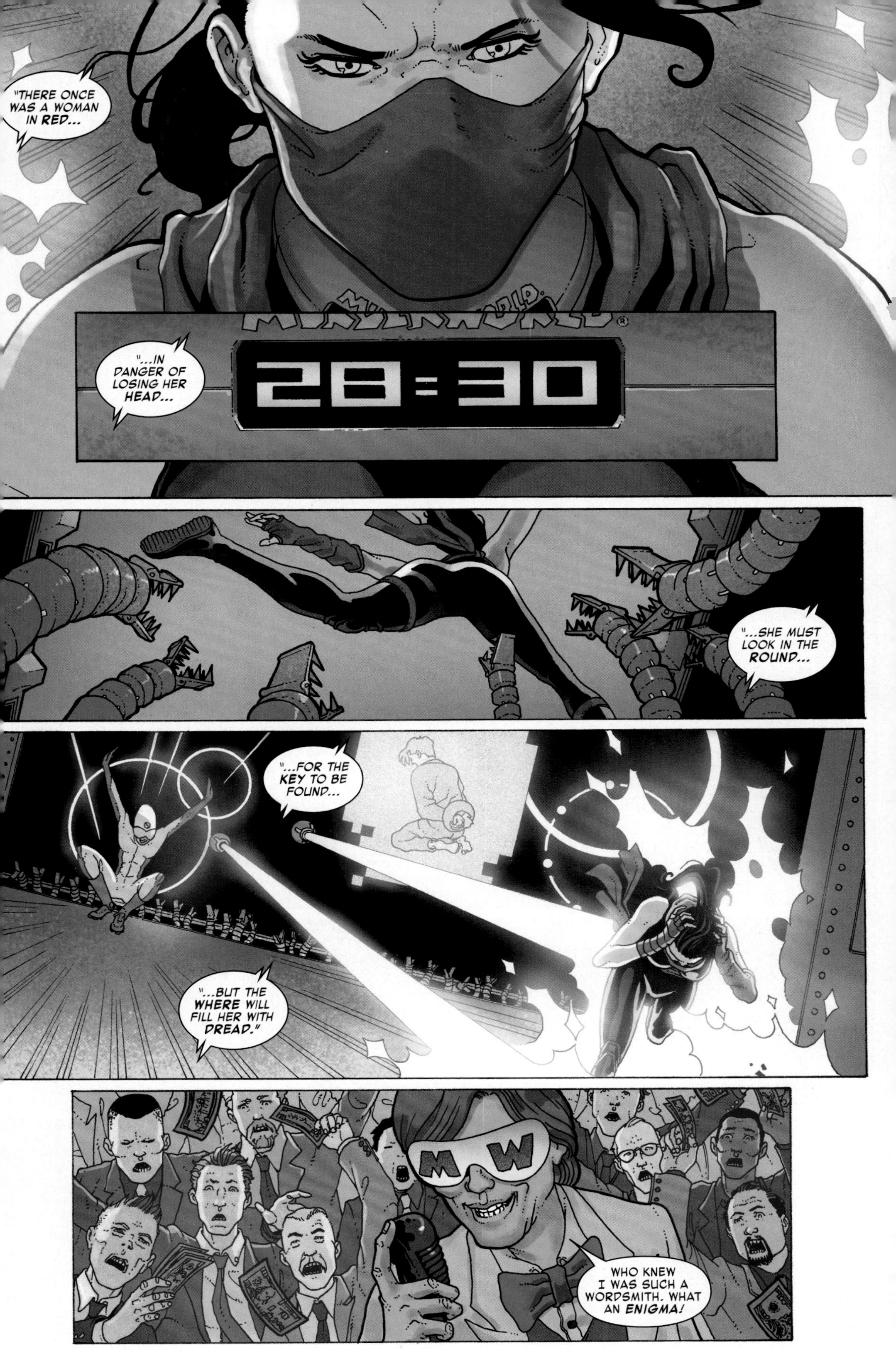
"THERE ONCE WAS A WOMAN IN RED...
"...IN DANGER OF LOSING HER HEAD...
28:30
"...SHE MUST LOOK IN THE ROUND...
"...FOR THE KEY TO BE FOUND...
"...BUT THE WHERE WILL FILL HER WITH DREAD."
MW
WHO KNEW I WAS SUCH A WORDSMITH. WHAT AN ENIGMA!

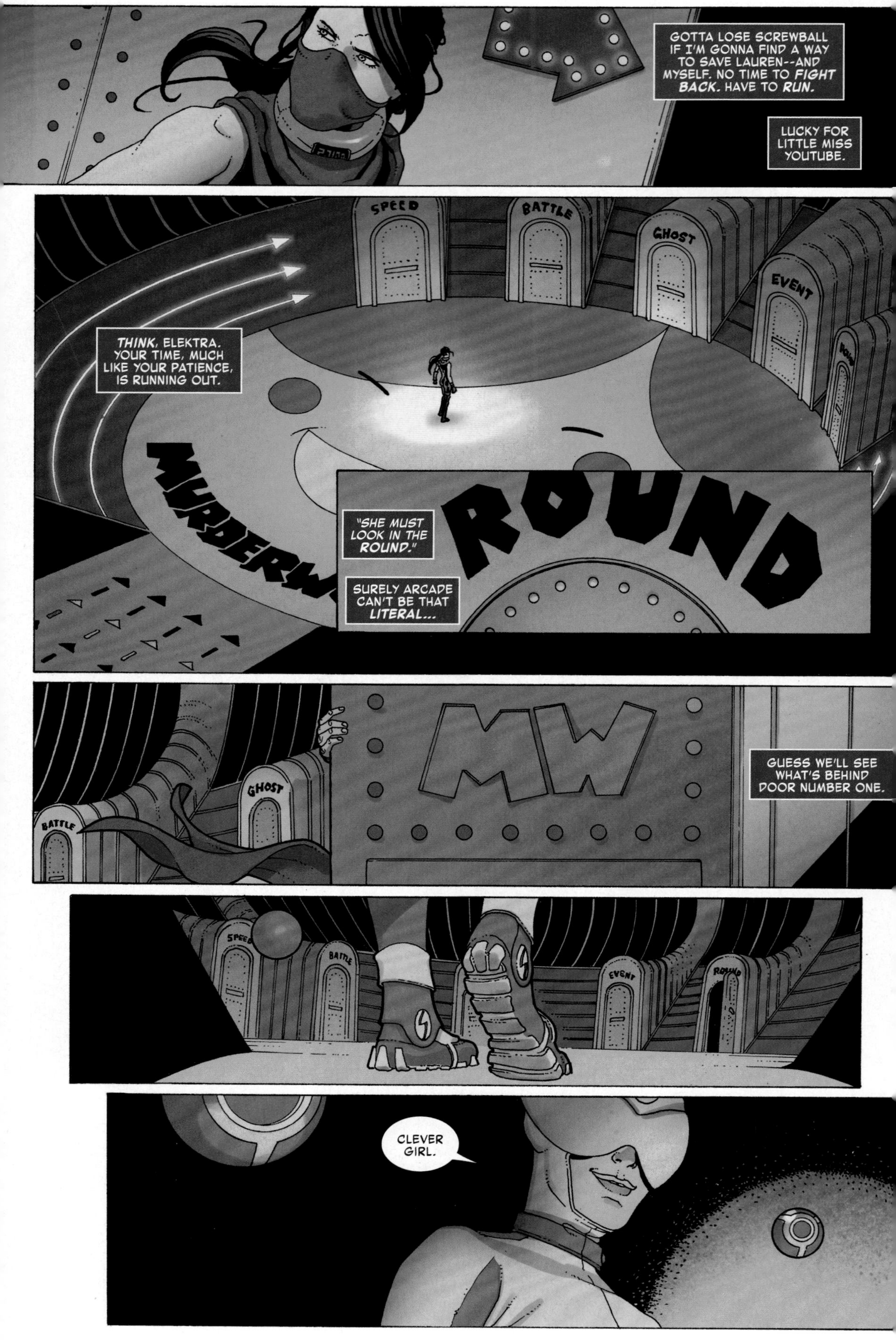
GOTTA LOSE SCREWBALL IF I'M GONNA FIND A WAY TO SAVE LAUREN--AND MYSELF. NO TIME TO FIGHT BACK. HAVE TO RUN.
LUCKY FOR LITTLE MISS YOUTUBE.
SPEED
BATTLE
GHOST
EVENT
ROUND
THINK, ELEKTRA. YOUR TIME, MUCH LIKE YOUR PATIENCE, IS RUNNING OUT.
MURDERW
ROUND
"SHE MUST LOOK IN THE ROUND."
SURELY ARCADE CAN'T BE THAT LITERAL...
MW
GHOST
BATTLE
GUESS WE'LL SEE WHAT'S BEHIND DOOR NUMBER ONE.
SPEED
BATTLE
EVENT
ROUND
CLEVER GIRL.

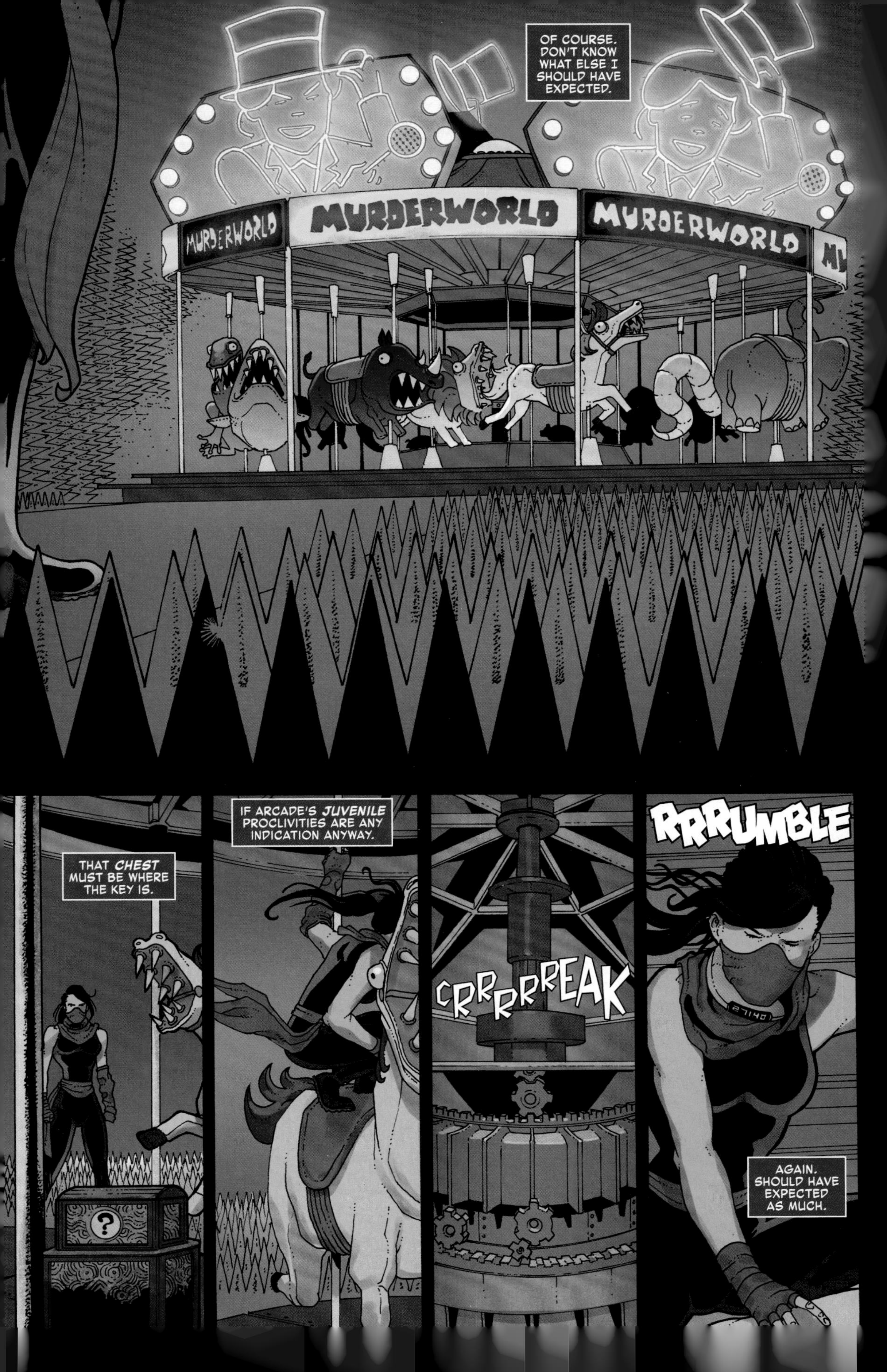
OF COURSE. DON'T KNOW WHAT ELSE I SHOULD HAVE EXPECTED.
MURDERWORLD
MURDERWORLD
MURDERWORLD
THAT CHEST MUST BE WHERE THE KEY IS.
IF ARCADE'S JUVENILE PROCLIVITIES ARE ANY INDICATION ANYWAY.
CRRRRREAK
RRRUMBLE
AGAIN. SHOULD HAVE EXPECTED AS MUCH.

JUST BECAUSE HE GAVE YOU A *HINT* DOESN'T MEAN HE'S GONNA MAKE IT *EASY.*

PICKING UP SPEED...

...MAKING IT HARD TO MOVE...

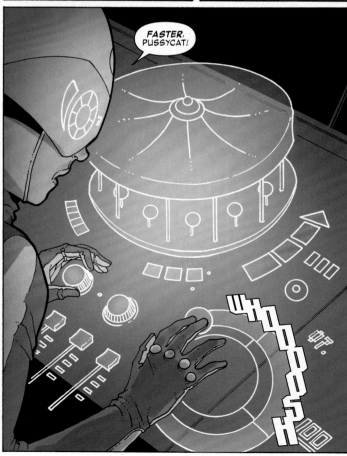

FASTER, PUSSYCAT!

DIE! DIE!

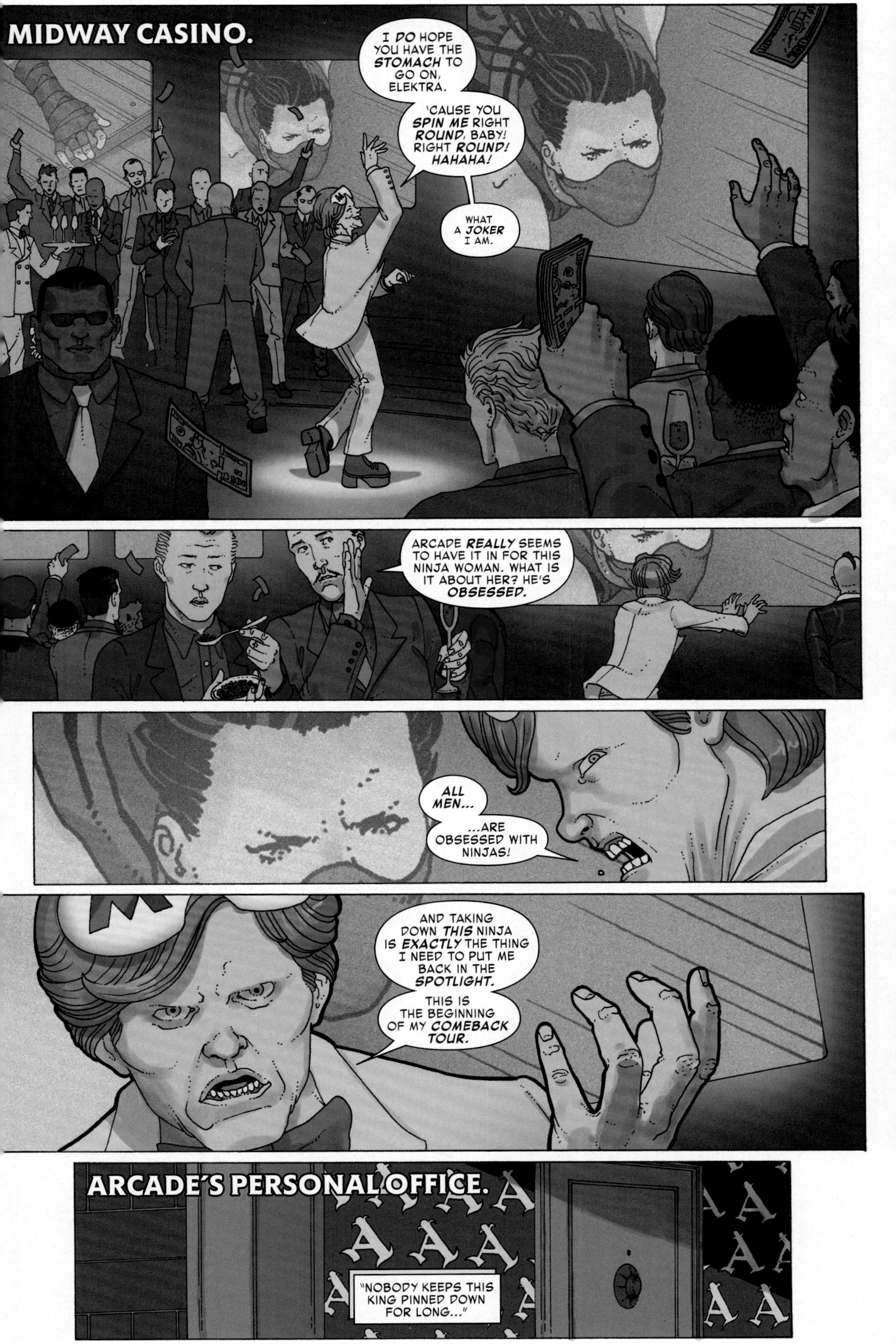
MIDWAY CASINO.
I DO HOPE YOU HAVE THE STOMACH TO GO ON, ELEKTRA.
'CAUSE YOU SPIN ME RIGHT ROUND, BABY! RIGHT ROUND! HAHAHA!
WHAT A JOKER I AM.
ARCADE REALLY SEEMS TO HAVE IT IN FOR THIS NINJA WOMAN. WHAT IS IT ABOUT HER? HE'S OBSESSED.
ALL MEN...
...ARE OBSESSED WITH NINJAS!
AND TAKING DOWN THIS NINJA IS EXACTLY THE THING I NEED TO PUT ME BACK IN THE SPOTLIGHT.
THIS IS THE BEGINNING OF MY COMEBACK TOUR.
ARCADE'S PERSONAL OFFICE.
"NOBODY KEEPS THIS KING PINNED DOWN FOR LONG..."

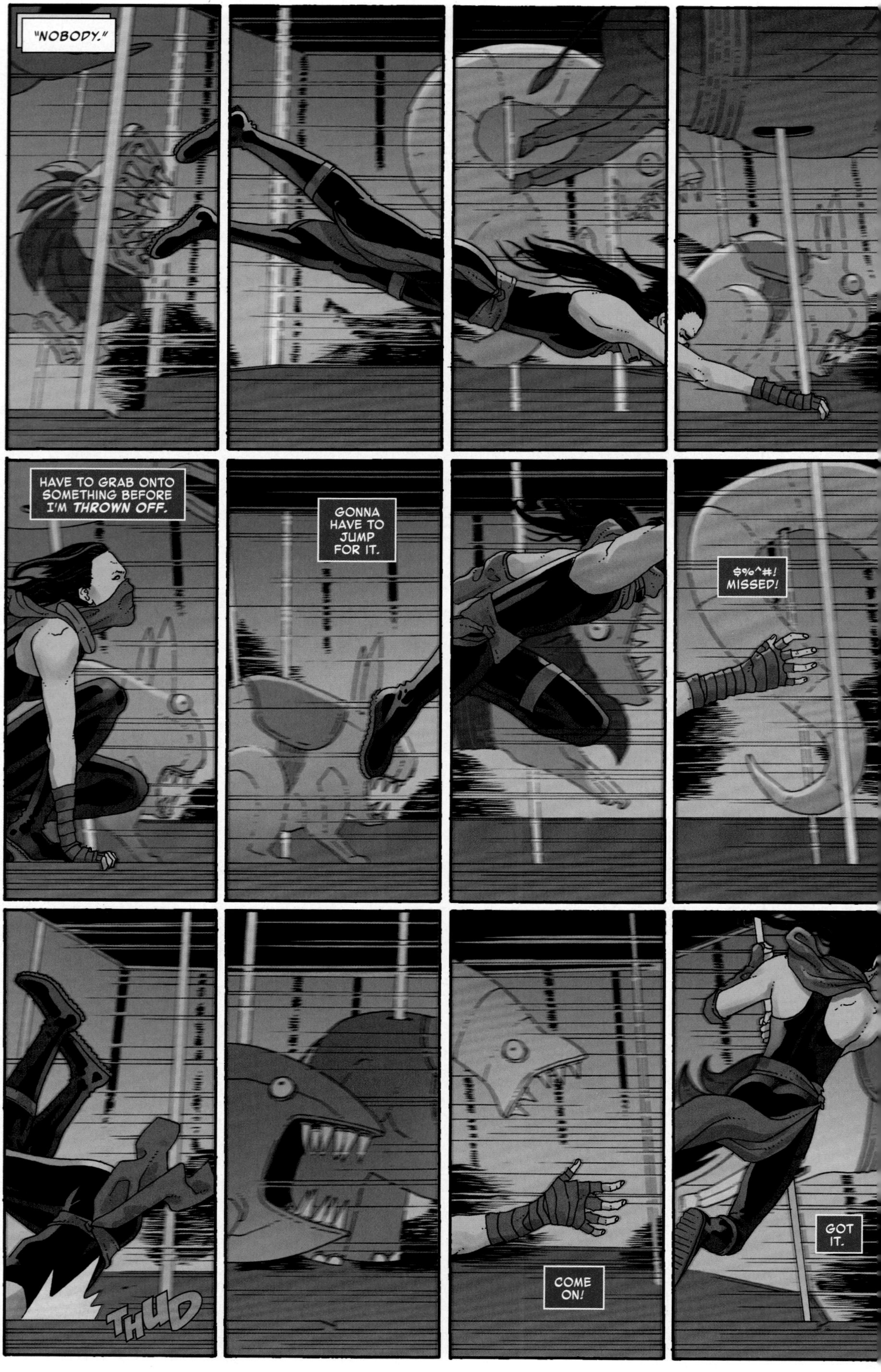
"NOBODY."
HAVE TO GRAB ONTO SOMETHING BEFORE I'M *THROWN OFF.*
GONNA HAVE TO JUMP FOR IT.
$%^#! MISSED!
THUD
COME ON!
GOT IT.

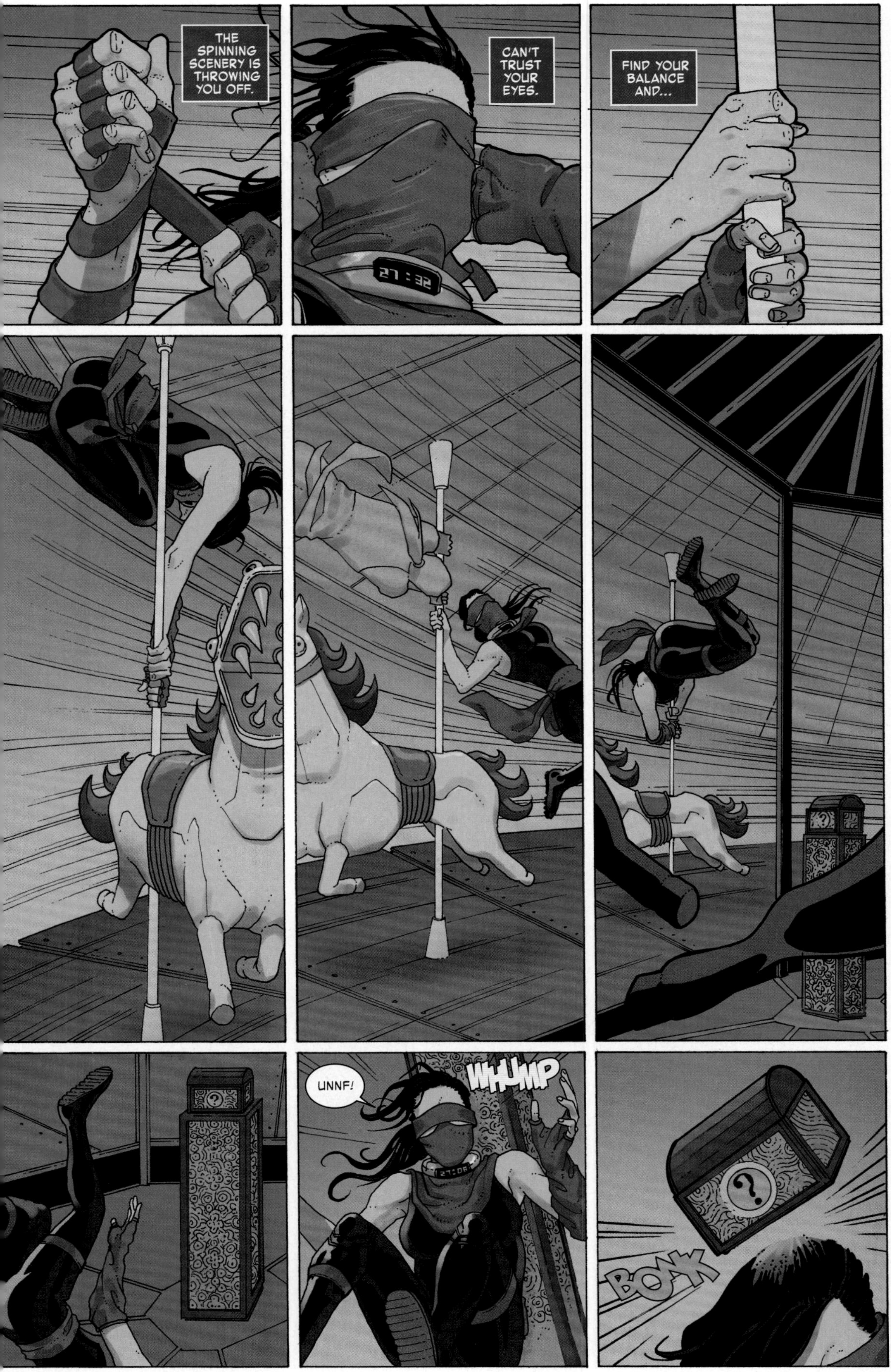
THE SPINNING SCENERY IS THROWING YOU OFF.
CAN'T TRUST YOUR EYES.
FIND YOUR BALANCE AND...
UNNF!
WHUMP
BONK

NOT THE MOST GRACEFUL--BUT I STILL GOT IT.

UH-OH! A MIMIC!

SORRY, PRINCESS, BUT THE KEY IS IN ANOTHER CASTLE.

SPROING

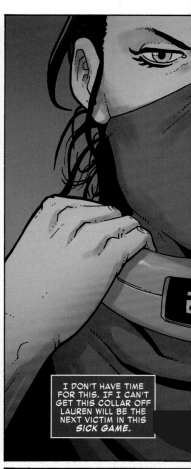

I DON'T HAVE TIME FOR THIS. IF I CAN'T GET THIS COLLAR OFF LAUREN WILL BE THE NEXT VICTIM IN THIS *SICK* GAME.

GETTING NERVOUS? DON'T LOSE YOUR HEAD.

ALLOW ME TO HOLD YOUR HAND A LITTLE MORE, THEN.

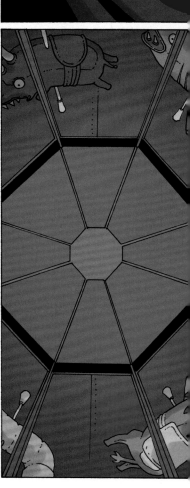

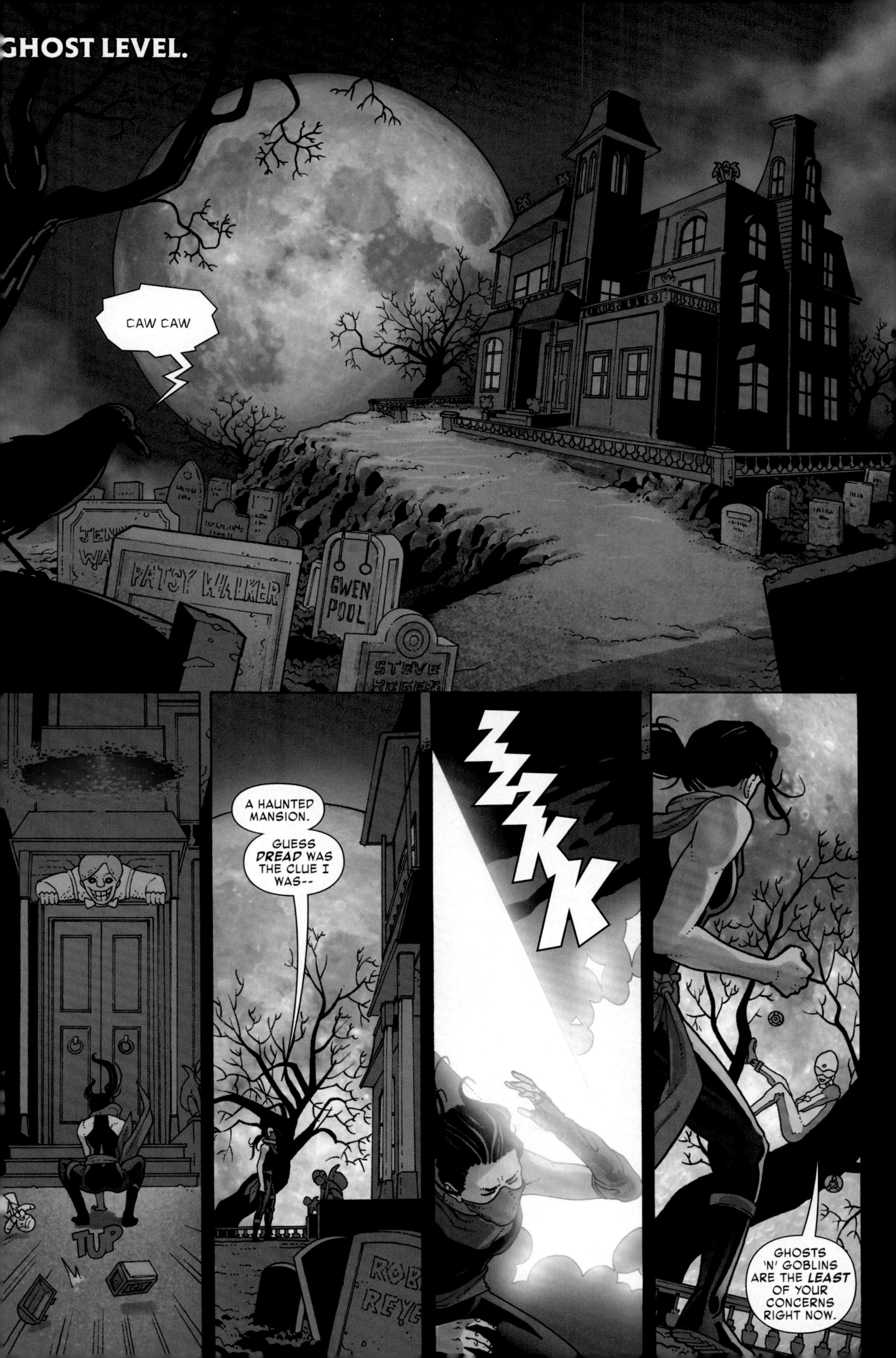
GHOST LEVEL.
CAW CAW
PATSY WALKER
GWEN POOL
STEVE
TUP
A HAUNTED MANSION.
GUESS *DREAD* WAS THE CLUE I WAS--
ZZKK
GHOSTS 'N' GOBLINS ARE THE *LEAST* OF YOUR CONCERNS RIGHT NOW.

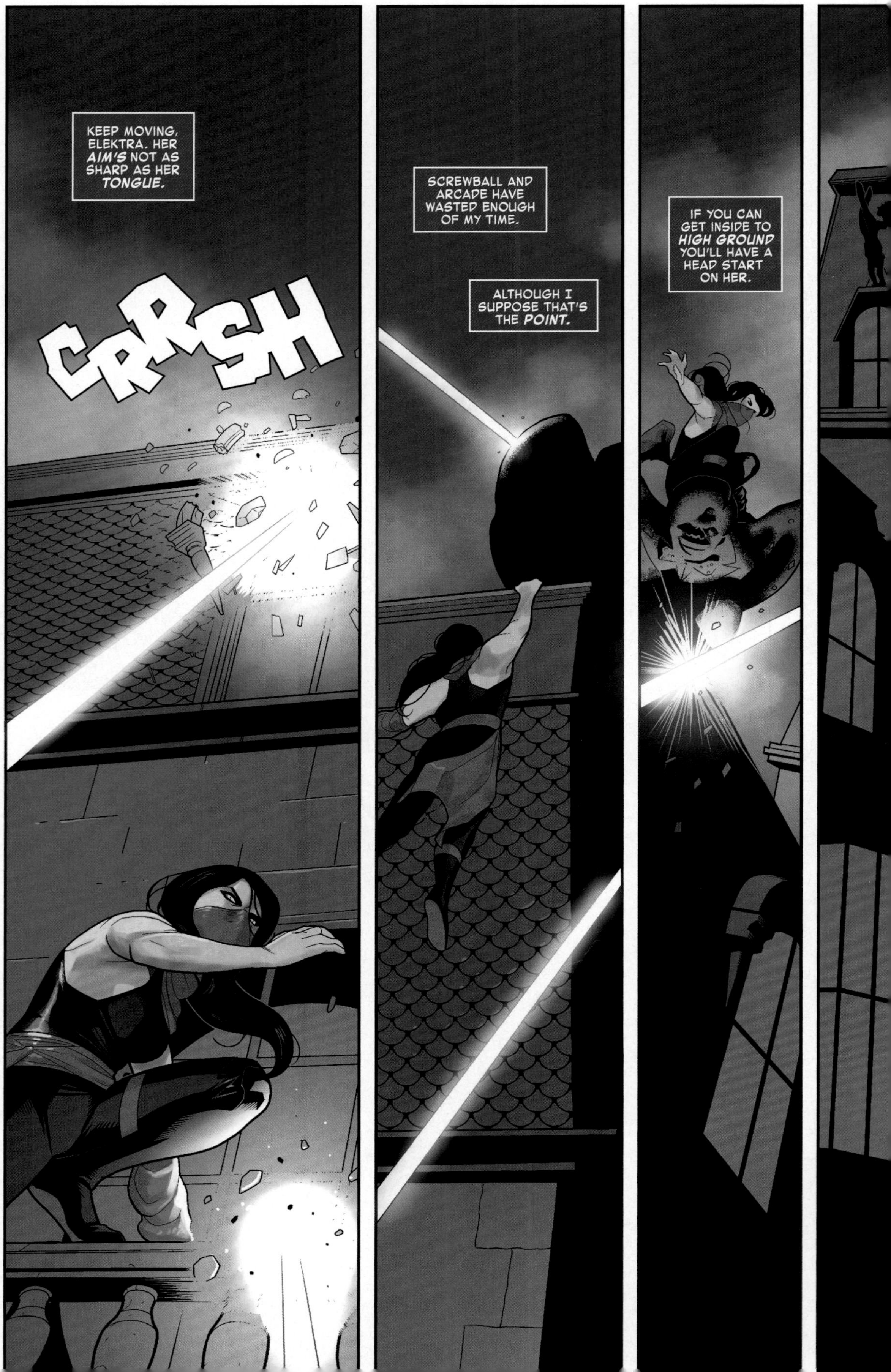
KEEP MOVING, ELEKTRA. HER *AIM'S* NOT AS SHARP AS HER *TONGUE.*
CRRSH
SCREWBALL AND ARCADE HAVE WASTED ENOUGH OF MY TIME.
ALTHOUGH I SUPPOSE THAT'S THE *POINT.*
IF YOU CAN GET INSIDE TO *HIGH GROUND* YOU'LL HAVE A HEAD START ON HER.

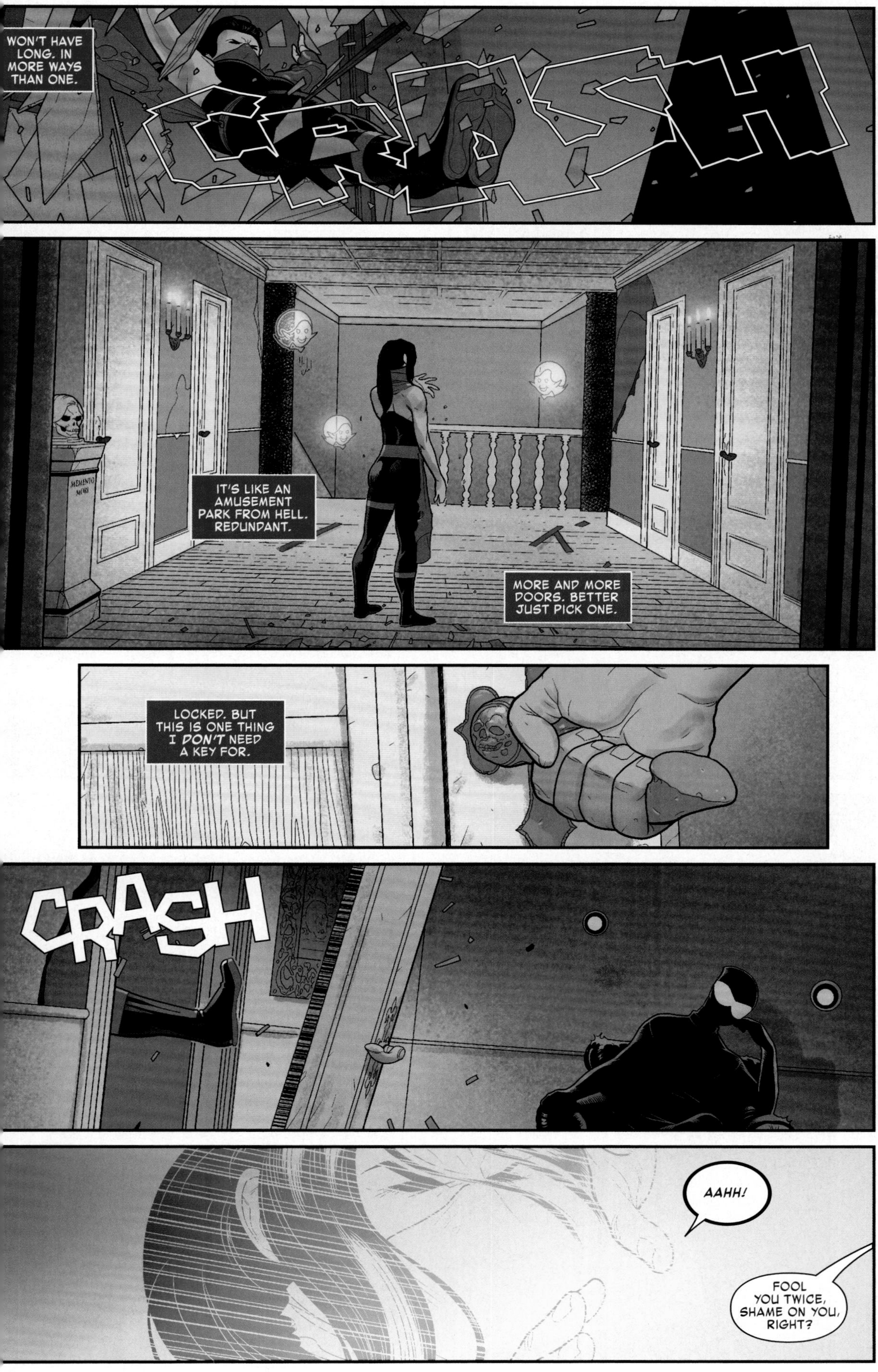

WON'T HAVE LONG. IN MORE WAYS THAN ONE.
CRASH
IT'S LIKE AN AMUSEMENT PARK FROM HELL. REDUNDANT.
MEMENTO MORI
MORE AND MORE DOORS. BETTER JUST PICK ONE.
LOCKED. BUT THIS IS ONE THING I DON'T NEED A KEY FOR.
CRASH
AAHH!
FOOL YOU TWICE, SHAME ON YOU, RIGHT?

GUESS THAT'S WHAT YOU GET FOR UNDERESTIMATING ME, *HUH?*

WELL, THIS AIN'T YOUR MOMMA'S *SCREWBALL.*

I GOT TIRED OF BEING *SMACKED AROUND* BY SPIDER-MAN. AND SPIDER-GIRL.

SO MANY FREAKING *SPIDER-PEOPLE* NOWADAYS.

**BAM**

ARCADE FOUND ME AND MADE ME AN OFFER I COULDN'T REFUSE.

I PLAY CAMERAMAN AND REFEREE IN HIS VEGAS *BATTLE ROYALE* FANTASY.

**WHAK**

SCREWBALL vs ELEKTRA - Action at the Mansion
TheRealScrewball
SUBSCRIBE

Live

171,586 Views

Elektroll
that's not Elektra! Elektra wears red!

Elektra Nachos
You know nothing, yo soy elektra

JohnnySkeptical
Mmm. I have the sneaky suspicion you're not Ele...

HE GIVES ME *TRAINING,* NEW TOYS, AND EXCLUSIVE *STREAMING* RIGHTS TO SELL AT A *HIGH PRICE.*

Disco Dazzler-Bedazzled by You [official video]

Starfox (2021) - Teaser Trailer (OFFICIAL)

Nick Fury: Agent of S.H.I.E.L.D.-The spy who left me one-eyed FULL MOVIE

Matt Owen's Top 10 Most Embarrassing Moments

Wheel of Impressions with Mimic (Cal Rankin)

Comicbook tutorial: Swipe Like a Pro-Juann Cabal style

IF *THIS* IS ALL YOU'VE GOT, THEN ARCADE SHOULD GET HIS MONEY BACK.

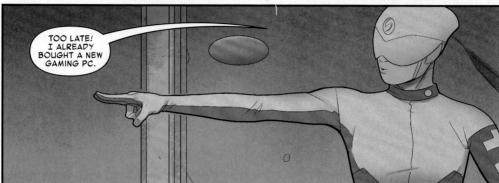

TOO LATE! I ALREADY BOUGHT A NEW GAMING PC.

YOU NERDS DESERVE EACH OTHER.

TSK TSK. HAVEN'T YOU BEEN PAYING ATTENTION?

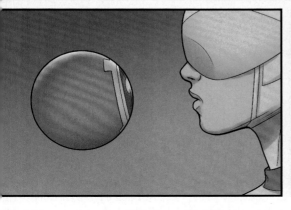

SMOOCH

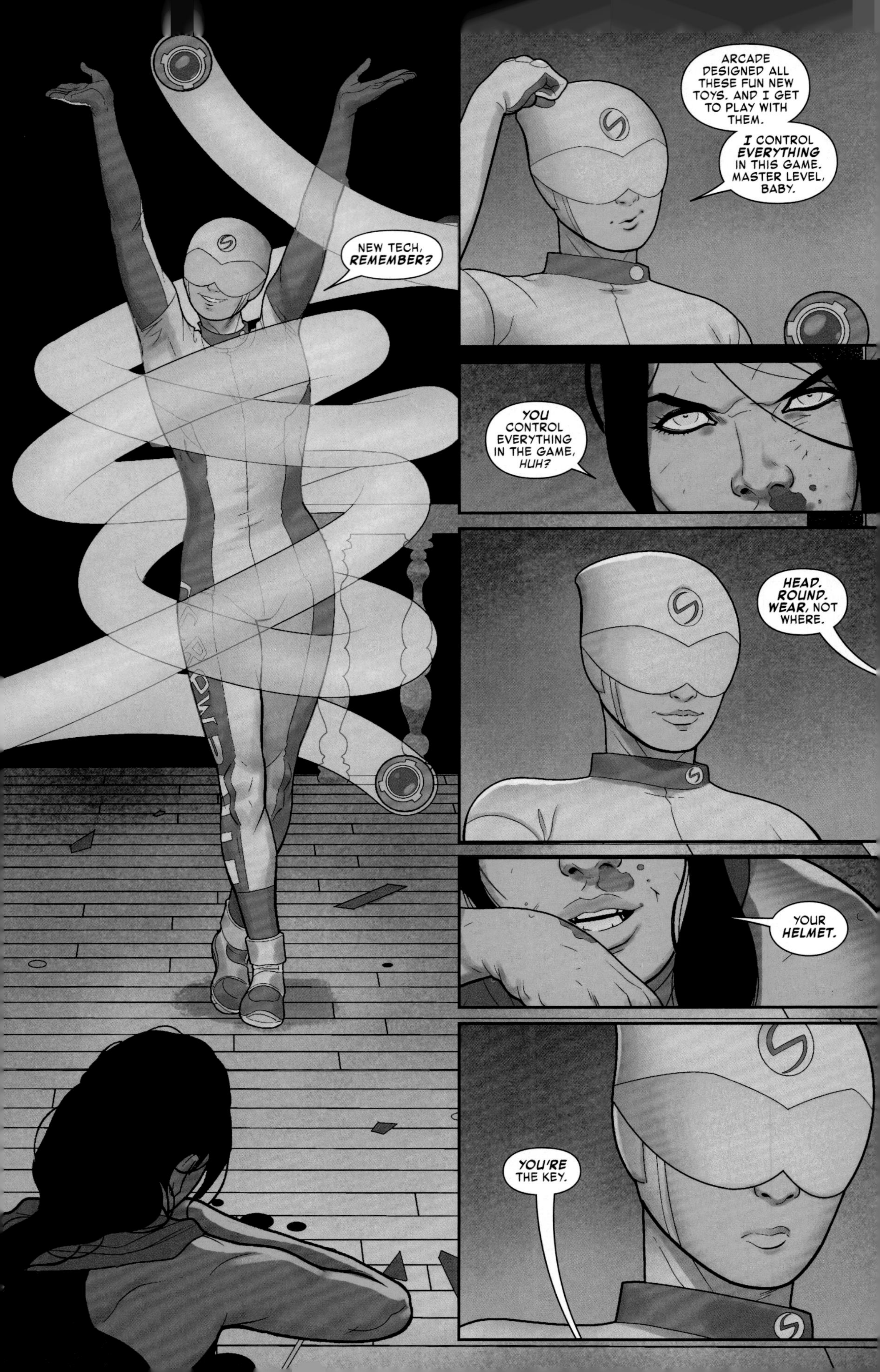

NEW TECH, REMEMBER?
ARCADE DESIGNED ALL THESE FUN NEW TOYS. AND I GET TO PLAY WITH THEM.
I CONTROL EVERYTHING IN THIS GAME. MASTER LEVEL, BABY.
YOU CONTROL EVERYTHING IN THE GAME, HUH?
HEAD. ROUND. WEAR, NOT WHERE.
YOUR HELMET.
YOU'RE THE KEY.

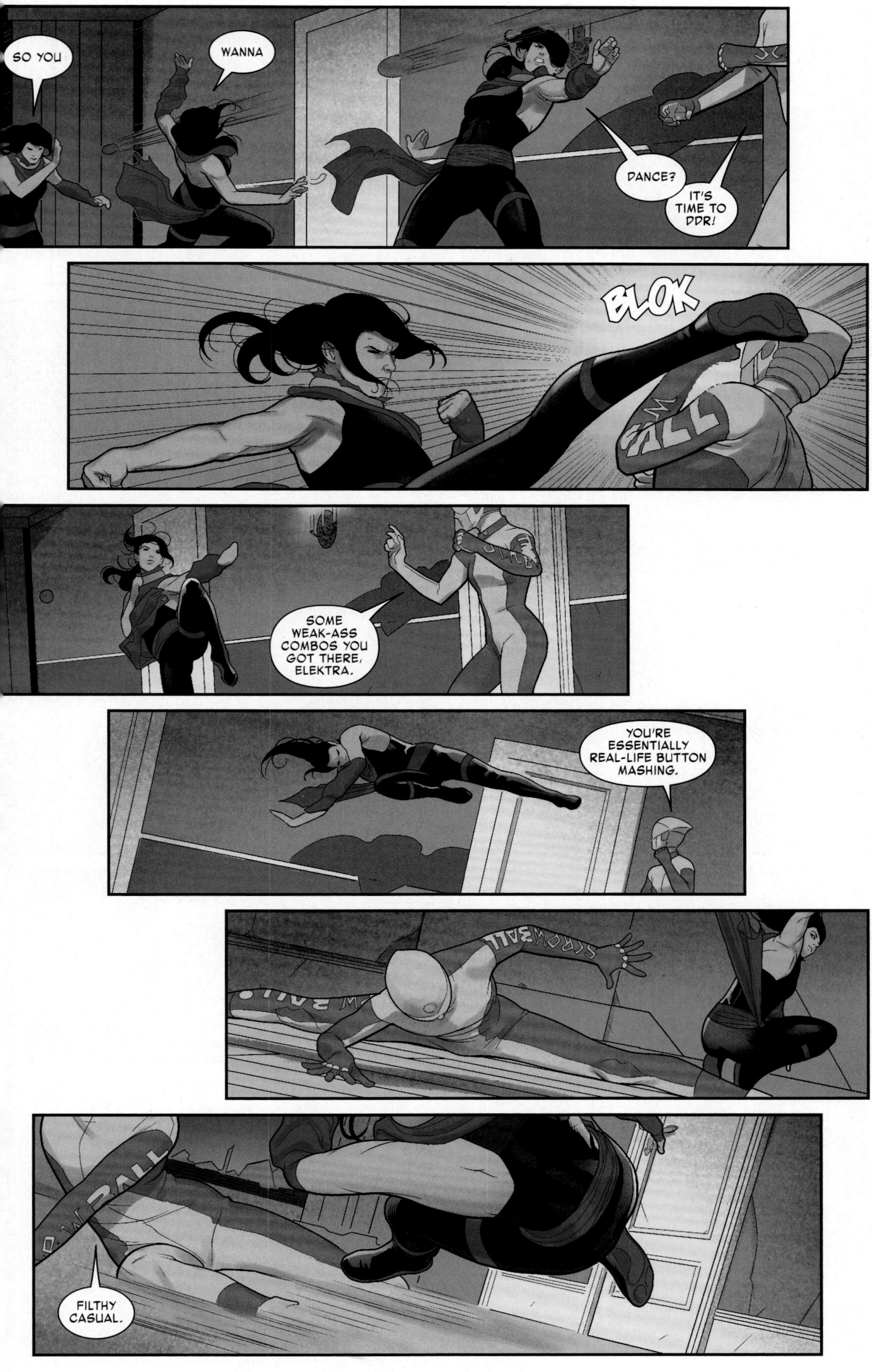
SO YOU
WANNA
DANCE?
IT'S TIME TO DDR!
BLOK
SOME WEAK-ASS COMBOS YOU GOT THERE, ELEKTRA.
YOU'RE ESSENTIALLY REAL-LIFE BUTTON MASHING.
FILTHY CASUAL.

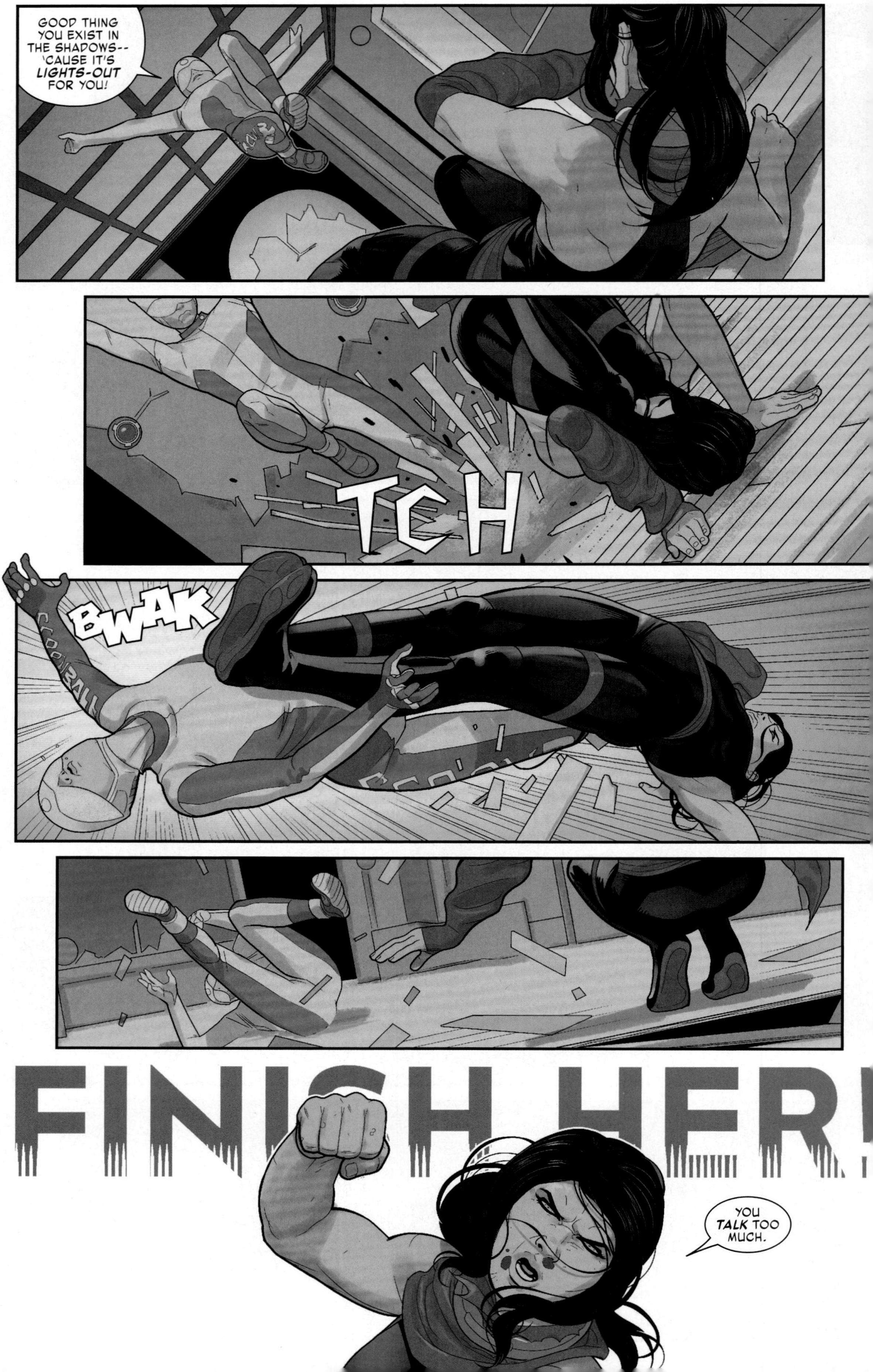
GOOD THING YOU EXIST IN THE SHADOWS-- 'CAUSE IT'S *LIGHTS-OUT* FOR YOU!
TCH
BWAK
FINISH HER!
YOU *TALK* TOO MUCH.

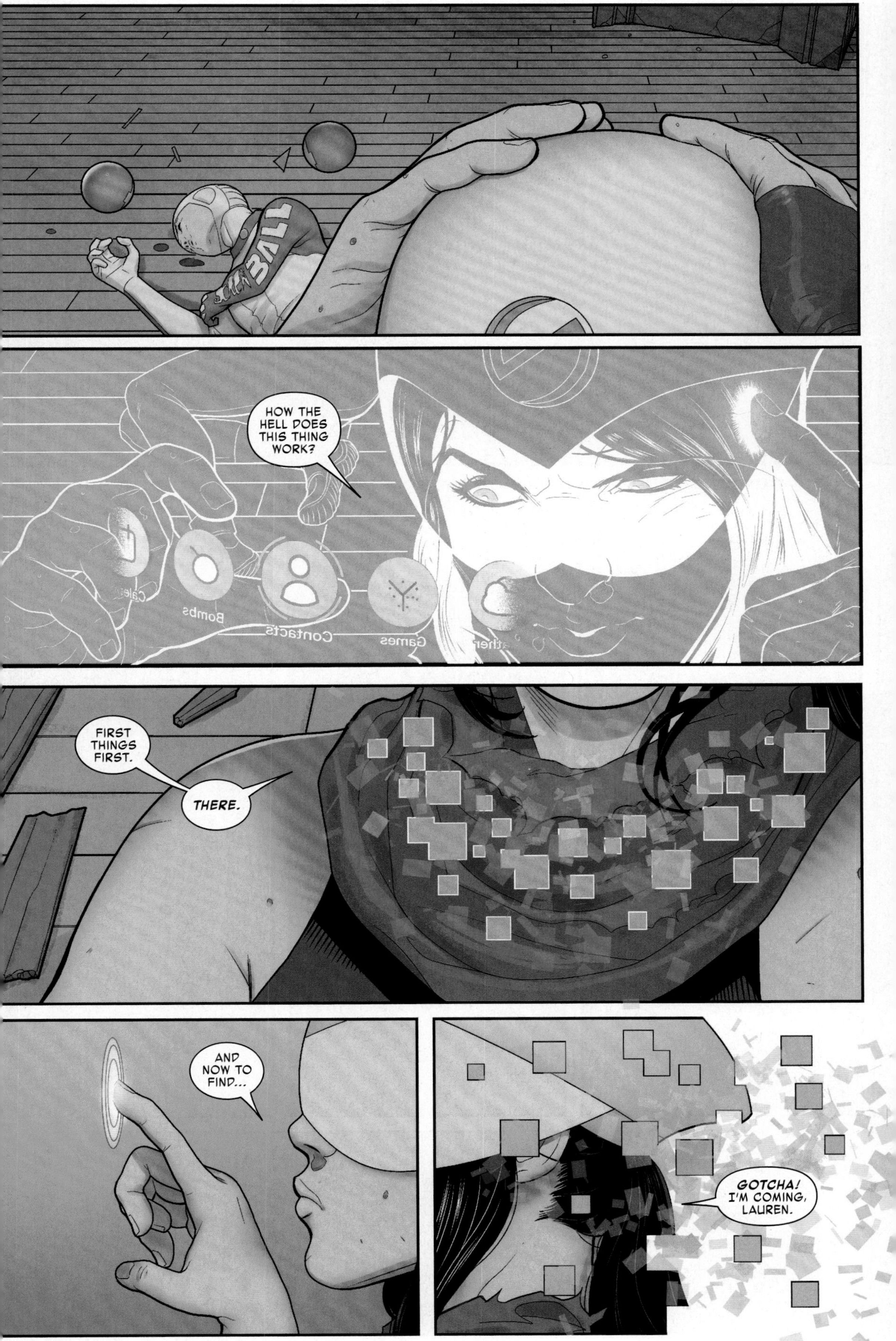
SOCCA BALL
HOW THE HELL DOES THIS THING WORK?
Bombs
Contacts
Games
FIRST THINGS FIRST.
THERE.
AND NOW TO FIND...
GOTCHA! I'M COMING, LAUREN.

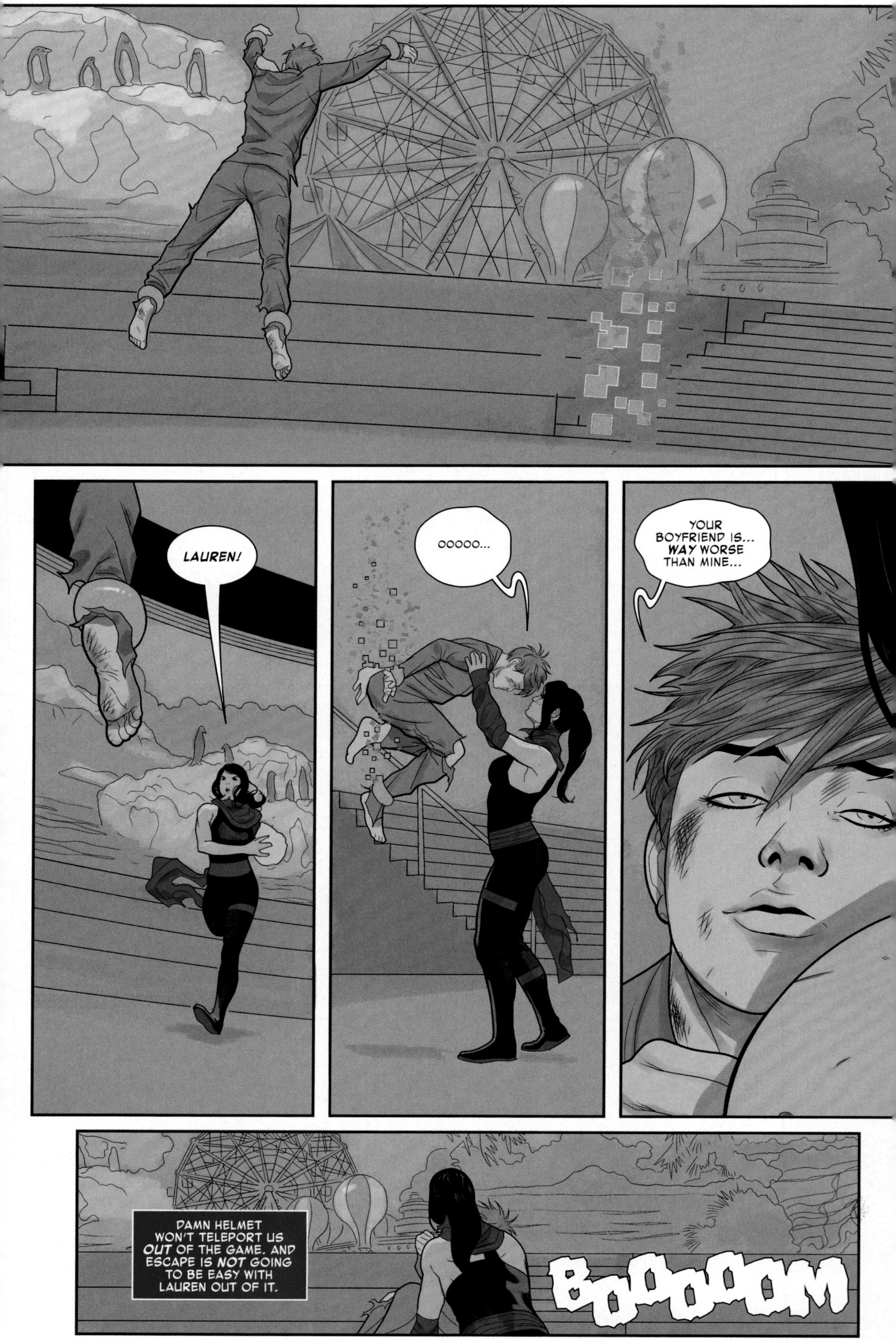
LAUREN!
OOOOO...
YOUR BOYFRIEND IS... WAY WORSE THAN MINE...
DAMN HELMET WON'T TELEPORT US OUT OF THE GAME. AND ESCAPE IS NOT GOING TO BE EASY WITH LAUREN OUT OF IT.
BOOOOOOM

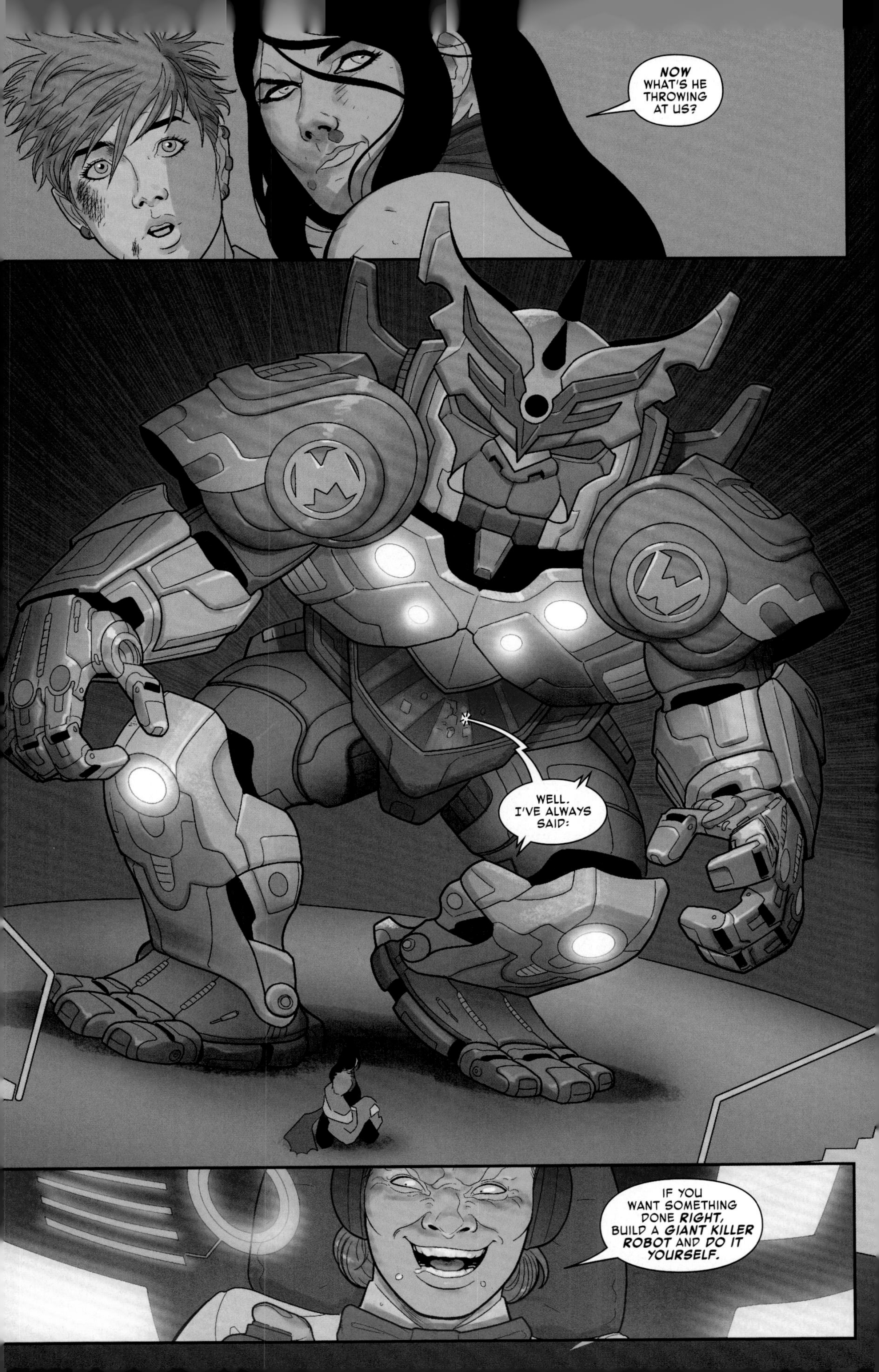
NOW WHAT'S HE THROWING AT US?
WELL. I'VE ALWAYS SAID:
IF YOU WANT SOMETHING DONE RIGHT, BUILD A GIANT KILLER ROBOT AND DO IT YOURSELF.

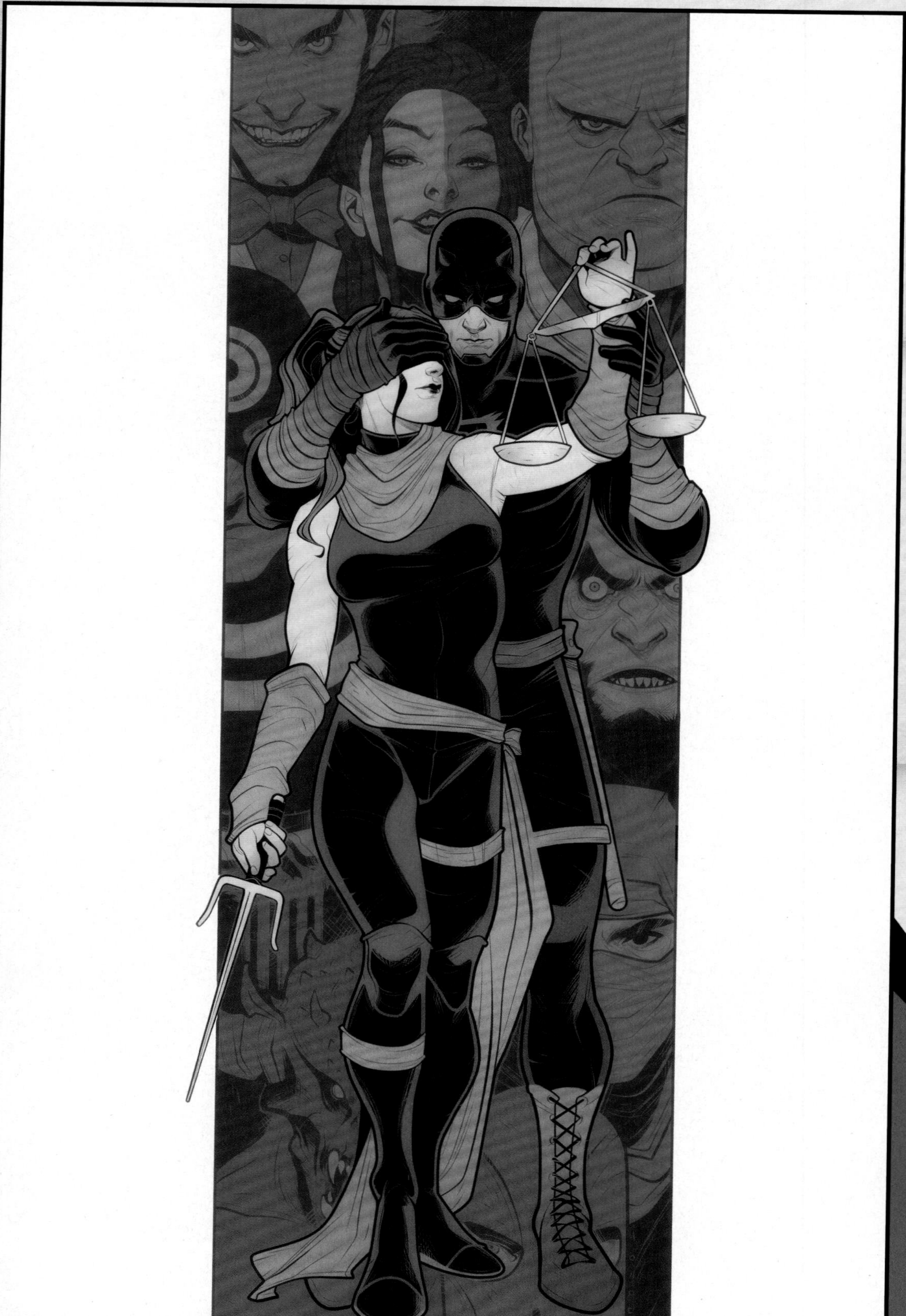

5

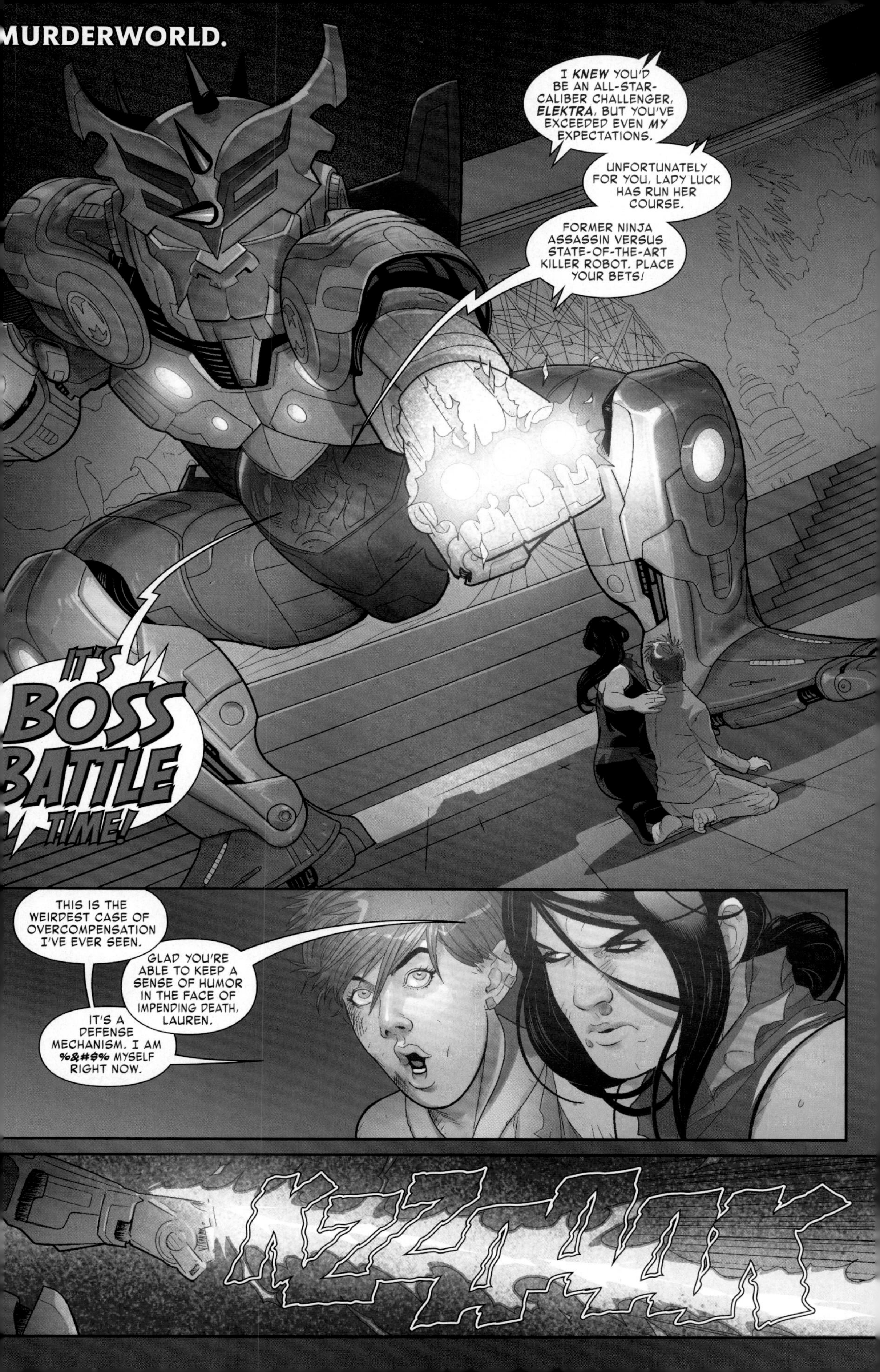
MURDERWORLD.
I KNEW YOU'D BE AN ALL-STAR-CALIBER CHALLENGER, ELEKTRA, BUT YOU'VE EXCEEDED EVEN MY EXPECTATIONS.
UNFORTUNATELY FOR YOU, LADY LUCK HAS RUN HER COURSE.
FORMER NINJA ASSASSIN VERSUS STATE-OF-THE-ART KILLER ROBOT. PLACE YOUR BETS!
IT'S BOSS BATTLE TIME!
THIS IS THE WEIRDEST CASE OF OVERCOMPENSATION I'VE EVER SEEN.
GLAD YOU'RE ABLE TO KEEP A SENSE OF HUMOR IN THE FACE OF IMPENDING DEATH, LAUREN.
IT'S A DEFENSE MECHANISM. I AM %&#$% MYSELF RIGHT NOW.
NZZTTTK

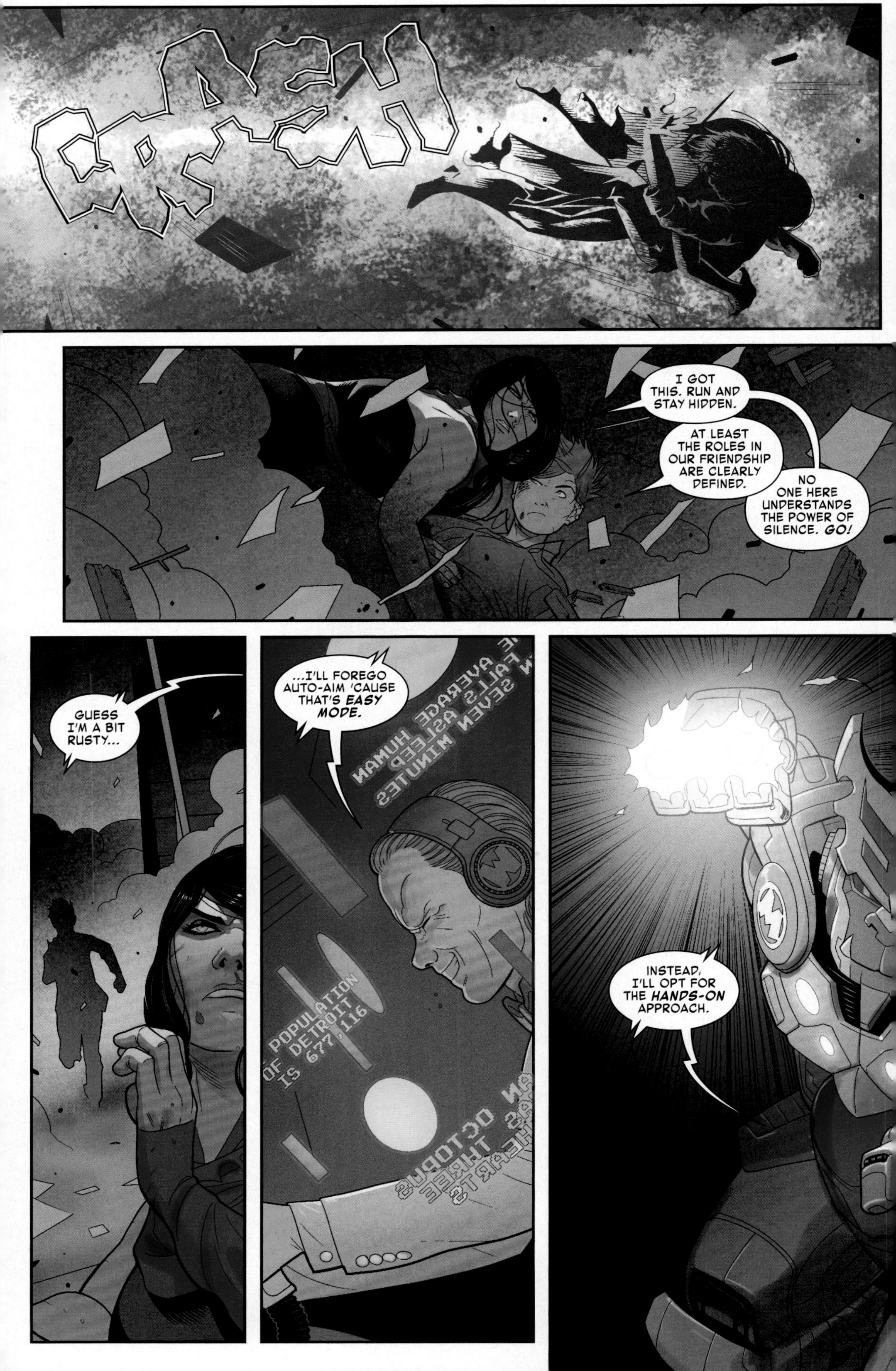
CRASH
I GOT THIS. RUN AND STAY HIDDEN.
AT LEAST THE ROLES IN OUR FRIENDSHIP ARE CLEARLY DEFINED.
NO ONE HERE UNDERSTANDS THE POWER OF SILENCE. *GO!*
GUESS I'M A BIT RUSTY...
...I'LL FOREGO AUTO-AIM 'CAUSE THAT'S *EASY MODE.*
POPULATION OF DETROIT IS 677,116
INSTEAD, I'LL OPT FOR THE *HANDS-ON* APPROACH.

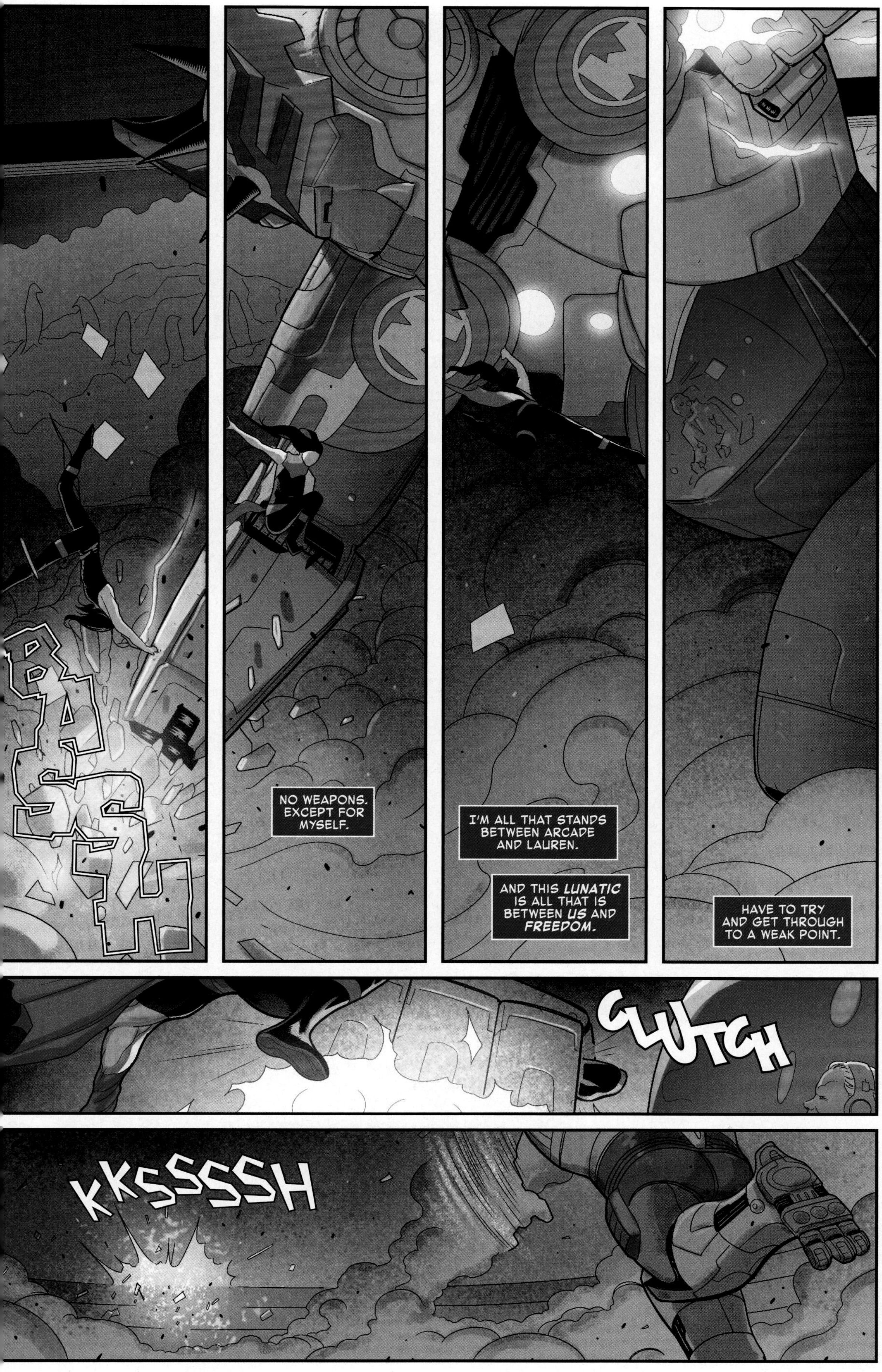
BASH
NO WEAPONS. EXCEPT FOR MYSELF.
I'M ALL THAT STANDS BETWEEN ARCADE AND LAUREN.
AND THIS *LUNATIC* IS ALL THAT IS BETWEEN *US* AND *FREEDOM*.
HAVE TO TRY AND GET THROUGH TO A WEAK POINT.
CLUTCH
KKSSSSH

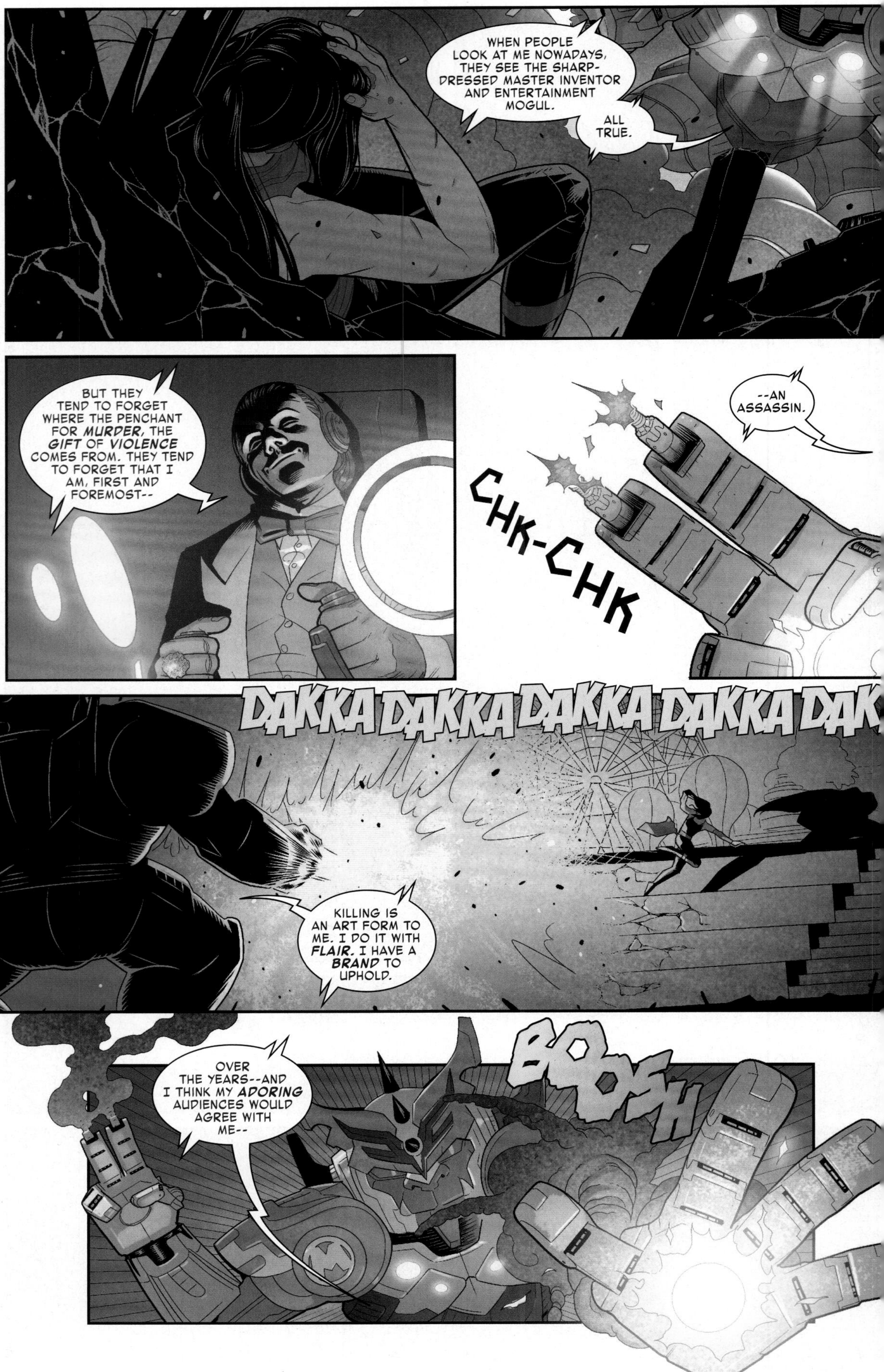
WHEN PEOPLE LOOK AT ME NOWADAYS, THEY SEE THE SHARP-DRESSED MASTER INVENTOR AND ENTERTAINMENT MOGUL.
ALL TRUE.
BUT THEY TEND TO FORGET WHERE THE PENCHANT FOR MURDER, THE GIFT OF VIOLENCE COMES FROM. THEY TEND TO FORGET THAT I AM, FIRST AND FOREMOST--
--AN ASSASSIN.
CHK-CHK
DAKKA DAKKA DAKKA DAKKA DAK
KILLING IS AN ART FORM TO ME. I DO IT WITH FLAIR. I HAVE A BRAND TO UPHOLD.
BOOSH
OVER THE YEARS--AND I THINK MY ADORING AUDIENCES WOULD AGREE WITH ME--

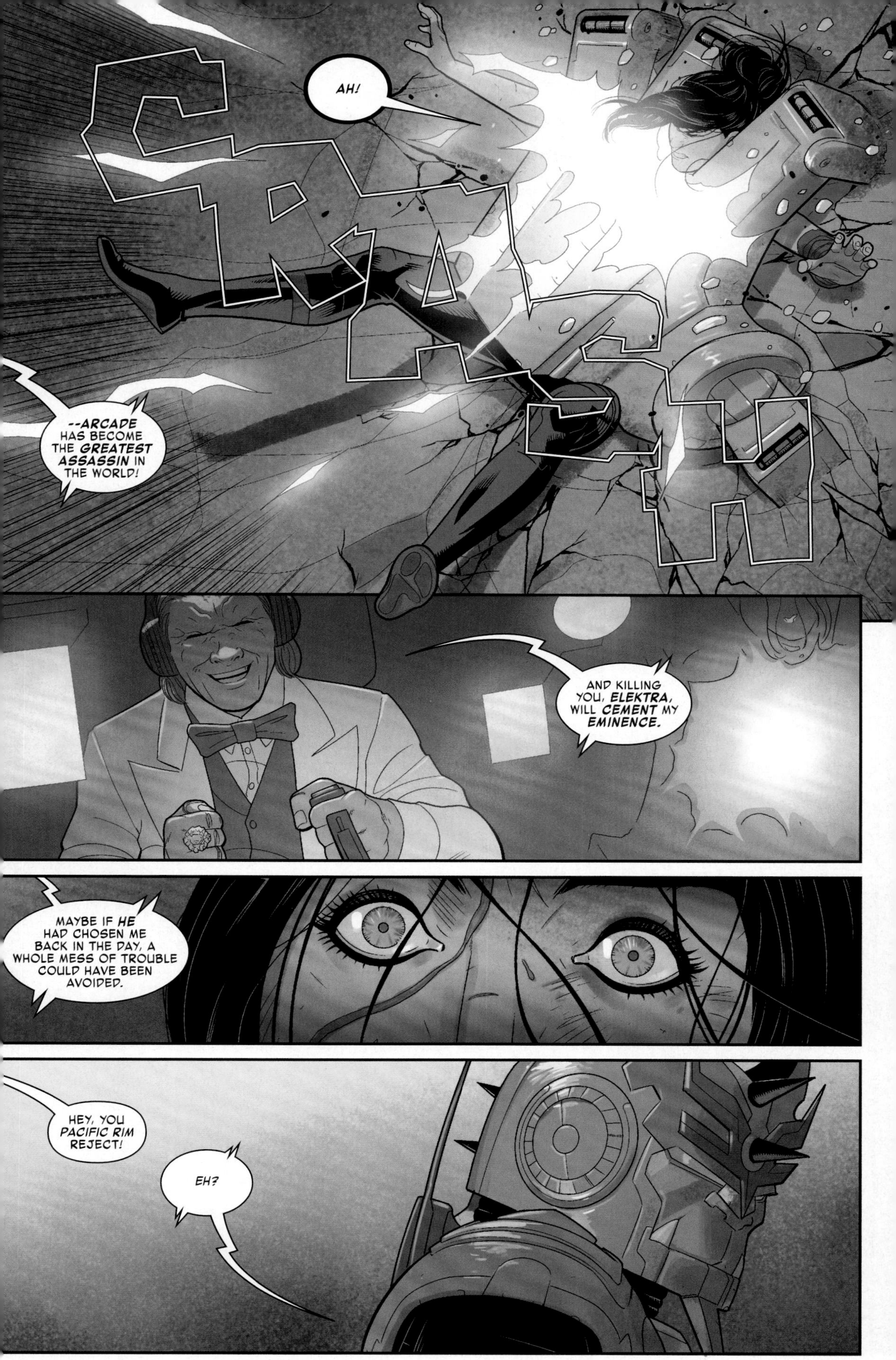
AH!
CRASH
--ARCADE HAS BECOME THE GREATEST ASSASSIN IN THE WORLD!
AND KILLING YOU, ELEKTRA, WILL CEMENT MY EMINENCE.
MAYBE IF HE HAD CHOSEN ME BACK IN THE DAY, A WHOLE MESS OF TROUBLE COULD HAVE BEEN AVOIDED.
HEY, YOU PACIFIC RIM REJECT!
EH?

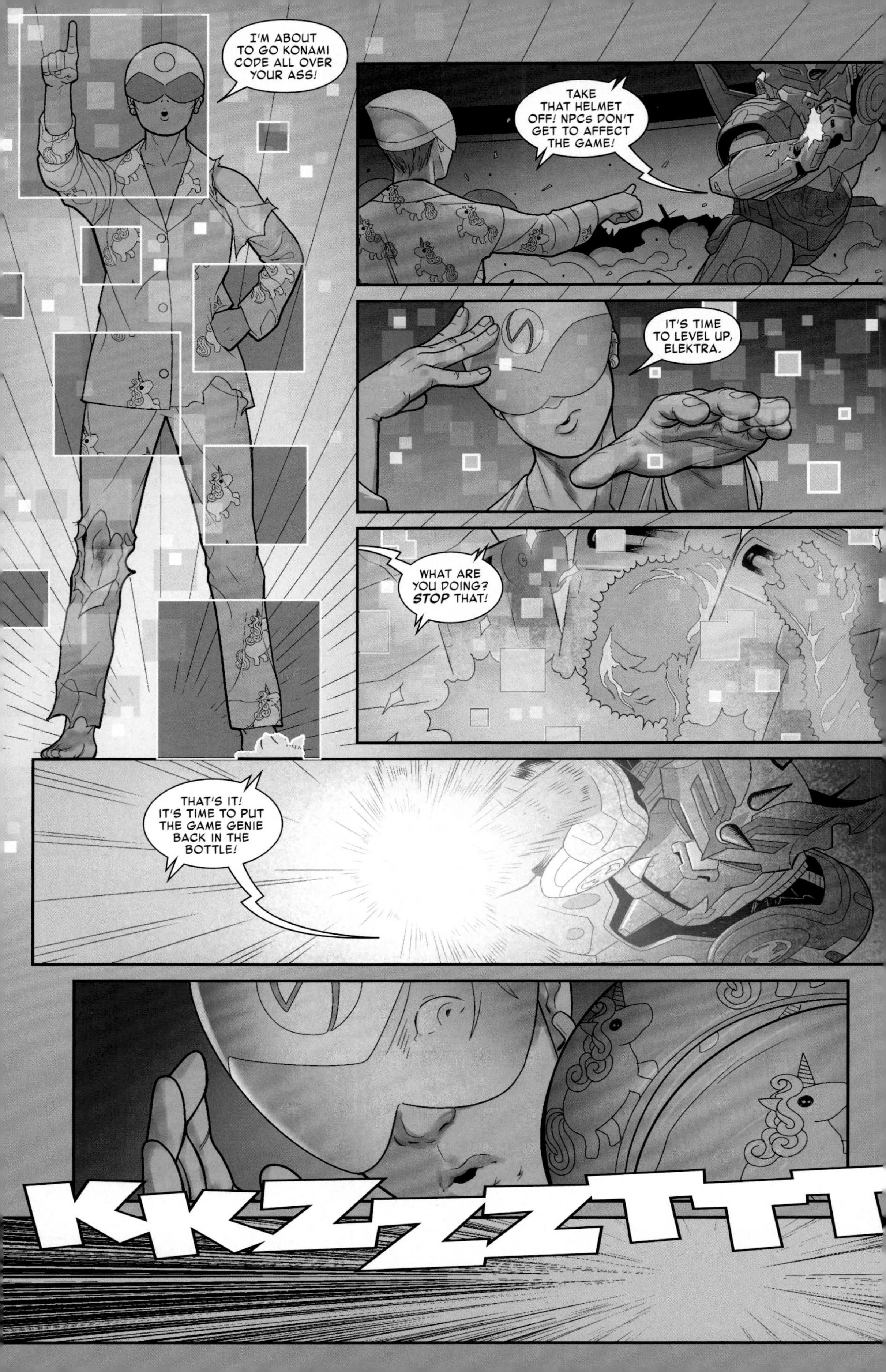
I'M ABOUT TO GO KONAMI CODE ALL OVER YOUR ASS!
TAKE THAT HELMET OFF! NPCs DON'T GET TO AFFECT THE GAME!
IT'S TIME TO LEVEL UP, ELEKTRA.
WHAT ARE YOU DOING? STOP THAT!
THAT'S IT! IT'S TIME TO PUT THE GAME GENIE BACK IN THE BOTTLE!
KKZZZTTT

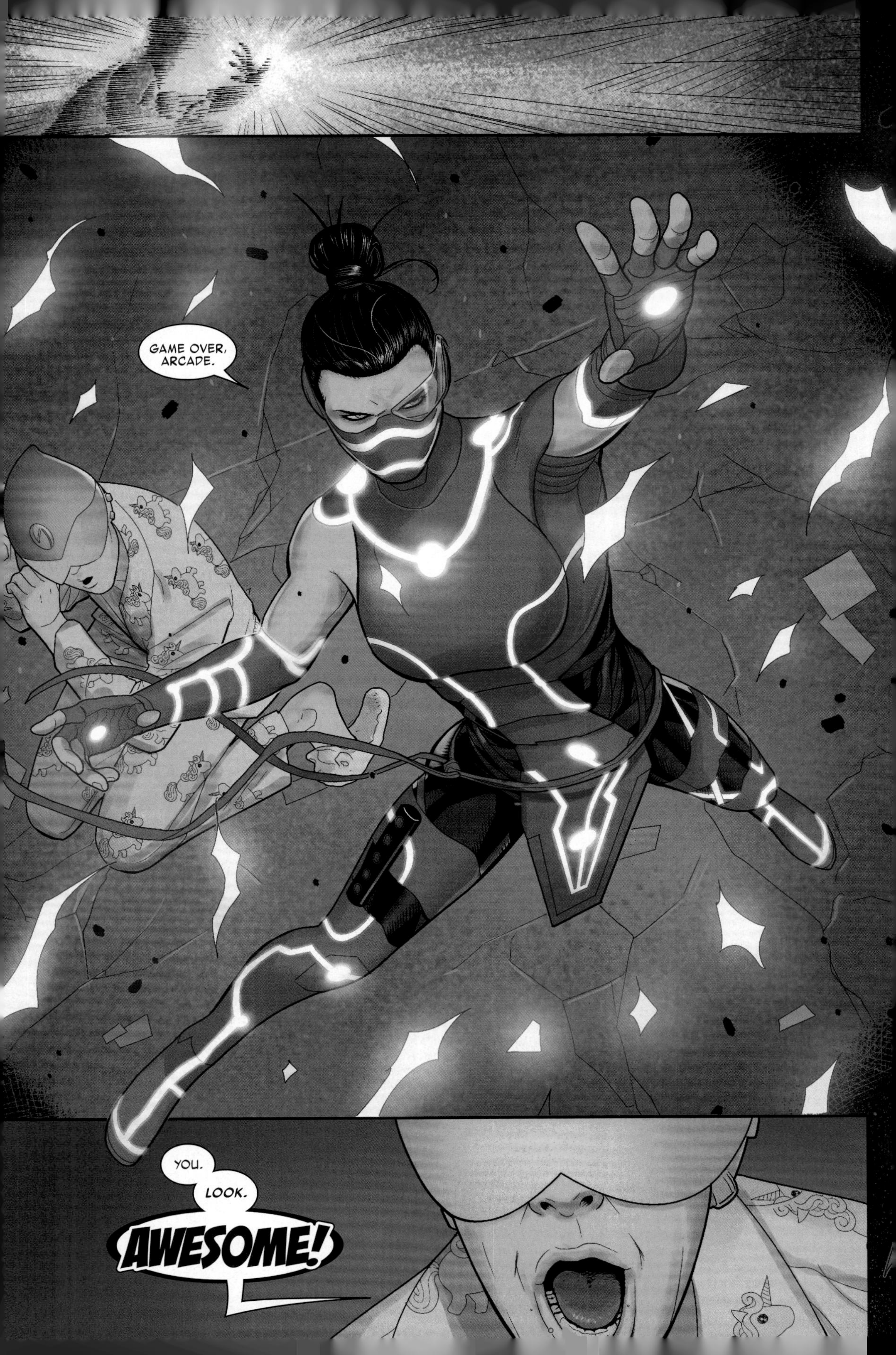
GAME OVER, ARCADE.
YOU.
LOOK.
AWESOME!

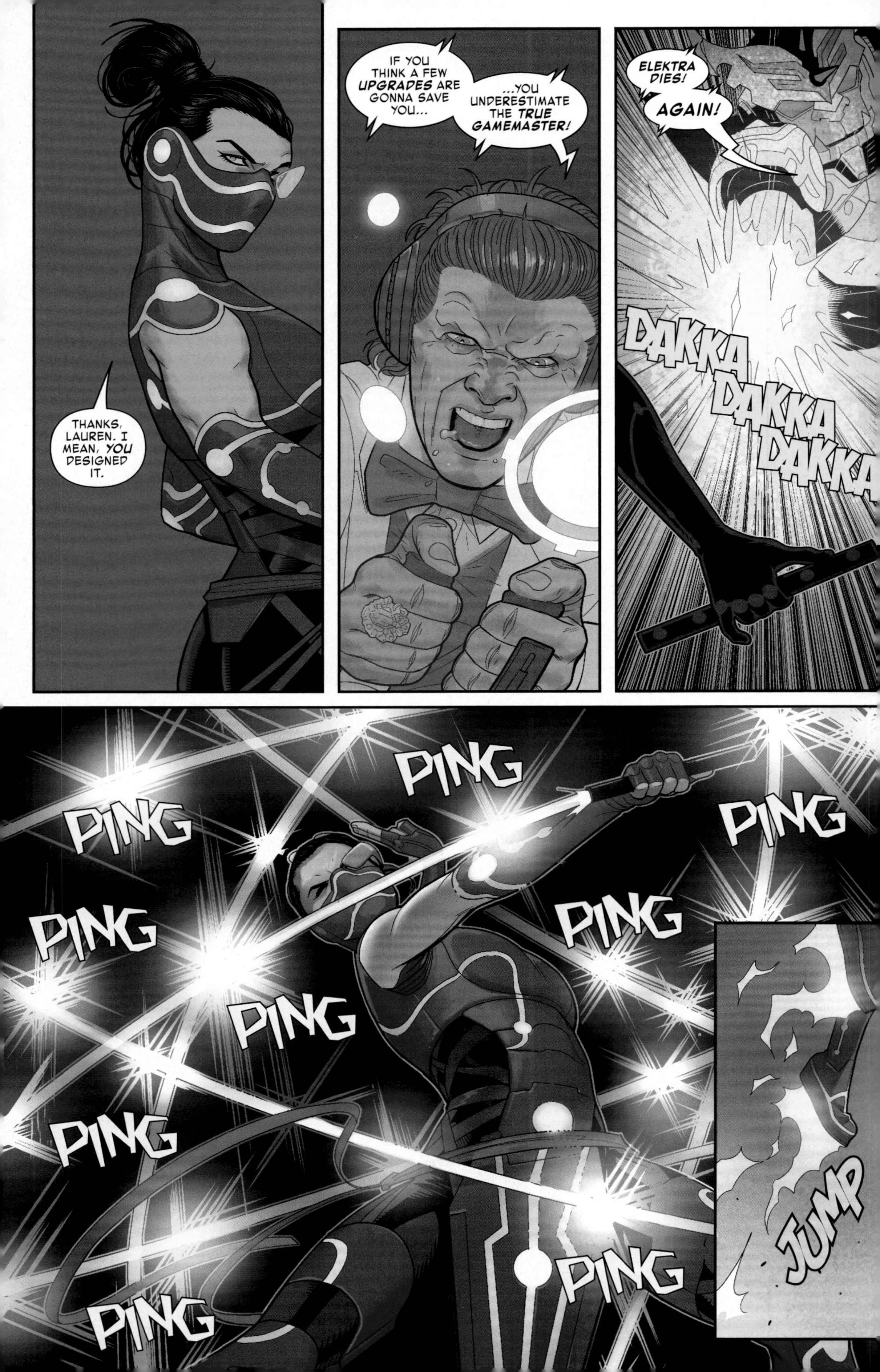
THANKS, LAUREN. I MEAN, YOU DESIGNED IT.
IF YOU THINK A FEW UPGRADES ARE GONNA SAVE YOU...
...YOU UNDERESTIMATE THE TRUE GAMEMASTER!
ELEKTRA DIES!
AGAIN!
DAKKA
DAKKA
DAKKA
PING
PING
PING
PING
PING
PING
PING
PING
PING
JUMP

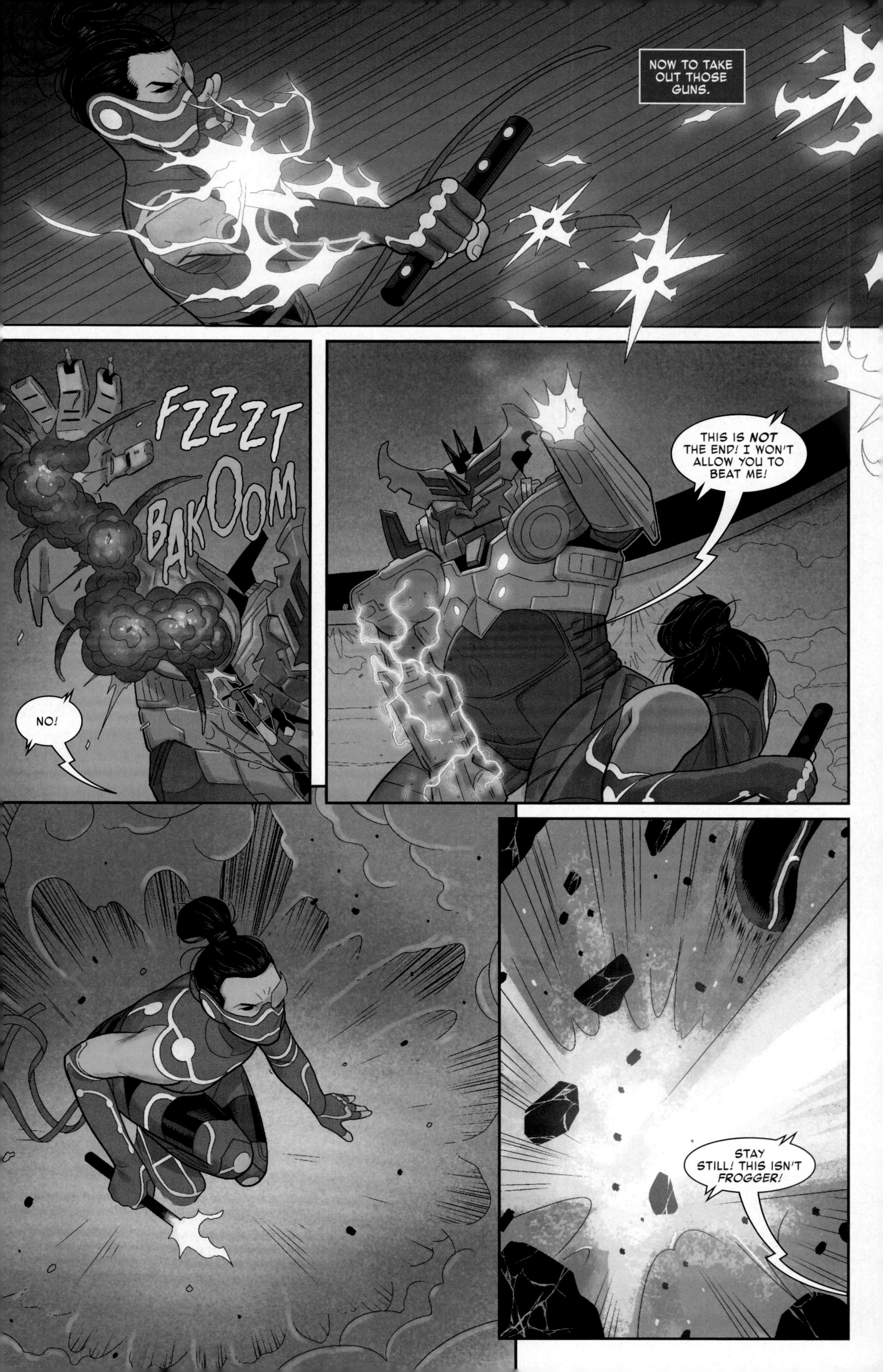
NOW TO TAKE OUT THOSE GUNS.
FZZZT
BAKOOM
NO!
THIS IS **NOT** THE END! I WON'T ALLOW YOU TO BEAT ME!
STAY STILL! THIS ISN'T *FROGGER!*

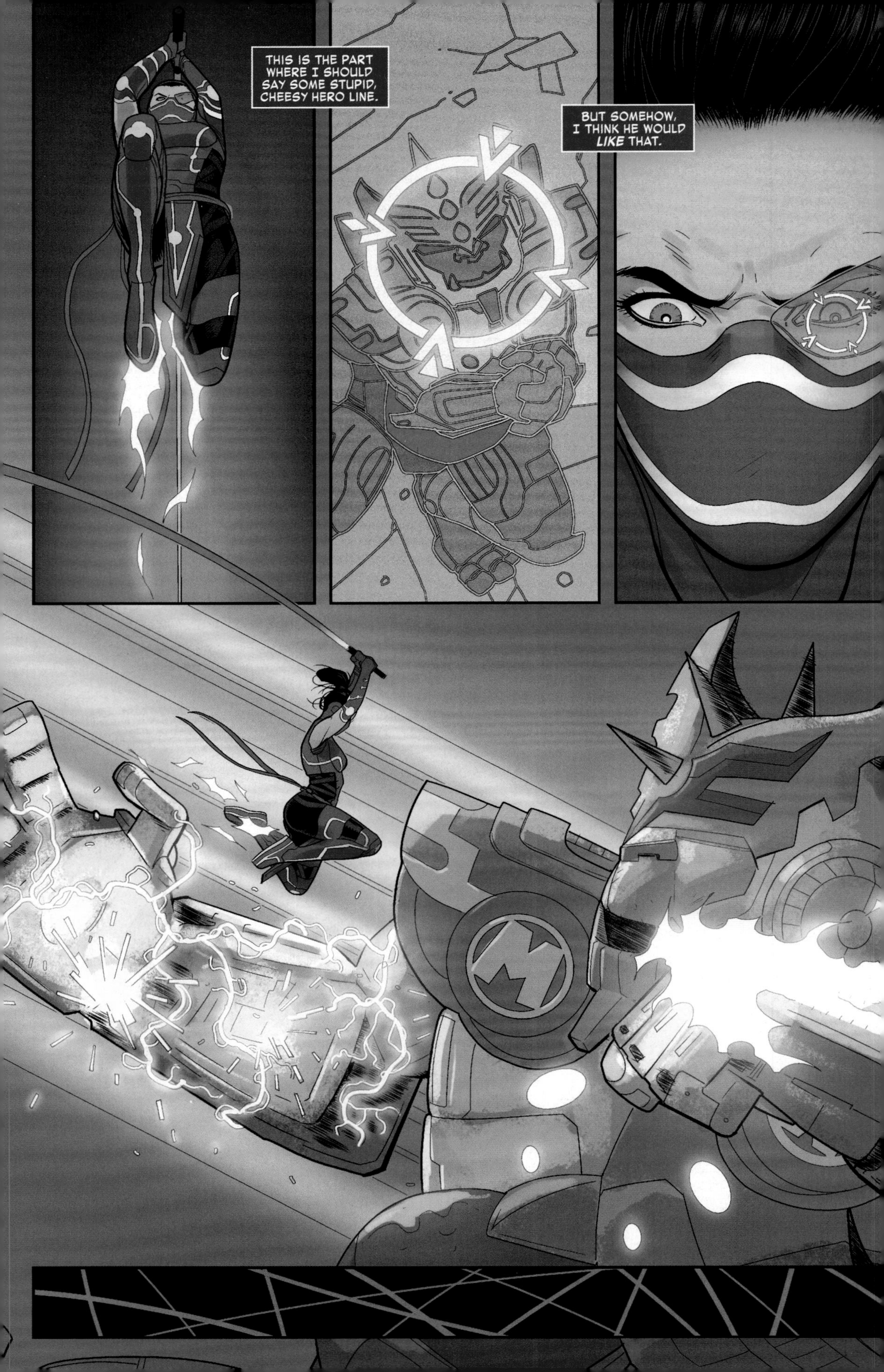
THIS IS THE PART WHERE I SHOULD SAY SOME STUPID, CHEESY HERO LINE.
BUT SOMEHOW, I THINK HE WOULD *LIKE* THAT.

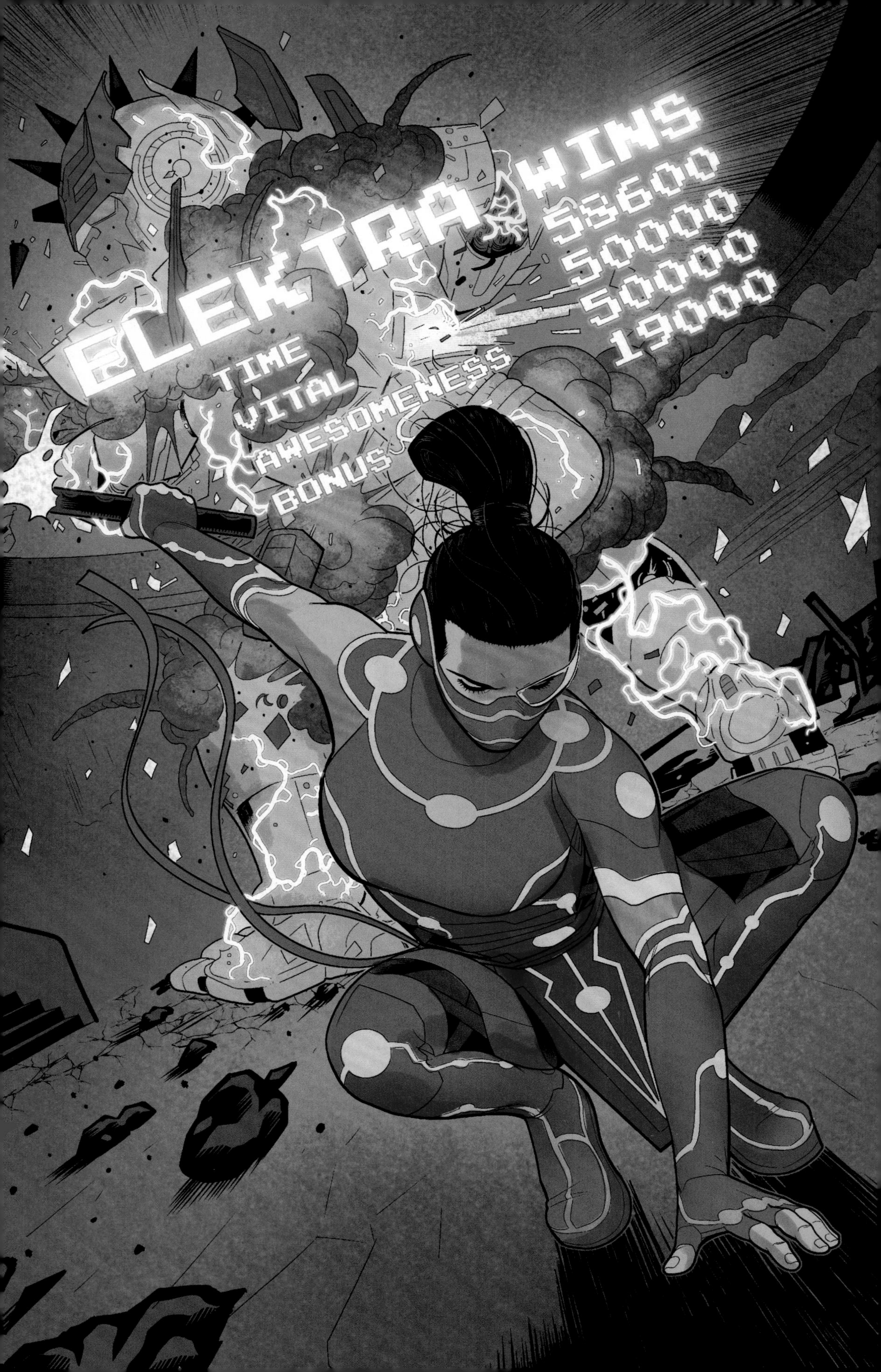
ELEKTRA WINS
TIME 53600
VITAL 50000
AWESOMENESS 50000
BONUS 19000

YES! SHE DID IT!

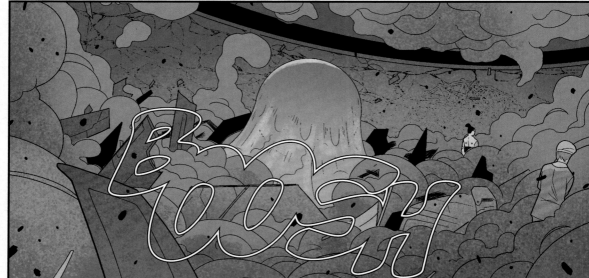

OR... NOT.

CONGRATS ON BEATING THE BOSS, ELEKTRA. UNFORTUNATELY FOR YOU, I HAVE ANOTHER LIFE LEFT TO PLAY.

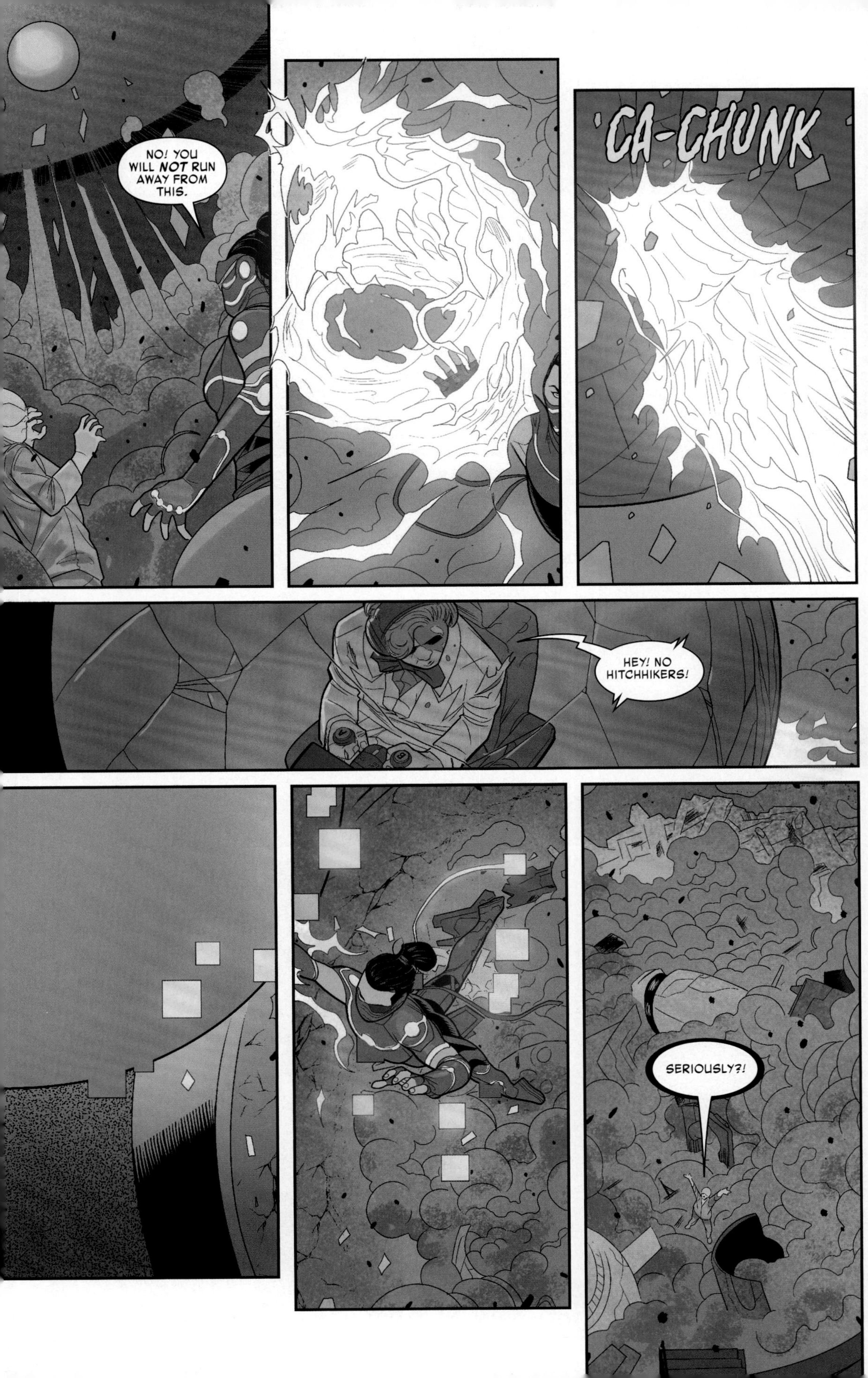
NO! YOU WILL NOT RUN AWAY FROM THIS.
CA-CHUNK
HEY! NO HITCHHIKERS!
SERIOUSLY?!

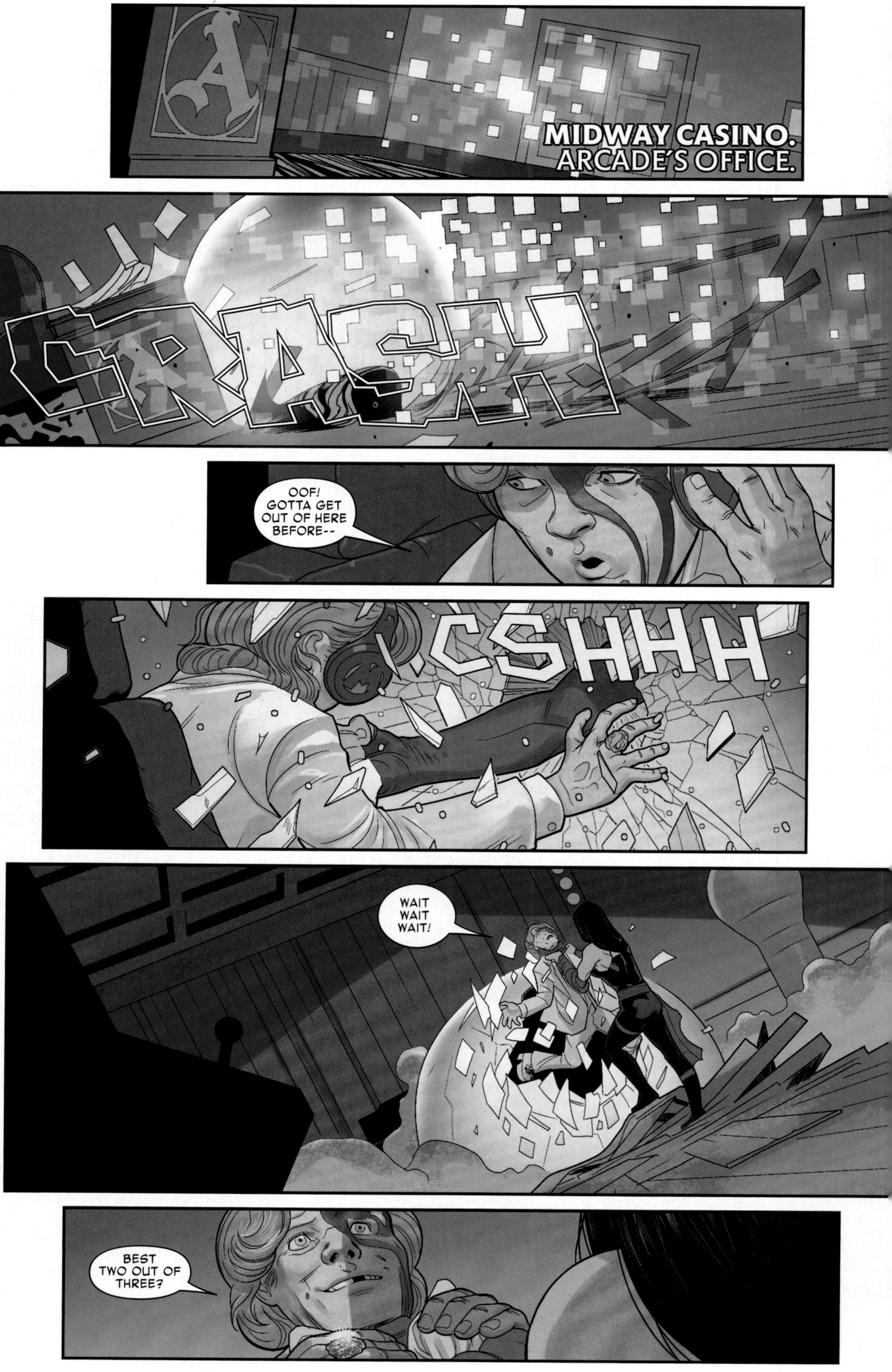
MIDWAY CASINO.
ARCADE'S OFFICE.
CRASH
OOF! GOTTA GET OUT OF HERE BEFORE--
CSHHH
WAIT WAIT WAIT!
BEST TWO OUT OF THREE?

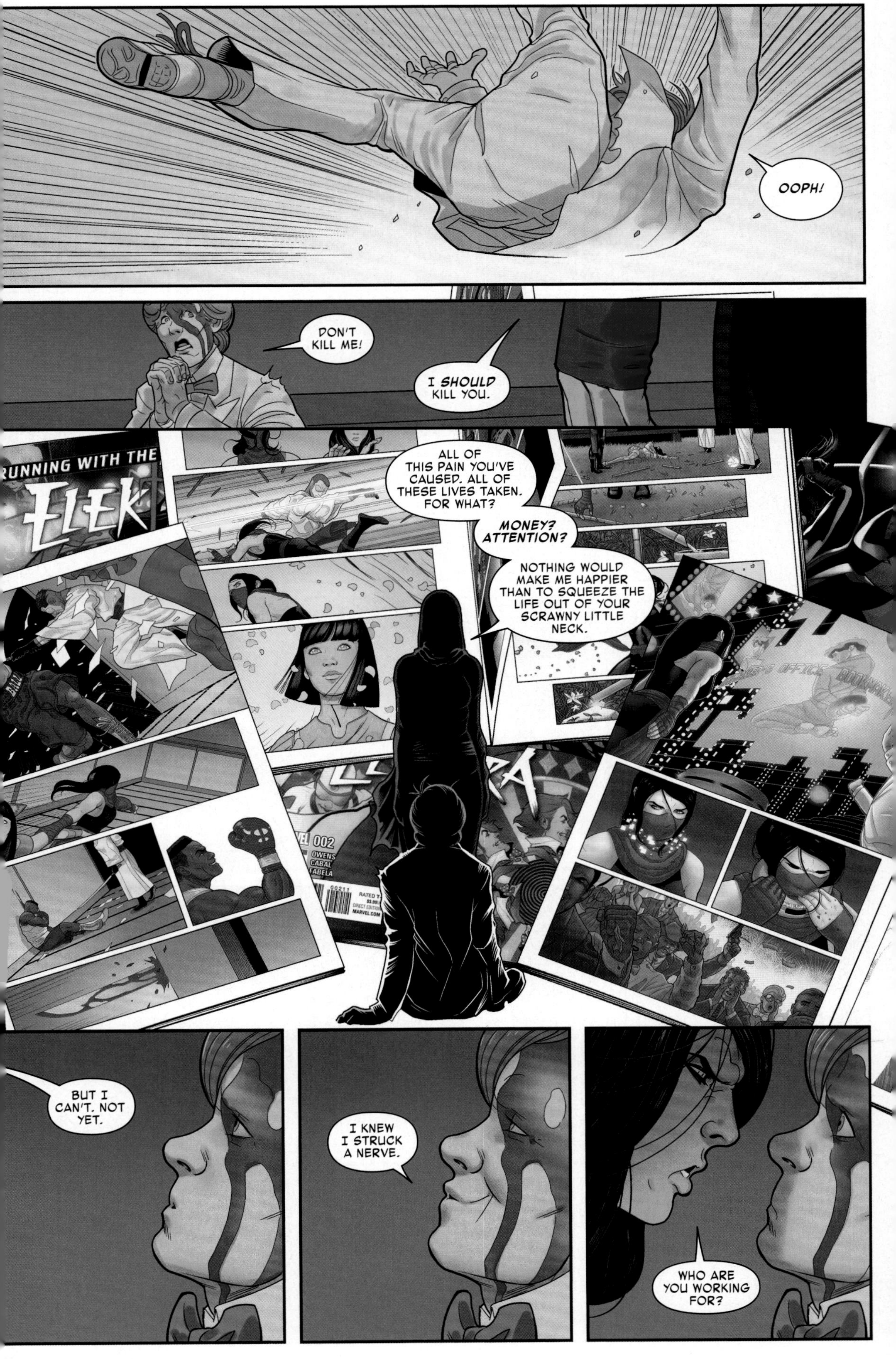
OOPH!
DON'T KILL ME!
I SHOULD KILL YOU.
RUNNING WITH THE
ALL OF THIS PAIN YOU'VE CAUSED. ALL OF THESE LIVES TAKEN. FOR WHAT?
MONEY? ATTENTION?
NOTHING WOULD MAKE ME HAPPIER THAN TO SQUEEZE THE LIFE OUT OF YOUR SCRAWNY LITTLE NECK.
BUT I CAN'T. NOT YET.
I KNEW I STRUCK A NERVE.
WHO ARE YOU WORKING FOR?

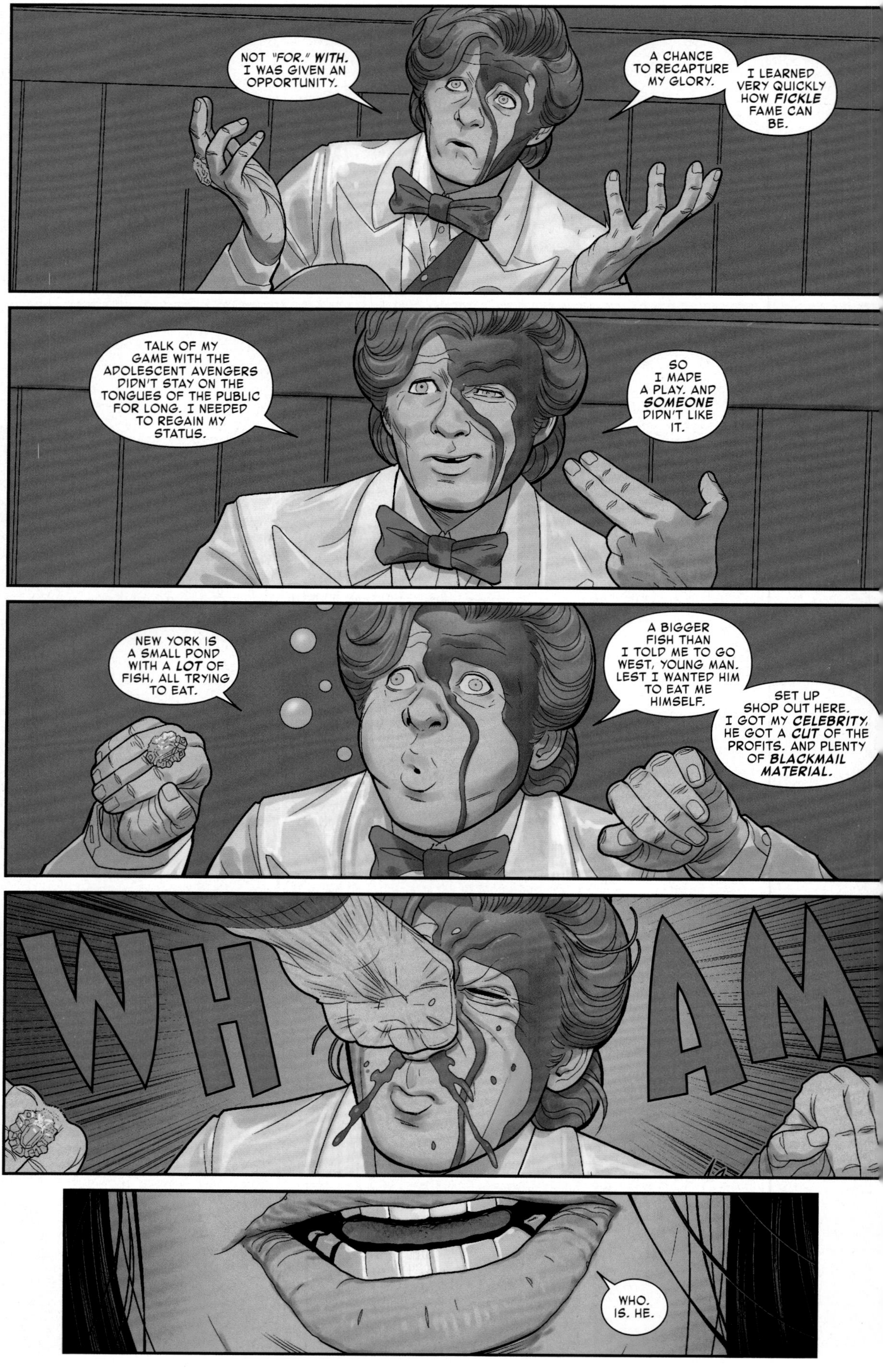
NOT "FOR." WITH. I WAS GIVEN AN OPPORTUNITY.
A CHANCE TO RECAPTURE MY GLORY.
I LEARNED VERY QUICKLY HOW FICKLE FAME CAN BE.
TALK OF MY GAME WITH THE ADOLESCENT AVENGERS DIDN'T STAY ON THE TONGUES OF THE PUBLIC FOR LONG. I NEEDED TO REGAIN MY STATUS.
SO I MADE A PLAY. AND SOMEONE DIDN'T LIKE IT.
NEW YORK IS A SMALL POND WITH A LOT OF FISH, ALL TRYING TO EAT.
A BIGGER FISH THAN I TOLD ME TO GO WEST, YOUNG MAN. LEST I WANTED HIM TO EAT ME HIMSELF.
SET UP SHOP OUT HERE. I GOT MY CELEBRITY, HE GOT A CUT OF THE PROFITS. AND PLENTY OF BLACKMAIL MATERIAL.
WHAM
WHO. IS. HE.